WINDS OF THE STEPPE

WALKING THE GREAT SILK ROAD FROM CENTRAL ASIA TO CHINA

BERNARD OLLIVIER

Translated from the French by Dan Golembeski

Skyhorse Publishing

Originally published in France as *Longue marche: À pied de la Méditerranée jusqu'en Chine par la route de la Soie. III.–Le vent des steppes* by Éditions Phébus, Paris.

English translation © 2020 by Dan Golembeski

The translator would like to express his thanks to Dr. Jennifer Wolter of Bowling Green State University for her insights and suggestions, and to Jon Arlan for his careful revisions and constructive comments. This translation was made possible by a 2017 National Endowment for the Arts Fellowship.

Skyhorse Publishing books may be purchased in bulk at special discounts for sales promotion, corporate gifts, fund-raising, or educational purposes. Special editions can also be created to specifications. For details, contact the Special Sales Department, Skyhorse Publishing, 307 West 36th Street, 11th Floor, New York, NY 10018 or info@skyhorsepublishing.com.

Skyhorse® and Skyhorse Publishing® are registered trademarks of Skyhorse Publishing, Inc.®, a Delaware corporation.

Visit our website at www.skyhorsepublishing.com.

10 9 8 7 6 5 4 3 2 1

Library of Congress Cataloging-in-Publication Data is available on file.

Maps: iStockphoto, Getty Images

Cover design by Brian Peterson
Cover photo credit: Getty Images

Print ISBN: 978-1-5107-4690-9
Ebook ISBN: 978-1-5107-4692-3

Printed in the United States of America

To Sofy

OTHER BOOKS BY THE SAME AUTHOR
AVAILABLE IN ENGLISH

Out of Istanbul: A Journey of Discovery along the Silk Road. Skyhorse Publishing, 2019.

Walking to Samarkand: The Great Silk Road from Persia to Central Asia. Skyhorse Publishing, 2020.

CONTENTS

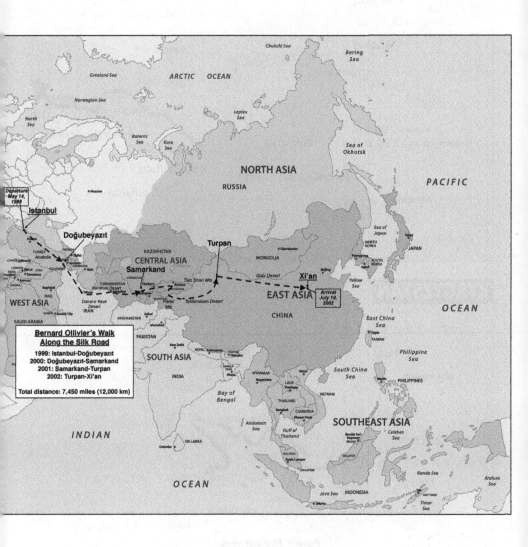

Greeland Sea

Norwegian Sea

ARCTIC OCEAN

Chukchi Sea

Bering Sea

North Sea

Barents Sea

Kara Sea

Laptev Sea

Sea of Okhotsk

NORTH ASIA

RUSSIA

PACIFIC

Sea of Japan

Departure May 14, 1999

Istanbul

Doğubeyazıt

TURKEY

Anatolia

Turpan

KAZAKHSTAN

CENTRAL ASIA

MONGOLIA

Ulaanbaatar

NORTH KOREA

Pyongyang

JAPAN

SOUTH KOREA

Samarkand

Tian Shan Mts

Gobi Desert

Xi'an

Yellow Sea

Beijing

OCEAN

WEST ASIA

Baghdad

IRAQ

Dasht-e Kavir Desert

IRAN

Karakum Desert

TURKMENISTAN

Pamir Mts

Taklamakan Desert

EAST ASIA

CHINA

Arrival July 10, 2002

East China Sea

TAIWAN

Taipei

SAUDI ARABIA

AFGHANISTAN

Kabul

PAKISTAN

Bernard Ollivier's Walk
Along the Silk Road

1999: Istanbul-Doğubeyazıt
2000: Doğubeyazıt-Samarkand
2001: Samarkand-Turpan
2002: Turpan-Xi'an

Total distance: 7,450 miles (12,000 km)

New Delhi

NEPAL

Kathmandu

BHUTAN Thimphu

SOUTH ASIA

INDIA

BANGLADESH

Dhaka

MYANMAR

Naypyidaw

Hanoi

LAOS

Vientiane

VIETNAM

South China Sea

Manila

PHILIPPINES

Philippine Sea

Bay of Bengal

THAILAND

Bangkok

CAMBODIA

Phnom Penh

SRI LANKA

Colombo

Andaman Sea

Gulf of Thailand

SOUTHEAST ASIA

Bandar Seri Begawan BRUNEI

Celebes Sea

INDIAN

MALAYSIA

Kuala Lumpur

SINGAPORE

Banda Sea

Arafura Sea

OCEAN

INDONESIA

Jakarta

Java Sea

EAST TIMOR

Timor Sea

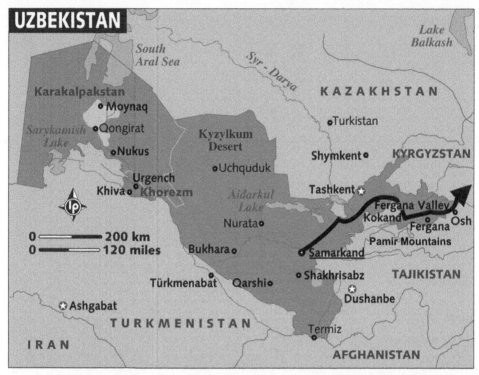

UZBEKISTAN

South Aral Sea

Sarykamish Lake

Karakalpakstan

Syr - Darya

KAZAKHSTAN

Moynaq

Qongirat

Nukus

Kyzylkum Desert

Uchquduk

Turkistan

Shymkent

KYRGYZSTAN

Urgench
Khiva Khorezm

Aidarkul Lake

Tashkent

Fergana Valley

Kokand

Fergana Osh

0 — 200 km
0 — 120 miles

Nurata

Bukhara

Samarkand

Pamir Mountains

Türkmenabat Qarshi

Shakhrisabz

TAJIKISTAN

Ashgabat

Dushanbe

TURKMENISTAN

Termiz

IRAN

AFGHANISTAN

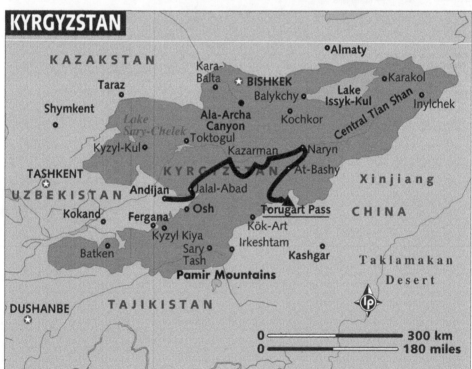

KYRGYZSTAN

KAZAKSTAN

Almaty

Kara-Balta

BISHKEK

Karakol

Taraz

Balykchy

Lake Issyk-Kul

Central Tian Shan

Inylchek

Shymkent

Lake Sary-Chelek

Ala-Archa Canyon

Kochkor

Kyzyl-Kul

Toktogul

Kazarman

Naryn

TASHKENT

KYRGYZSTAN

At-Bashy

Xinjiang

UZBEKISTAN

Andijan

Jalal-Abad

Osh

Torugart Pass

CHINA

Kokand

Fergana

Kök-Art

Kyzyl Kiya

Irkeshtam

Kashgar

Taklamakan Desert

Batken

Sary Tash

Pamir Mountains

DUSHANBE

TAJIKISTAN

0 — 300 km
0 — 180 miles

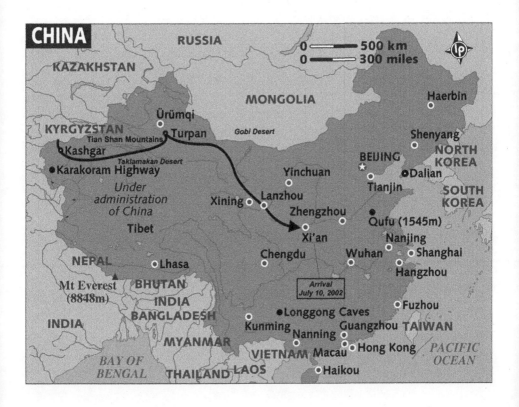

PART I—THE HEIGHTS OF THE PAMIRS
THIRD VOYAGE

(Summer–Autumn 2001)

I

LEAVING

Leaving, they say, is the hardest thing to do. But leaving yet again is harder still.

After starting out from Samarkand, Uzbekistan, two days ago, here I am back on the Great Silk Road, which has obsessed, delighted, and terrified me for two years now. My body protests: aching muscles, legs that refuse to go the distance, a feeling of unquenchable thirst brought on by the sudden heat, and nights filled with erotic dreams as my sex drive tries to hold out against the imposed fast. Despite what they say, the first step is not always the toughest. In the beginning, *every single mile* is torture. But most agonizing of all is tearing myself away from those I love. Yes—dollar-hungry cops and robbers, the frozen heights of the Pamir Mountains I'll have to cross, and the Taklamakan Desert (meaning in Uyghur, "the place from which one never returns")—all that will be my lot over the course of the 120 days of my 2001 walk. But no nightmare will be worse than the terrible isolation I'll have to endure all the way to Turfan,* that burning oasis, which the Chinese have nicknamed the "Land of Fire." I never get used to being alone. Still, today, more than ever before, I find myself craving the adventures, encounters, and joys that this intoxicating road has lavished upon me so far.

It's been two days since I took leave of the Chukurovs, my friends in Samarkand. Sabira, attentive soul that she is, did nothing to make

---

* Known also as Turpan.

my departure any easier, quite the contrary. Preoccupied with all the hardships I would soon face, she pampered me in her cozy home on the outskirts of town, gorging me with food: a large bowl full of fruit from their garden, copious servings of green tea, and revitalizing *plov*—Uzbekistan's national dish, consisting of rice, vegetables, and meat. Though I had eaten my fill, she insisted on extra helpings. "It's good for the heart!" she repeated with each additional spoonful, her kind, grandmotherly eyes smiling out from behind thick-lensed glasses obscuring much of her face. To help get me ready for the hell I'm heading into, she had transformed her patio into a little piece of paradise. As darkness fell, her granddaughters, Yulduz and Malika, and her son, Faroukh, kept me company around a basket of melt-in-your-mouth cherries. I had brought with me a copy of my book telling of my walk in the year 2000, and of the warm welcome their family had given me.* Mounikha Vakhidova, who assisted me during my stay in Samarkand last year, translated my account of it for them. Sabira was moved to tears: "While my husband was alive (he had been a literary critic celebrated throughout the Soviet Union), fifty authors from around the world stopped by our house each year. But none of them ever put my name in a book!"

Winter had been ruthless this year with temperatures dropping to -13°F. Pipes burst in the walls. A spring drought caused wells to dry up. People living outside the city limits have no more water and the apricots have ripened a month earlier than usual. The day before yesterday, things got even worse. The *chilla*, a period of scorching heat lasting forty days, suddenly hit. In two or three days, the *sarafon* will follow: lasting a full month, it's the hottest wave of summer heat, and, with its flaming arrows, it could very well prevent me from walking.

---

* *Longue marche: à pied de la Méditerranée jusqu'en Chine par la route de la Soie. II. Vers Samarcande* (Paris: Phébus, 2001). The English translation is available as *Walking to Samarkand: The Great Silk Road from Persia to Central Asia* (New York: Skyhorse Publishing, 2020).

I've chosen the worst possible time to get underway. But did I really have a choice? I had to decide whether to bake at the outset of my journey and head into the Fergana Valley at the hottest time of the year, or to leave much earlier and arrive in the Taklamakan Desert at the worst possible moment. Turfan, my final destination, is the hottest place in all China—though the entire country experiences blistering summer heat. I've made up my mind to sweat it out at the beginning so as to have cooler weather at the end. It's that childhood dilemma we have to deal with all of our lives: which should we eat first, the bread or the chocolate? To top it all off, I have to time my journey so that I reach the Pamir Mountains no later than August or early September, to avoid the possibility of snowstorms as winter draws near and reach my destination before mountain passes close down in this region known as the "roof of the world."

I added my last few pounds on the eve of my departure in Mounikha Vakhidova's small apartment. She speaks excellent French, delightfully rolling her R's. In this convivial Tower of Babel, each of her friends—some Tajik, some Uzbek—speaks in his or her native tongue since everyone understands both. The children, meanwhile, play and call to one another in Russian, and Mounikha and I speak French. When Central Asians sit down to a meal, the order in which the dishes are served matters little. Guests happily move from meats to vegetables, from sweet to savory without the slightest transition. It's a meal in which everyone nibbles at will: meat dumplings, grilled cauliflower, carrots, strained *fromage blanc* with basil and dill (known as *chaka*), green beans, onions, chicken, potatoes, *dolmas*, stuffed peppers, kabobs, and on and on.

It's truly a miracle I found it in me to get going again. Sabira set up a *karavot* for me out in her lush, cool garden. A *karavot* is a kind of platform on which you can eat, chat with friends, and sleep. I lie down and contemplate all the trees now heavy with fruit: a peach tree, a cherry, a plum, a mulberry, an apricot, a fig, a quince, a grapevine, and more. A vision of nirvana that I etch into my memory so that I'll be able to feast on it later on when I face rocky mountain slopes and desert sands. The next morning, even before I'm completely awake, I'm gorging on onion-filled *tikva* flatbreads, *pirozhki*, cheese, honey, and the delicious apricot jam that Sabira prepared the night before, and which I slather on *lepyoshka* (Uzbek bread). In a country that probably produces the best apricots in the entire world—*o'rik*—none of the fruit is lost: the kernels—*donak shorak*—are dried in the oven where they burst open, yielding superior almonds. Sabira slips a few into my backpack. It's a waste of time trying to tell her that I already bought some at the bazaar, along with a few handfuls of raisins: she knows hers are better.

As I make ready to face the road, I help myself to seconds from each dish since "it's good for the heart." Will I meet interesting people again this year? A pathway of cultures and friendships, of history and violence, of conquest, trade, fortunes, and plunder, the Silk Road has revealed itself slowly to me, step by step over the 3,730 miles (6,000 kilometers) I've traveled since starting out from Istanbul. I'm halfway through the journey. For the third year in a row, I'm off to set my bootprints in the sand and sun-softened asphalt. In four months, after crossing the fertile Fergana Valley, the highlands of Kyrgyzstan, and the Taklamakan Desert, I'll reach Turfan. But will I make it to the end? I'm sixty-three: maybe I'll run out of steam? Today, June 28, in the soothing warmth of the morning out on the Chukurovs' terrace, my head reeling, I have my doubts.

While the sun seems to linger just below the horizon, I prepare my belongings in silence, having already said my goodbyes last night. But that was assuming my kind hosts would let me leave without a word. . . . One by one, their eyes still full of sleep, they surround me. We all remain silent then, turning our palms up toward the sky, Sabira recites a short prayer, at the end of which we all perform the *fatiha*, the "amen" of Central Asian Muslims, which is also done when getting up from a meal, and which is performed by running one's hands down over the face, from forehead to chin.

And then, so as to tear myself away from the warmth of their friendship, I make a quick getaway, leaving Samarkand by way of the road heading north. I leave a little sand from my boots on their living room floor. But Sabira won't bother with the broom today, for then her friend might never return.

The route I'm taking is not the most direct, far from it. I'm going to kick off my walk this year by making a detour of at least ninety miles. The original route zigzags back and forth between the borders of Tajikistan and Uzbekistan. But if I want to dodge both the bullets of the Kalashnikov-wielding mujahideen and the Uzbek Army's big guns, I'll have to steer clear. Officially, nothing's going on. But travel agencies have been ordered not to send tourists into the Fergana Valley, especially in the Bekabad region where fundamentalist bullets are flying these days for the greater glory of Allah. Whatever's going on, I've been warned: all the borders are closed, there's no getting into Tajikistan. So, traveling north, I'll first reach the city of Angren, then turn east heading over the Kamchik Pass, which tops out at an altitude of 2,300 meters (7,550 feet). With the *sarafon*—the heat wave—it will be no walk in the park. And I'm not even sure, in this thin strip of land linking Uzbekistan's two regions bisected by Tajikistan, that I'll be able to steer clear of small bands of fundamentalists that train in Afghanistan and make incursions into the country every summer.

I've learned to cope with hot weather: I've brought three plastic water bladders, for a total of twelve liters, and I wrap my head in my kaffiyeh to avoid losing too much water. "Ulysses" follows on my heels. My friend Marcel Lemaître—a man with no need to go running the world over in search of wisdom since he already has an abundance of it within—gave me a hand transforming an old golf push cart that had been gathering dust in my attic, and which is now going to take over from EVNI,* my old two-wheeled traveling

---

* Translator's Note (TN): EVNI stands for the French words *Étrange véhicule non-identifié* (Strange, Unidentified Vehicle), the French equivalent of UFO (Unidentified Flying Object). Like Ulysses, Ollivier built EVNI so that he could pull his gear and water through the desert, rather than carry it on his back.

companion that I gave away to some kids in Samarkand last year. Wielding his magic blowtorch, Marcel reworked the compact, foldable contraption. Ulysses, with whom I hope to complete this "odyssey," will carry my twelve liters of water, my backpack stuffed with only the clothing I need, my more substantial first-aid kit this year, and some food. I've packed my camping gear in a duffel bag and hope to use it as little as possible, as I always prefer meeting people at a hotel or, better yet, staying with locals. Marcel and I had the good idea—or so we thought—of keeping Ulysses's original rubber-disk wheels, since that way, I'd never have a flat tire.

Quite the miscalculation. Only four days into my walk, as I'm nearing my layover city of Jizzakh under a sun burning the "Steppe of Hunger" as the Russians called it to a crisp, a suspicious noise makes me turn around. One of Ulysses's tires has literally melted on the scorching ground and is breaking apart. I fasten the pieces back together with some string, but just two hundred yards farther on, my cart's rolling on a rim. This doesn't bode well. If this is what happens on a good road, what will happen on mountain footpaths and desert trails? I fold Ulysses up for the two or three miles left between here and the city. The two of us hop into a crowded bus, under the unblinking gaze of fifty pairs of eyes.

From April 1931 to February 1932, an expedition of French explorers known as the caravan of the *Croisière Jaune*—the "Yellow Journey"—made its way across Asia. Two convoys, one starting at each end of the route, planned to meet up in the middle: one group headed east out of Beirut, and the other west from the Chinese coastline. The latter group, which included the famous paleontologist Pierre Teilhard de Chardin, was forced to interrupt its advance: its vehicles' rubber treads had begun to melt. Before the caravan could push on again, the old ones had to be replaced with new ones from Europe. The incident occurred after only ninety-three miles: Ulysses broke down after seventy-five! The thought of emulating such illustrious predecessors lifts my spirits. See, Bernard? You're not so pathetic after all! And neither is your friend Marcel!

The hotel (*gostinitsa*) where I find a room is part guesthouse, part den of thieves. A state-owned hotel during the communist regime, it was "privatized"; that is to say, the manager took it over for himself. His large family, a dozen idlers, lives at his expense. One of his sons, a scruffy, lank thirty-year-old with the bulging eyes of a toad, abruptly comes up to me an hour after my arrival:

"What's your room number?"

"Ask your sister, she's the one who checked me in."

"She doesn't want to tell me."

Now that he so naively informed me that he intends to poke around my little room, the following morning, I put padlocks on all my backpack pockets. In the evening, upon my return, I find them broken. The thief climbed up onto the balcony. All he took were a few of my notes, which I immediately piece back together. Everything that might have been of interest to him—my cash, camera, and GPS—I had on my person, as I always do. The following night, I get back into the habit of sleeping within easy reach of my open knife.

There's no running water above the third floor, but they've devised a solution: a poor old platinum-blond slave woman smelling of cheap perfume delivers bottles of water up to us so that we can void the toilets. The water is so muddy looking that I forgo washing up.

Another son has given himself an exotic name for this country: Juan. He looks less like a pirate than his brother, but drinks more heavily. All things considered, I prefer this one to the other, and we hit it off. He barely touches the *plov* I invite him to share with me, but he downs bottles of beer at the speed of light, caressing the waitress's bum each time she brings him another. He promises to drive me to the city's bazaar at 8:00 tomorrow morning where, he tells me, I'll find everything I need to get Ulysses back into working order. Before leaving, he introduces me to Grisha and Misha, two Russians who maintain the hotel's hot water heater, an enormous block of rust with plenty of leaks that might easily date from the days of Tamerlane.

At 10:00 a.m. the next day, after spending two hours waking Juan—who had kept right on drinking after bidding me farewell—we all hop into Juan's car: Micha, Grisha, Juan, and I. It's a stolen vehicle. We have to enter through the back doors, given that the front ones are jammed shut. The rascal starts the engine by touching two wires together in the steering column, and Juan, who fears that one day he'll run into the former owner, has slipped an enormous knife, practically a machete, alongside the shift lever so that he can defend "his property."

The two Russians are silent and business-like. Grisha has a very Slavic face. So much vodka has made him look older than his real age of fifty. He has white hair, raven-black eyebrows, and a pleasant smile. Micha is younger; he has a mop of black hair gone prematurely white at the temples, a svelte if not skinny body, and he puffs non-stop on a cigarette rolled in newspaper that goes out almost as soon as it's lit. They quickly find a pair of wheels about the same size as the ones currently on Ulysses, and which also have solid tires. But we spend all afternoon getting them to fit. Sitting on his haunches, Juan watches with great interest as we work. It's a banner day in the life of a man with too much time on his hands, and who drinks out of boredom. Grisha takes the original wheel that survived the drama back to his house and returns it to me in the evening, all patched up so I can use it as a spare. Now I can get going again, although none of this has me very reassured, for Ulysses is clearly not suited to the roads I'll be traveling in Kyrgyzstan and China.

At four in the morning, the thermometer reads 90°F. At noon, dazed from the heat, I have a hard time finishing the lavish dish the restaurant owner sets down in front of me as he proclaims the price: three hundred so'm. When I leave some meat around a bone, he hands me fifty so'm back: he'll sell the leftovers to another customer. I try to get him to keep the money, but he's an even more stubborn soul than I. While waiting for the heat to subside, I exchange a few words with him about the weather and local customs.

"How do you recognize the most beautiful bride in our country?" he asks, playing the smart aleck.

When I draw a blank, he explains:

"The one who cannot walk because she's weighed down with jewels!"

Prior to the days of the Soviets, a woman could be repudiated for any reason. Her jewels, inherited from her mother, were therefore her only worldly possessions and her sole safety net and source of independence, should she need it. So she always kept them on her person. Although repudiation is now a thing of the past, brides continue the tradition by donning all their jewelry for the wedding. It's most often made of silver.

I stop to chat with some little old men preparing *plov* in the cool shade of a mulberry tree. With goatees and traditional square *do'ppi* caps on their heads, chiseled faces and shiny boots, they make me think of characters from Joseph Kessel's "The Horsemen," minus their steeds and brawn.*

In the village of Pakhtakor, Komal quite literally bumps right into me. He's a strapping lad some thirty years old and has no doubt whatsoever that his English is very good. The arrival of a foreigner is quite an event for him. It's the chance he's been waiting for to prove that his people are the most hospitable anywhere in the world. It just so happens that today, the only thing I want welcoming me is a bed to sleep in. Clobbered by the heat, my body is still not used to the demands I'm making of it. I'm worn out and, too tired to be hungry, all I want to do is sleep.

But Komal has other plans for me. He's the nicest but most intrusive man I've ever met. He first invites half the village to come

---

* Joseph Kessel, *The Horsemen*, translated by Patrick O'Brien (New York: Farrar, Straus, and Giroux, 1968). Originally published as *Les Cavaliers* (Paris: Gallimard, 1967). TN: An adventure film based on the novel also entitled *The Horsemen* was released in the United States in 1971. Directed by John Frankenheimer, the film stars Omar Sharif and Jack Palance.

parading through the inn I checked into, so everyone can see him conversing in English with the foreigner. In the meantime, he had someone cook up a Pantagruelian plate of *plov* for me. I swallow a few grains of rice, one or two chunks of meat, then make as though I'm ready to head back to my room. But he bars the way: "Come on! Let's go check out the evening market!"

The evening market is held in a small square and consists of a fellow grilling *shashlik*—those thin, greasy kebabs—and three women selling flatbreads that they're carting around in baby carriages. Seeing how disappointed I am, Komal wants to make up for it. He drags me over to a concert hall where a rock band from Tashkent has hit the stage. The "musicians" are blasting their guitars for ten lifeless boys and fifteen teenage girls, all chaperoned by their mothers. Upon seeing my rather limited interest, he leads me to the town's nightclub, which, he makes a point of telling me, is run by a former prostitute. It's actually an odd sort of bistro fitted out with several curtained alcoves. From behind the curtains I hear laughter and whispering: but fear not, the former lady of the night keeps a careful watch over the young ladies' virtue.

Figuring that all the cultural excitement must have aroused my appetite, Komal orders a *shish kebab*—skewers of meat cooked in an aromatic sauce and served with broth and carrots. It's nearly midnight. I beg him to let me go to bed. We head back through narrow dirt streets plunged in total darkness, blithely stepping in all the rubbish everyone impulsively tosses out their front door. Komal's afraid that I might fall, and grabs me by the arm. He also finds that that way he can lead me every now and then to another door and introduce me to more of his friends. There's no way we can refuse when they invite us in for tea, for that would be an inexcusable faux pas. I'm ready to collapse. Suddenly, my friend exclaims:

"Come to think of it, I never gave you time to wash up! Let's head over to the bathhouse. It's run by a friend of mine."

He drags me to a sauna where the heat is so intense I can hardly breath. Scoured clean but even more wiped out, if that's even possible,

I get ready to make a mad dash for the hotel. Once again, Komal bars the way: "You have to meet a friend of mine who's an engineer!"

As we drink what I hope is our last tea, our host tells me that he works nights for the railroad, pulling twelve-hour watches.

"Twelve hours straight, making sure trains are on the right track?! But isn't that practically asking for an accident?"

"Not at all. There hasn't been a single night train for five years. I while away the hours studying English. By the way, what do you think?"

I think that the day he stops pronouncing English as if it were Uzbek, it might be comprehensible. But since I'm a nice guy, I offer an encouraging smile.

We finally get back to the hotel and I head straight to my room. I haven't completely taken off all my clothes when Komal bursts in without knocking, as is the custom here.

"There are some people in the dining room who have never seen a foreigner! They really want to meet you. I'd be so happy if you'd come by, just for a minute." Asleep on my feet, I follow him. The dozen or so revelers I meet downstairs have already had far too much vodka. But to celebrate the event, they order a bottle of Uzbek *shampan* and, hollering, ask my opinion of it. It's awful. But since my politeness knows no bounds, I tell them that it's just as good as French champagne. Delighted, they order another bottle and force me to down a second glass. Serves me right: we pay for every lie we tell.

It's nearly 1:00 in the morning when I finally fall into a deep sleep . . . only to be woken by someone shaking me and from music blasting from loudspeakers. A rather drunk woman is standing there, insisting that she wants to dance with me. I brush her off, but ten times over the course of an hour, Komal's friends come into the room, inspect Ulysses, and say a few words. It's impossible to close the door, for there's no key and no inside latch. I'm borderline comatose. Around 2:00, the loud voices stop but the music continues to blare. At my wit's end, I get up and poke around the deserted house. I finally discover the sound system in an empty room with a jazz tape spinning away in it, the volume at its highest setting. Komal's in the courtyard, seated on a chair.

"You told me you have to get up early. So I'm trying not to fall asleep so that I can wake you at dawn. But if I don't have the music, I won't be able to stay awake!"

Hell, as we all know, is paved with good intentions.

I unplug the stereo and take a two-hour nap, which hardly even counts. When I head off, Komal is sound asleep on his chair. I'm careful not to wake him. But around 9:00, he catches up with me on his bicycle, telling me that he's going to introduce me to some friends in the city where I'm planning to spend the night. I tell him to go back to Pakhtakor. Gently, but firmly. With him along, I'd die from exhaustion in no time at all.

The landscape is uniformly flat. What was once the "Steppe of Hunger" is more fertile today thanks to an intricate network of irrigation canals. The apricot trees are groaning under the weight of the fruit. Much of it has fallen to the ground, creating what looks like a yellow carpet around the trunks.

After dark, I find safe haven in a mosque. It's actually an abandoned factory onto which has been grafted a zinc, dome-shaped structure, surmounted by a crescent, also made of zinc. The imam who takes me in asks me not to mention his name to anyone. In Uzbekistan, Muslims keep the lowest possible profile. The communist regime has converted to democracy in words only, having kept the same police force and the same brutal tactics. But he most fears religious authorities, since they're the only ones who could do him harm or foster the emergence of a fundamentalist movement like the one now plaguing neighboring Afghanistan, solidly held by the Taliban, the "students of religion."

Up to this point, I've been traveling north, but I'm about to run into the Kazakh border. The region's national boundaries were drawn up by Stalin, who was good at governing by dividing. He made the "republics" interlock so closely that their populations are constantly border hopping. As long as the Central Asian republics remained de facto provinces of Moscow, that was of little consequence. But since emerging as independent states, things have gotten complicated. Some parts of Uzbek territory exist as enclaves within Kyrgyzstan, twelve, even twenty miles beyond the Uzbek border. The only way to get from Samarkand to Tashkent is to cross thirty miles of Kazakh territory. Motorists don't even slow down at the border and customs officials, who are Russian soldiers, make no attempt stop them.

In the village of Gagarin, I ask what my status would be as a pedestrian. Since I'd have to spend one night in Kazakhstan, I'd need a visa, and that, it turns out, can only be obtained in Tashkent. Under the best of circumstances, I'd have it in three weeks! That's clearly not an option. I'm therefore going to have to make yet another detour, skirting the border before heading back up toward Angren. Just thinking about all this exhausts me, so I settle into a shady patio and order a lukewarm beer to take a closer look at my maps. A burly fellow plumps himself down in front of me. His tank top shows off his arms, which are like those of a wrestler and covered in blue tattoos, while a thick, sooty mustache makes up for his bald, shiny head. He jingles a set of keys under my nose and points to his taxi, then cuts me off as though he were speaking to a child or some simple-minded fool:

"I'm Ashur Mouhamadief. They told me what you're doing and that you plan to get going again and walk forty kilometers. No, come on, just look at yourself! You seem tired, you're dirty. You need a bath and a bed. Come to my house. Svetlana will wash your things and make you something to eat."

My first inclination is to send him packing, but he has a warm smile and a twinkle in his eye. I grab a glass, set it in front of him, and pour him half my beer. A few minutes later, with Ulysses safe in the trunk of his car, Ashur stops in front of a large, drive-in gate and honks the horn authoritatively. A girl in her late teens, with long legs dangling from an ultra-short skirt, opens the gate for us and flashes me a radiant smile.

"That's Zarina, my daughter," Ashur says soberly—but I sense the pride in his voice. Another charming teen approaches, and he introduces her as well: Simona.

A little later, Svetlana arrives from the train station where she works. The three blond-haired women have stunning eyes, a mixture of cerulean blue and jade green. Eyes that are downright heavenly. The girls are thrilled to have a guest from abroad. Ashur tries to play the unsentimental parent, but you can see that he's more than just a little proud. In Central Asia, Russian men never marry local women, but the reverse is quite common, so I'm not surprised that Ashur—who is Tajik—has married a woman of Slavic origins. In no time at all, sweet Svetlana has handed me some of her husband's clothes and sent me into a steam room where I give myself a good scrubbing; meanwhile, she and her daughters busy themselves with the meal. Floating in Ashur's clothes while mine dry out on a line, I sit down for lunch. The fare is delicious, but most satisfying of all is the vision of these divine faces. When we've finished eating, my host invites me to get into his taxi along with Zarina and youthful, angelic Simona. Their mother has to stay home to can large pickles, feed the eight pigs in the backyard, and harvest the eggs laid by the chickens now scratching about in the alleyways of their vegetable garden. We traverse the sunbaked city and pull up in front of a house surrounded by high walls. An Uzbek woman comes out to greet us under the courtyard trees.

"My wife."

"But . . . Svetlana?"

"I have two wives!"

This is his legal wife. Although Ashur's religion is perfectly fine with him having several spouses, it's forbidden under Uzbek law. But no one seems to be bothered by the situation. In his second family, Ashur not only has three more daughters, but a little boy as well who has clearly understood that it was for *him* that all these women and his father were waiting. He already has the look and mannerisms of a little tyrant.

On the way back, Ashur tells me how happy he is to have me stay with him. A number of years ago, he says, he was a bulldozer driver in Kazakhstan, living in a shack in abject conditions along with a half dozen other workers. One day, when he was suffering from a particularly bad case of the blues, a Kazakh invited him home to wash up, rest, and launder his clothes. He was endlessly grateful and swore that, were the opportunity to ever arise, he would return the favor, in payment of what he considered to be a debt. I myself am that opportunity and he's grateful to Allah for it! His own experience understandably allows him to grasp just how much his warm welcome is joy to my soul.

Out on the patio, as night begins to fall, I chat with kind Zarina, endowed with a captivating smile and eyes like the sea and sky. I ask her how old she is.

"Seventeen. In two years, I'll be married."

"Do you have a boyfriend?"

"No, my father won't let me date boys."

I pity the lads.

"Will your father choose your husband for you?"

"That's our tradition."

She tells me that she has a crush on one of her university classmates. Meanwhile, she attends law school and helps her mother with the housework. They can't look to Ashur for that, for he's a man and, as such, doesn't have to lift a finger around the house.

"And if your husband were to take a second wife, what would you say to that?"

She shrugs her lovely bronzed shoulders: "Nothing. That's our tradition."

We stop talking, the both of us lost in thought. I look at this very pretty young woman and think to myself how nature so often smiles favorably when two ethnicities are involved.

I leave before sunup, clean as a whistle and reenergized by Ashur and Svetlana's warm welcome, which remains in my thoughts for a time as I make my way down the road. I walk joyfully. Pleasant encounters like this boost my morale. I've been rebuilding strength for a week now. My leg muscles are increasing in size from all the exercise, and my body's adjusting to the heat. A few strong bursts of endorphins—that natural drug all walkers love—and I'm singing as I walk along the Kazakh border, flagged here by metal fences like the ones used for chicken coops back home.

The conversation I had with Zarina confirms my understanding that, although the Muslim faith lost ground when communist or Christian Russians took over, Islamic culture is still strongly present between the Amu Darya and the Syr Darya rivers, especially in terms of social structure.

Beginning in 712 CE, the year the Arabs captured Samarkand, Islam progressively grew to become the region's only religion, all the way up to the early twentieth century. Prior to their arrival, however, both Zoroastrianism (which was a state religion in Persia) and Nestorianism were well established.

The conquerors, realizing just how important trade and money were between the two rivers, decreed that anyone who converted to Islam would be exempt from taxation. A brilliant idea—too brilliant, in fact! So many people renounced their former religion that, in just a few short years, the treasury ran dry. So they decided to levy a new tax, resulting in public outcry and unrest that finally settled down around the year 750.

II

UMAR

At noon, I stop in a small *choyxona*—a teahouse—and order a cup of tea. The manager, a woman, comes over to sit down at my table and says, in French: *"Je m'appelle Sadinsa."* That's all she remembers from the courses she once took in Andijan, the town she grew up in. She then brings me a dozen dishes I didn't order and encourages me to do them justice while pointing out, this time in Russian, that "it's free."

In the evening, in the village of Mirzachol, I observe that pleasure is an excellent fuel: for the first time since Samarkand, I've traveled thirty pain-free miles! The *choyxona* that I settle on is run by four women: a mother and her three daughters. They laugh, sing, babble on, and speak to me at length in Uzbek, without my grasping a single word. Madina, the youngest, introduces me to her daughter Malakhad, a little baby spoiled rotten by her aunts and grandmother. Pointing to the child, Madina runs her index finger across her eyebrow. When I show that I don't understand, she then places her finger under her nose and says *"Papa, nyet."* A single mother! That's a crime here, one made all the more serious since the young woman refuses to reveal the name of the "culprit."

I catch a glimpse of the father a little before I fall asleep out on the terrace where they've set up a bed for me. He tiptoes up to the house, scratches at the door, then heads back out before dawn. Madina, who noticed that I was awake, sends me a knowing wink. What a strange country this is, where Ashur can show off his two wives, but, just one village over, a man has to hide in order to sleep with the mother of his

19

child! Just before leaving, as I'm getting ready to take my hostesses' picture, five or six men and teenage boys sipping tea come over and plant themselves front and center. I chase the men away and, believe me, the women are delighted! My word, it's nice to be honored this way, and by a foreigner to boot!

I'm approaching the Syr Darya, one of Central Asia's largest rivers. Like the Amu Darya, which I crossed last year, it flows into the Aral Sea. The two rivers bracket a vast and rich territory that the Romans named *Transoxiana* and the Arabs *Mā Warā' an-Nahr*. A hundred yards or so before the bridge spanning the river, I come to a police roadblock. Until now, I haven't had my papers checked. But I've learned from past experience: Uzbek cops are eager for dollars and those of the Fergana Valley, or so say all the guidebooks, are down-right thugs. They once went so far as to remove one unfortunate tourist's clothes just to get at his greenbacks. Consequently, when they motion me to stand in line along with all the drivers waiting their turn in front of the canvas shelter, I'm already on my guard. Last year, I had to stand my ground against policemen who tried to force me into the station, behind closed doors. They clearly hoped to rob me. But this year has been a surprise, for those I've run into thus far have seemed almost indifferent. They're no doubt going to make up for that now!

The unhappy drivers all know they'll have to pay. So they hold their vehicles' papers in one hand, and the banknotes to give to the cops in the other. The cops' boss, an expressionless roly-poly, is com-fortably ensconced in an armchair beneath a canvas tarp for pro-tection from the sun, but which does nothing to prevent him from sweating profusely as he collects the bills and places them in stacks on a table in front of him. He entrusts non-cash donations to a sub-ordinate, who wanders off now and again to stash them away in a small building out back. The boss must have felt that the people he was robbing were being disrespectful by simply standing there and looking him up and down; so he had a piece of fabric hung in front of him at eye-level such that, in order to speak with him, the drivers have to peek underneath it, crouching down, perhaps even kneeling. All forms of the abuse of power disgust me, and this one more than most. I'm furious.

By the time my turn comes around I've made up my mind: the swine won't get me to bend a knee! I'm tense, nervous, and outraged by this touch of sophistication that humiliates those being fleeced. I bypass the hanging cloth, approach the roly-poly from the side, and toss him my passport. He looks at me, picks up the document without going through it, hands it back to me, and motions to one of his minions to let me go. The police have clearly been instructed to leave foreigners alone. The podgy cop knows perfectly well that I alone have more money than all the others he's making bow down before his highness. If he doesn't try to wrest a banknote from me, it must be that he's been given strict orders not to. Have Uzbek policemen stopped going after tourists' dollars as they once did? Have the country's leaders finally understood that, if they let that happen, they're killing the goose that lays the golden eggs?

The Syr Darya is nothing at all like its alter ego, the Amu Darya. That was a furious sea; this is a pond. A trickle of clear water lies idly between two high banks lined with poplar trees. Kingfishers are searching for minnows. The water diversion projects must, for the most part, take place upstream. The drought that Faroukh mentioned may also explain why the water is so low.

On the opposite bank, I worry for a moment that my papers are about to be checked yet again. A dozen uniformed police officers are seated at tables under the trees. But it's a *choyxona*! The house specialty is fried fish and given the time of day, I can't resist. At a table near mine, an inquisitive couple asks me about my journey. We chat, then the man gets up, goes over to the police officers, and says a few words to their boss, another roly-poly. I'm beginning to think that there's either something about their rank that quickly fattens them up or that bosses are chosen on the basis of weight. They return together, followed shortly thereafter by the other cops. The top dog asks me a thousand questions and I finish my meal having to obstinately refuse the many offers to buy me yet another round of fish! Their money probably comes from plundering, too. But though I try to give them the cold shoulder, nothing can dampen their enthusiasm. Two of them take out cameras and insist that I pose with their comrades for a souvenir photo. The boss does a double-take when, after he asks, I tell him my age. To put his mind at rest, he wants to see my passport. He thinks he's reading my last name, but goes to the wrong line: "Bernard, André, Michel . . ." Then, in the same breath, he asks me for my autograph, which—so as not to confuse him—I sign: "Bernard, André, Michel." When I ask to pay, the tavern keeper tells me that the bill has already been settled. Robber-cops on the left bank, generous cops on the right: there's definitely no lack of contrasts in this country!

Yet this string of kind acts is still not over, for, two days later, in the little village of Almalyk, three police officers, tipped off by the local grapevine, come to my hotel that evening . . . to wish me a good night. You see what I mean?

They're not the only ones who show me a little kindness. A man I chat with briefly offers me a large watermelon. His village used to be called "Socialism." It was renamed "Pakhtakor." I ask him why they didn't choose "Kapitalizm," which gets him laughing. He explains that these days, people are wary of politics here. Miss Nafissa, a young woman with a deep dimple in her chin, comes over carrying two teakettles. There's warm water in one so that I can wash my clothes, and cold water in the other, so that I can rinse them. Water is scarce. Only because I'm a foreigner am I allowed to waste it. Thank you, sweet Nafissa!

Irrigated cotton fields and freshly harvested wheat cut high on the stem. Rising from the horizon of this flat, featureless landscape are the treeless mountains I'll soon have to climb. I stop to watch a family busy at work in a field. A young man is perched atop a horse harnessed to an ard. His father has the horse firmly by the hand so that the furrow will be straight. Two children—a boy and a girl—are throwing seeds into the gaping wound. Behind them, a woman armed with a rake, which she moves in precise sweeps, covers them back up. Beneath a tree, a woman and her daughter, busily preparing food, invite me for tea and enthuse over my "achievement." I lack the words to tell them that my walk is easy as compared to the work that they have to do, out in the fields where the blazing sun burns their bare skin.

As the miles go by, I abandon along my route all the questioning and regrets of those first few days. Very gently, I've entered into the rhythm of a journey that, step by step, will lead me to the highest peaks of the Pamirs.

My collection of memorable encounters continues to grow. I'd like you to meet fifteen-year-old Ulugbek, who works from dawn till dusk in a *choyxona*. He used to dream of going to college and traveling. But he's the oldest of five siblings, and they all have to be fed and sent to school. So seven days a week, never surrendering his boyish smile, he runs from table to table serving meals and hundreds of liters of tea. Every now and again, his boss gives him a day off. A dream.

And then there's Khusniddin Renkulov, who grabs hold of me the moment he spots me on the road. He snatches Ulysses from my grasp and guides us to his restaurant. The last foreigner he saw was a Danish cyclist in 1999. But that story is now old hat, so he's delighted to have new one he can share—mine. Meanwhile, he recounts his.

He once traveled to France—to Bordeaux—where he spent three or four days as part of a Communist Party delegation. On the return trip, he had a three-hour layover between flights. He headed out of Orly Airport and walked like a madman without stopping. He wanted to see the French capital. "Paris is beautiful, but I never saw the Eiffel Tower," he tells me, lifting his eyes to the heavens. I don't have the heart to inform him that he probably never got any farther than the suburbs of Antony or Kremlin-Bicêtre! During the Soviet-Afghan War, Khusniddin was on board a Russian tank when it was struck and incinerated by a Stinger missile. He was the only survivor, waking up after being in a coma for twenty-one days, but he was badly injured. He was granted a three-penny pension, not enough to live on. So he opened the restaurant we're in, where he works eighteen-hour days. He takes no pride in that, but nor does he have any regrets: he has nothing else to do and he's an insomniac. And he has to be able to afford school tuition for two sons and a daughter, as well as the three packs of cigarettes he smokes every day. He tells me not to camp near Kamtchik Pass: they've laid mines in the area to trap mujahideen soldiers who train with the Taliban in Afghanistan. While he was busy telling me of his misfortunes, he prepared a plate of *gouyash* for me: buckwheat flour, carrots, and eggplant puree, topped with two fried eggs.

Lovely Diliara waits tables in a restaurant named Buyuk Ipak Yo'li (The Great Silk Road), where I feel obligated to stop. Her smiles and charms are somewhat self-serving: since there's always some chance that a knight in shining armor might carry her off to the paradise of the West, no efforts should be spared. Yes, he's sixty-three years old, but no one's perfect! She has serious competition, however, in the person of Fatima, who works here, too. She tries her luck by slipping me a little piece of paper with her address on it. If I drop by her place, she promises to wash my shirt. So I check into a hotel.

Delba Abdulayeva is deputy mayor of Angren, a city of 170,000 inhabitants that sprang up on the "Steppe of Hunger" fifty years ago after the discovery of a large deposit of coal. I was taken to see her since she's the only person at city hall who speaks a foreign language. Before entering politics some twenty years ago, she taught English. I'd like to find a computer so I can check my email. She promises to do what she can, but, in the meantime, she calls over two journalists from the *Angrenskaya Pravda* who put me through a long, drawn-out interview. Delba tells me that, just ten years ago, brainwashed by propaganda like everyone else, she thought that all Westerners were egotistical, idiotic monsters. "We believed that only *we* could have good intentions," she confesses, while marveling at the fact that the

two or three Europeans she actually has met don't fit the stereotype
that had been instilled in her.

"Uzbek democracy is special. The mayor was ousted."

"By whom?"

"The *Hakim*."

The *Hakim* she's referring to is at once the chief executive and a
kind of all-powerful prefect in the province where Angren is located.*

"Are you going to elect a new mayor?"

"Yes."

"Are there candidates?"

"Not yet, the *Hakim* will nominate one soon."

"Just one?"

"Yes."

"And what if he doesn't receive a majority of votes?"

"That has never happened. But if it did, the *Hakim* would simply
nominate another."

I get lost in Angren's bazaar. The women farmers, perched atop stone
tables surrounded by their carefully scrubbed vegetables, laugh in a
show of gold teeth. Making his way past Russian women in tailored
outfits, and Uzbeks, Tajiks, and Kazakhs in baggy, colorful robes, is
an old, hunch-backed *aksakal* in a long, gray frock coat, cinched at
the waist by a garish scarf.†

Delba comes by to pick me up at the *gostinitsa* where I checked
into the most expensive suite, the one costing a dollar and a half a
night. For that price, I have at my disposal plenty of plastic bottles
filled with water, which do the job of the toilet's broken flusher. The
shower has only one tap: no one bothered to install a pretend faucet
for hot water. The deputy mayor informs me that she has located
a computer with an Internet connection in one of the city offices.

---

* TN: Each province in Uzbekistan has its own *Hakim*.
† TN: An *aksakal* (also spelled *oqsoqol* or *aqsaqal*)—meaning "white beard" in Turkic
languages—is a respected male elder.

So off we go, trying as best as we can not to walk in the sun. The place sits across from a church abuzz with Uzbek children eager to enjoy what's being handed out to them—cheap candy and video-cassettes—the rather obvious goal of which is to convince them all to convert to Christianity. I discover that the institution is financed by Korean-Americans. Which just goes to show that diplomacy, like God, works in mysterious ways.

As I leave Angren, I know that I'll be leaving behind the immense plain I've been traveling since leaving Samarkand and will face the first real challenge of my journey: the Kamchik Pass, which rises at its peak to 2,300 meters (7,550 feet). Uzbekistan is shaped a bit like an opera lorgnette: two larger areas of land connected in the north by a narrow pass. Uzbek authorities realized that the current route linking the two parts of its national territory by way of Tajikistan was a vulnerability. So, at great expense, it has decided to open a new route through the land bridge; it climbs into the mountains between the Kazakh border to the north and the Tajik border in the south. Enormous construction vehicles are currently blasting through the rock.

Around noon, without warning, Ulysses's tow bar snaps clean in two. I try to repair it with my walking stick, but to no avail. Seeing what time of day it is, I make for a *choyxona* a thousand feet down the road and order a meal: I want to eat first, to keep my spirits up despite the mishap. I have no idea how I'm going to resolve the matter. But Kamal, who's having lunch at the next table over, knows exactly what to do. Before I'm even done eating, he has Ulysses in the bed of his truck. He then drives us six miles back the way I've already come, to where a welder interrupts his work on an ailing bulldozer and sets about reinforcing my cart with a steel rod big enough to jack up the Great Pyramid of Giza. All done in the blink of an eye: he's a true "para-mechanic"! While our blacksmith is busy at work, I notice that cracks are already starting to form in what were supposed to be indestructible tires. The night before, I redid my calculations:

if I stick to my current walking schedule, I'll arrive at the Kyrgyz border two days *after* my visa expires. Cursed visa! I'm going to have to leapfrog a few stages, especially seeing that I now need to plan on taking an extra day in order to weld some honest-to-goodness wheels onto Ulysses's frame. What an awful idea it was to throw myself into such a perilous adventure!

That's precisely what I'm thinking as I nostalgically start dreaming of my rosebushes back in Normandy. Why do I have to deal with these bureaucrats who get to decide, on a piece of paper, whether or not I'm allowed to visit their countries' wonders for thirty full days, but not a single day more? It's as if they were forcing me to visit their country the way Khusniddin had to visit Paris: in three hours, with an eye to his watch!

Pleased that Ulysses's operation went smoothly, Kamal and I dive into the lake that supplies Angren with water. "Dive into" is a bit of an exaggeration. The water level is rather low—which suits my savior just fine since he doesn't know how to swim and so just splashes around in a large puddle. The dual challenge now facing me has me increasingly worried: cutting two stages out of my itinerary *and* fixing Ulysses. I have no choice but to switch to larger wheels with inflatable tires, which will better withstand the heat and the bumps.

At the base of the slope leading to the mountain pass, the owner of an inn refuses to serve me dinner. "Everything I have is for the military," he tells me, in a tone that admits no exceptions. The army is all around, jittery and inquisitorial. Every mile or so, soldiers watch me with sharp, suspicious eyes and want to see my papers; they circle around Ulysses but refrain nevertheless from searching my bags despite how much they would obviously like to. They fear an infiltration of "terrorists," and this strip of land is indeed an ideal location for them, with Tajikistan to the south and Kazakhstan to the north, each less than a day's hike away. There will be no blessing for the innkeeper. Since he holds a monopoly here, I start uphill on an empty stomach. Fortunately for me I filled my water bags earlier that day, since, although it's late, I'm already dripping in sweat.

With darkness beginning to fall, I decide to pitch my tent beside Hilola's cabin.

Hilola is forty years old and must have once been quite beautiful. Today, she's worn out, aged before her time. She sells juice and cigarettes to passing trucks and cars from her shack, but the road is so steep at her location that few stop. Hilola has her twenty-three-year-old son with her to lend her a helping hand (doing what, for heaven's sake?), and her twelve- or thirteen-year-old daughter who does the cooking. Slouched in a chair, she speaks in a monotone, plaintive voice. When it's time to eat, some kids come running like devils out of nowhere, a few as naked as the day they were born, but covered in dirt from head to toe!

"Are they all yours?"

"I have twenty."

"Twenty children??!!"

"I have two others in my belly. That's enough!"

She tells me with a sarcastic smile that Karimov, the country's president, decorated her because she has the largest family in all Uzbekistan! With twins on the way, she'll be shoring up her "record."

"*Zharko! Zharko!*" (Hot! Hot!). In the early hours of the morning, the father of Hilola's children returns home, sponging his forehead. He stopped by for a quick visit during the night, then drove away again with his eldest son in a car that, by some miracle, is holding together, although not without emitting loud squeals of protest. The vehicle is packed to the roof with old oil and tar drums. When he's not busy making babies with his wife, the fellow occupies himself by making things out of scrap metal. He pretty much repeats the same words over and over: "*Zharko! Zharko!*" But what about his pregnant wife, doesn't the heat bother her, too? It doesn't seem to have even crossed his mind. It depresses me beyond all reason to have stopped here. Misery—when it is forced on people like this, though everyone knows that nothing can be done about it—always breaks my spirit. As compared with such embryonic existences, the life of a mayfly seems almost enviable.

I've resumed the climb to the top of Kamchik Pass, stopping only for police checks. I climb slowly, taking small steps, towing Ulysses with both hands, leaning over the asphalt, which has already begun to soften even though the sun is only just over the horizon. The salt tablets I suck on seem to have no effect; my clothes, once stiff from all the dirt, are now soft from all the sweat, but the salt in them stings my skin wherever it's raw from friction, especially at my hips, and between my thighs and buttocks. With each minute like an eternity, it takes me five hours to finally reach the top. A tunnel has been dug about 150 feet below the pass's natural summit. Two soldiers ask to see my papers but don't bother to study them too hard. They won't let me through; they have to consult with their boss first. Sitting on a stone, I pass the time looking out over the broiling plain, which stretches as far as the eye can see. The eye plunges into the deep, barren valley and catches on the snow-capped peaks flanking it, both on the Kazakh and Tajik sides. I'm chomping at the bit. I'd like to head back down the other slope as quickly as possible, but the soldiers don't seem to be joking around. They finally return accompanied by a junior officer with three gold teeth; he thumbs through my passport once again, then looks me over at such close range that I could probably tell you the brand of vodka he has been drinking since breakfast. He finally gives the two soldiers their orders, and they lead me away, one to my right and one to my left, their assault rifles tightly in their hands. I try to make small talk but get no reply. When we reach the middle of the tunnel, two other soldiers come to meet us and take charge of me. At the other end, they show my passport to another boss who pages through it for such a long time that he'll soon have memorized the entire thing! Finally, they hand it back and I rush off. Other soldiers are standing around, most of whom have only a knife for a weapon. A fort overlooks the road; two men in a mirador are keeping watch. I figured I'd seen my last police checkpoint. Unfortunately, twenty yards farther on, a police officer stops me.

"Passport."

"But I just . . ."

"Passport!"

It's best not to argue, these are panicky men. Patience, Bernard! And that's the right decision, for everything goes smoothly.

With Ulysses pushing me from behind, I'm off as if I had wheels, too. I know that I'll pay dearly for this later on, since heading down-hill is especially hard on the legs, but I don't give a damn. I want to polish off as much road as I can. As I'm hurtling down the steep incline, I catch my first glimpse of the vast, flat Fergana Valley in the fading daylight. For Silk Road travelers, this valley was unavoidable: it was a little piece of paradise before they faced the brutal, ice-covered slopes of the Pamir Mountains, followed by the burning sands of the Taklamakan Desert. Above all, for a large number of merchants who would not cross over into China, it marked the end— or rather the halfway point—of their journey. Before long, near the Stone Tower described in the second century in Ptolemy's *Geography*, they would be able to sell or trade their merchandise, then, as wealthy men, head back to the comforts of home. The Fergana's opulence was legendary, and news of its superior horses had spread to the very ends of the known world. Which, moreover, would eventually wind up causing it a fair bit of trouble.

I camp in the middle of a field and at noon the following day I stop for lunch beneath a tree, in front of an inn where tables have been set out wherever there's a little shade. On the back of a map, I sketch out the changes I'd like to make to my two-wheeler so that I'll be able to explain them to a bicycle merchant in Kokand. After my meal, I'm slow getting started again. Yesterday's descent, just as I feared, ruined my legs. Tremendous fatigue, made worse by the intensity of the sun that bakes everything it touches, starts gently nudging me into an irrepressible siesta, when a man next to me—a big, lanky devil with such disheveled hair that you'd think he had a handful of hay on his head—asks:

"What's that drawing?"

Central Asian men are unabashedly curious and ask the darnedest questions. I'd rather sleep than discuss my mechanical troubles, but the man has an honest look about him that I like. So I explain. The devil of a man gives it some thought for a moment, takes a closer look at Ulysses, then jumps on his bicycle, blurting back in my direction:

"I live two kilometers from here, in Chinabad! I'm Umar. Stop by to see me, we'll have melon!"

Yeah whatever. I have neither the time nor the inclination to eat melon, especially with this deadline hanging over my head and my visa's expiration date seemingly flashing before my eyes like an endless daymare. I sleep for half an hour, then hurry back onto the burning road, having already completely forgotten the unwelcome meddler. But, as I'm making my way through Chinabad, there he is, sitting at the crossroads, with a melon in one hand and a large knife in the other.

"I was waiting for you! Come on, my house is just fifty meters further."

"But I'm in a hurry and . . ."

"It won't take long."

His voice is calm, reassuring, warm. How can I refuse? I follow him, while promising myself all the while to leave as soon as I've had his slice of watermelon. Through a large door, we step into a kind of junk-filled hangar that's almost as disorganized as my own attic back home, and it makes me really like the man. An old kid's bike hangs on the wall. He points to it:

"Your cart's wheels!"

Hand tools of all sizes lie about here and there in the dust; a bench grinder with bare electrical wires hanging out of it and a greasy electric welding device covered in leprous paint are the only pieces of machinery. With one sweeping blow of his knife, Umar splits the melon in half. He cuts a slice off and hands it to me; then, pointing to a bench taken from a dissembled truck in a corner of his workshop, says:

"Make yourself comfortable, I'll fix it for you. It won't take long."

After all, whether here or in Kokand, what difference does it make? I take out my sketches, but Umar doesn't seem interested. He appears to know exactly what he wants to do and how he's going to do it. He goes out to the far end of the yard where he rummages noisily through a pile of old junk metal, then returns with a few iron rods covered in rust. A boy runs up to shake my hand. It's Laziz, Umar's son, a little fourteen-year-old fellow with a determined, sincere, and warm-hearted look in his eyes. The T-shirt he's wearing probably hasn't been washed since the start of the year, and he shuffles about in a pair of old rubber slippers held together with string. His father quickly gets him up to speed. He goes over and takes down the bike—*his* bike—then proceeds to remove the wheels. He checks the hubs and tightens up the spokes with the same mindful efficiency of his father who, in just a few short minutes, has chopped Ulysses's old wheels off, making me shudder in fear: did he really understand what I wanted? His son seems to read the look on my face.

"My dad used to teach shop at a junior high school in Kokand."

The former teacher cuts, welds, and bends the iron rods almost without taking measurements. He's one of those tinkering geniuses who forms a mental picture of what he wants to do, then applies it with a cool head and steady hand. The electric arc throws dazzling light into the workshop's darkest corners. For nearly two hours, father and son work nonstop; then, in a few short minutes, the different pieces of the puzzle come together, and then ta-dah! there's my Ulysses, fitted with two wheels that measure about two feet in diameter. Perched atop its high legs, my cart looks as elegant—and as fragile—as a sulky. My doubts as to its sturdiness must be written on my face, for Umar, with a spring surprising for a man his age, suddenly leaps up and does a little dance on my traveling companion.

"With this little guy, you can head safely into the mountains!"

We celebrate by slicing into another melon and downing two pots of tea. As we're doing that, Laziz builds a fire.

"You're my guest for dinner. It's too late for you to get going again, so you'll spend the night here."

And he points to a *karavot* beneath the arbor—one of those platforms for sitting and sleeping.

Within a half hour, he puts together a mutton dish smothered in a velvety brown sauce, which we wolf down in a blink. For dessert, Laziz climbs onto a chair and takes down three large clusters of powder-blue grapes dangling over our heads. Umar is gifted at creating whatever atmosphere he wants, whether for work or relaxation. After focusing all his attention on welding, he's now at ease, mindful of his guest. He tells me that one of his greatest wishes would be to come to see me in Paris and visit the Louvre, and he asks me a thousand questions about it. As for me, I'm relieved. Ulysses is up and running and I shouldn't have any trouble tackling the valley and, more importantly, the Kyrgyz Mountains.

Suddenly the garden door opens, and a policeman walks in. I tense up. Ten police checks in one day is more than enough, thank you very much! Please tell me they haven't come looking for me even here! Umar reassures me. I have nothing to fear from this fellow. He's here almost every evening to try to beat my host at chess. They set up their pieces while Laziz, in twenty moves, neatly eliminates me. His father emerges victorious, as he nearly always does, and the son and policeman play a final game just for fun, which ends in a loss for Laziz. The policeman laughs, revealing a mouthful of gold. At times I find myself wondering whether, in Central Asia, every baby's first tooth is made of gold!

Lying on my mechanically-inclined host's *karavot*, gazing up at the stars peeking through the grape leaves, I doze off with my mind at ease, and get a good night's sleep. In the morning, Umar shows up with a big steaming teapot. He rose before dawn, loaded all my gear onto Ulysses, and ran a few tests. All I have left to do is pay him, but I expect it will be a struggle.

"How much do I owe you?"

"Just send me the photos you took, that's all."

"I want to pay you. Not for your labor, but for the huge favor you did me."

He hesitates, then goes along with the idea. He asks me for the equivalent of two dollars. I give him a twenty-dollar bill. Under his tousled mop of hair—I have no doubt that there's not a single comb to be found anywhere in the house—his face turns beet red.

"Pay me in so'm."

Laziz comes to my rescue. He knows a moneychanger at the bazaar, it won't a problem. His father asks: how much money is that? Laziz explains that it's more or less what his father earns in one month. Umar places the note down in front of me: he won't take it.

I eventually have to give the money to Laziz. I hug his father and set off again: I find a melon sitting atop Ulysses—a gift from my amazing handyman! This miraculous encounter lets me skip Kokand, a city that, though steeped in history, is of little interest today. In the eighteenth and nineteenth centuries, it was the home of a khanate as brutal, obscurantist, and despotic as those of Bukhara and Khiva. The three cities, moreover, spent much of their time battling one another. Kokand's downtown was considered at one time to be among the greatest religious centers of all Central Asia with nearly sixty madrasas (Qur'anic schools) and, depending on the source, between five and six hundred mosques.

The wealth of these cities dates back two thousand years. In the first century BCE, the Xiongnu, a nomadic people living in northern China, made repeated attacks on the Empire, whose riches fascinated them: they referred to it as the "great shining" civilization. Emperor Wudi, who needed a cavalry worth its salt, sent, to that end, a delegation tasked with purchasing Fergana Valley horses. He had heard about its famous steeds from Zhang Qian, who had traveled West in search of allies, and was the first to "open" the Silk Road from the Chinese side.

Powerful and reputed for their stamina, the horses of this valley beyond the Pamir were heartier than the ponies of the steppe, which Wudi's own army used, just like those of his enemies. The emperor's need for horses was all the more critical since his last campaign against the Huns had cost him one hundred thousand animals. Carried away by their imaginations and stories told by travelers, the Chinese transformed the Fergana horse into a mythical creature, calling it the "dragon-horse" or "heavenly-horse." It was said to have been born of a mare that had paired off with a dragon. It had hard, wear-resistant hooves that didn't require shoeing, and a peculiar characteristic that fired their imagination: it sweated blood! It was later discovered that the cause of this small loss of blood was actually a tiny parasite that lived in the horses' skin.

The King of Dayuan and the rulers of the Fergana wanted to avoid running afoul of the Mongols (who were nearby) and did not feel threatened by the Chinese (who were far away). So they refused to sell him their steeds. That angered Wudi. An army of sixty thousand men with quartermasters and servants set off for the valley. With them, they took what they'd need to prepare a few snacks: one hundred thousand cattle and nearly fifty thousand horses, camels, and mules. Half of this army, nearly thirty thousand men, reached the fertile valley, and its inhabitants took refuge within their city's high walls. Hoping to get the besieged population to concede defeat out of thirst, the Chinese generals, who had brought their civil engineers with them, diverted the river from which the city drew its water. In forty days, the resistance was crushed; the conquerors stormed into the main square and decapitated its military leaders. But opposition leaders hunkered down in the central fort and threatened, should they be attacked, to slay their best animals before killing themselves. Furthermore, it was rumored that some allies were on their way and that Roman engineers had already reached the fort to drill wells and end the water shortage. So negotiations got underway. The Chinese left with several dozen of the finest specimens of "heavenly" horses and three thousand lower-grade stallions and mares.

Special stud farms were set up. The price Wudi had to pay was high: of the sixty thousand men who had set out, only ten thousand returned to Xi'an. But Wudi had acquired a weapon that he believed would allow him to keep the nomads at bay. And crucially, he now also possessed the horses that would accompany him on his journey to the heavens.[*]

The second crisis to strike Kokand was more recent. At the end of the nineteenth century, the Fergana Valley was invaded by the Czar and transformed into a vast, lush field of cotton. In 1917, as the Bolshevik Revolution was proving triumphant, some of Kokand's inhabitants threw off Russian control and established an Islamic republic. The Red Army's response was incredibly violent: tens of thousands of inhabitants were put to the sword, the city was pillaged, and its religious buildings burned or knocked down. It would never recover. Today, all that remains for visitors is the palace of the last Khan—a puppet leader set up by the Russians—who starved the valley so that he could build a residence for himself containing some one hundred and ten rooms.

I leave the road heading south I've been following and, upon reaching the first houses, turn east. In the evening, an Afghan named Misha offers to put me up. He's a fine example of a small-minded, alcohol-driven junior officer. He opened a bistro. That's where I have my dinner, while immersing my terribly aching feet in a sewage channel running along the road and from which everyone is drawing the water they need, while at the same time tossing in whatever they want to get rid of. Misha, meanwhile, who was practically sober when I arrived, downs two bottles of vodka with a fellow veteran of the Soviet-Afghan war. Then, stone drunk, he decrees that I'll be sleeping at his place and totters off, dragging Ulysses through the streets of the small town.

Inside his home, he bullies his wife and daughters, terrorizes his son, puts on his uniform to impress me, then jumps on his bicycle and heads off in search of an English teacher whom he has translate in full all the great feats of arms he accomplished in Afghanistan. I sleep outside, beset by a cloud of mosquitoes, contemplating a few rats as they make their nightly rounds and use my bed as a traffic circle.

---

[*] Luce Boulnois, *La Route de la Soie: Dieux, Guerriers et Marchands* (Geneva: Éditions Olizane, 2001).

III

THE PENDULUM OF HISTORY

Although I just ordered my meal in a *choyxona* directly across from his white house, built in a typical Soviet colonial style, Talib tells me that it's out of the question for me to dine or sleep anywhere other than at his place. The man stands out of the crowd here. Dirtiness is the rule, not the exception, and everyone—myself included—wears clothes stained and spotted a thousand times over; Talib, however, is a living commercial for laundry detergent. It may be 8:00 p.m. but his face, which ought to be covered in black stubble, is clean shaven. His cap and linen peacoat are spotless. Although he insists that I sleep inside, I decide to pitch my tent out on his immense wood balcony: there, I'll be both safe from mosquitoes and able to enjoy the cool night air. We eat outside in the company of his two sons near a fire where his wife and daughters are busy at work. He's a man of few words and almost never gives an order; but, in response to some imperceptible hand signal or change in expression, everyone carries out his wishes. He must be as intransigent with his entourage as he is with his attire. He insists on conducting the *qaytarma* ceremonial himself, which entails pouring tea into the cup, then back into the teapot three separate times. The first cup represents evil, danger, and fire. The second, the water to neutralize those elements. The third cup is the good one and can be served to the guest.

Knocked out from the headlong pace at which I'm walking, I fall asleep during dinner, still seated at the table, my belly stuffed

37

with *pelmeni*—mini ravioli squares filled with lamb and pumpkin. At 4:30 a.m., when I open my tent, Talib is there; he's freshly shaven and is wearing a new cap and a pristine, just-ironed peacoat. Were I to do as he tells me, I'd have to stay here another day, an entire week, perhaps even a full month! His curiosity and kindness are infinite. I'm going to have to put up a fight in order to leave, and, while drinking the tea he brought me and slurping on a slice of melon with juice as sweet as ambrosia, I form an alliance with his sons, telling them about my journey's deadlines and how I have to reach the border by a certain date. Nevertheless:

"You will come see my melon plantation."

"Thank you, Talib, but I have to get going. You see, I have . . ."

"Ah, ah, ah! Don't tell me you're in such a hurry that . . ."

"I also have to make the most of the cool hours of the day. You wouldn't want me to be out walking in the noon heat, now would you?"

"No, but you can put that off until tomorrow. We'll go have a look at my plantation, my melon plants and fruit trees, then I want you to visit our magnificent mosque; after all that, we'll lunch with friends."

"Talib, I have to get going now!"

He's speechless. He's not used to having people challenge his wishes, let alone his orders. He's a bit shocked, as if I were a sparrow that had just pooped on his vest. I turn to his sons. They plead on my behalf, but unsuccessfully, for Talib remains staunchly opposed to my leaving.

"You know as well as I do that I have to respect your country's laws. You surely don't want me to be arrested with an expired visa! Come on, now: I'll take a picture of you and your sons, then I'll be on my way."

A bit stiff, he finally agrees to the photo. And since I drew a link between it and my imminent departure, he comes close to conceding defeat.

"Okay. We'll just tour my melon plantation then."

"The nearest one only, right?"

"That's not the nicest one. I have another, ten minutes away. . . ."

"No, this one, Talib. I'm sure the melons here are excellent."

An hour goes by. When I'm finally freed of my host's binding friendship and am able to get back on the road, the sun's up and it's already 90°F according to my watch thermometer. Everywhere I look, there are fields of cotton, punctuated here and there with a few poplar trees. Spurred on by a good night's sleep, I walk at a brisk pace, and by 1:00 p.m., I'm at my intended stopover point. That's still not good enough if I want to get across the border on time. So I wolf down a huge plate of noodles and, as soon as the sun feels a bit less lethal, get back underway. In the *choyxona* where I stop, the owner recites from memory, in Russian, the names of all of Alexandre Dumas's works and recounts, without skipping a single chapter, the story of the "*Graf* of Monte-Cristo." Though I interrupt his accounts with "*Ya znayu, ya znayu*" (I know, I know), he doesn't let up one bit and I have to suffer through to the end. Last year, one of his customers saw Sylvain Tesson and Priscilla Telmon pass this way on horse.*
I'm unable to resist tossing out a little French machismo:

"Seeing Priscilla, you surely noticed that Uzbekistan isn't the only country with pretty women?"

He's sorry but he failed to notice Priscilla's beauty: on account of the heat and dust, her head was wrapped in a *cheche*, like mine often is.

He slips away, only to come back fifteen minutes later with a brand-new dagger, which he offers me as a gift "for my protection." I spend some time convincing him that my Laguiole† is all I need, that

---

* *La Chevauchée des steppes: 3 000 km à cheval à travers l'Asie centrale* (Paris: Robert Laffont, 2001). TN: In France, Sylvain Tesson and Priscilla Telmon are well-known travel writers, reporters, and environmentalist activists. Telmon worked briefly as a fashion model before embarking on a career as an independent journalist and photographer. From 1999 to 2000, she crossed Central Asia on horseback in the company of Sylvain Tesson, a journey described in the book Ollivier cites here.

† TN: A French-made pocket folding knife.

I don't want to carry a weapon, and that I cannot accept any gifts, or I'll have to replace Ulysses with an ox-drawn cart! Then I dash off a little farther to set up camp in a dense forest. It's surprising to find a plantation of trees here, given that even the tiniest plots of land are used to grow cotton.

By running all the red lights, I reach Andijan two days ahead of schedule. It's hot as hell. Naked children, their skin the color of chestnuts, climb out of the irrigation canals, then jump right back in before they're stung by the sun. Little girls are jumping in too, but with their clothes on. Long, looping lines wait patiently out in front of ice cream stands and soda shops.

The hotel I check into is strange, out of place; at any rate, I've never seen anything like it since starting out from Istanbul. Just imagine: the carpet is clean, and there's a faucet marked with a red dot that delivers hot water, and another emblazoned with a blue dot that provides abundant cold water! There are window screens to keep out mosquitoes without any holes in them, and the sheets were changed after the last guest left. What's more, instead of dollars, they charge me in the national currency, and the rate is fair. It's all so inconceivable that I decide to sacrifice one of the two days just gained on my timetable so that I can take full advantage of all this cleanliness. I also have to fatten myself up. I'm losing weight far too quickly and have never fully recovered from all the fatigue I accumulated crossing Kamchik Pass.

I hire a taxi and head to the bazaar with Ulysses's wheels in hand, hoping to purchase new tires and inner tubes. Those that Laziz has for sale are very artistic patchworks of rubber and repair patches. I've had two flats since leaving Umar and his son, and each time, thank goodness, I wasn't far from a *vulkanizatsiya*'s shop. There are plenty of tire repairmen along the road, and they're not hurting for business.

At the bazaar, with the help of my taxi driver, with whom I've struck up a friendship, I buy some Russian tires. He advises against Chinese tires, which cost less but won't last as long. So Russian tires it is!

In this region, there are two hidden bombs: they're fully armed and ready to explode if left unattended. The first is that of nationality; the second, that of water. The problem of borders and nationality poses a "Balkan" threat. In the days of Stalin, this was an inconsequential matter. What difference did it make whether a particular city, artificially located in Uzbekistan, happened to have a Tajik majority? Inhabitants were all members of the glorious Soviet Union. From its offices in Moscow, the regime kept order with an iron fist, while giving preferential treatment to Russians, who wielded all the power here. They had the upper hand, landing apartments and jobs at the locals' expense. When the Union fell apart, the new leaders, though weaned on internationalism, found nothing better to do than fall back on extremist nationalism. And here, that's totally absurd. There are nearly eighty different nationalities in Kyrgyzstan alone. Intermingled by history, the Uzbek, Tajik, Kyrgyz, Kazakh, and Turkmen peoples knew no borders. They had been forced to abandon their nomadic ways and put down roots in one place or another at the whim of history, work opportunities, voluntary displacements, or forced deportations, as in the case of the Tatars, or the Korean minority, which resettled for the most part here in Uzbekistan. When civil war broke out in Afghanistan, millions of refugees crossed the border, driving up the pressure. With the exception of the Russians, almost all of Uzbekistan's inhabitants, regardless of ethnicity, share the same religion and values. But who is to say whether, in the event of an economic crisis or some other crisis, someone would not begin to impose distinctions? In Osh Province, where, in 1990, a decision was made to give precedence to one of the two ethnic groups, violent incidents immediately caused a rift between Uzbeks and Tajiks, resulting in nearly three hundred deaths.

Large numbers of Russians have been emigrating ever since the Uzbek government decreed that any person unable to speak the national language would be barred from employment in the public sector. In Amir Timur Square in Tashkent, I saw Russians, the country's former rulers, standing in public view in alleyways wearing little cardboard signs around their necks indicating the surface area and price—in dollars—of their apartments, in the hope of fleeing as quickly as possible back to Russia. An old Ukrainian woman told me that she wanted nothing more than to go back to die in the village where her parents were buried. These are the *pieds noirs* of Central Asia.* Why would they bother to learn the local language? On the contrary, it was up to the locals to learn Russian, which they did. But then, the great pendulum of history swung the other way. Everywhere, in each former Soviet republic, the explosives have been planted. All that's missing is the detonator.

The issue of water is no less worrisome. Back at my hotel, I dine with Geoff, an American expert in hydrological issues, and Nina, his associate and significant other, a tall Russian blond with pale eyes—those gray-green eyes that seem to stare into infinity, and which leave you speechless. Take a look once again—or run to see them if perchance you never have—at *The Wedding* by Pavel Lounguine and Chris Marker's documentary of narrated stills, *If I Had Four Dromedaries.*† Ah! Those Russian eyes that can make you say all kinds of crazy things! But Geoff is a serious fellow and, for the moment, he's not thinking about Nina's eyes. He explains at length why he was sent here. Here's the nutshell version: in 1861, when the Civil War broke out in North America, the world could no longer rely on the southern states for their cotton. That's when the Russians began to promote growing it here. Cotton requires sun and water, a great deal of water. Water comes down from the Pamirs and the immense Tian Shan range—the "Celestial Mountains" as the Chinese call them—by way of two rivers, the Amu Darya and the Syr Darya. In order to meet the ever-increasing demand for this "white gold," the Soviet

---

* TN: Persons of European ancestry who lived in Algeria during the French colonial period, especially those who returned to Europe after Algerian independence in 1962.
† Released in 2000, Свадьба (*Svadba* or *The Wedding*) is a Russian film directed by Pavel Lounguine. *Si j'avais quatre dromadaires* (*If I Had Four Dromedaries*) is a 1966 French-German documentary directed by French filmmaker Chris Marker.

regime indiscriminately pumped water out of the two rivers and, in the process, caused an ecological catastrophe: the draining of the Aral Sea. Once again, so long as the Muscovite Bear had only to bare its teeth, water was shared among "comrades." Today, it's a free-for-all. Cutting off someone's water supply is tantamount to murder. Geoff laments this fact, but, he says, regardless of the consequences for those downstream, "when the *Hakim* tells us to shut off the water, we lower the floodgates." Adding to this political problem is another, more technical one: just ten years ago, the economics of a mutualized market differed greatly from those of today. For example, for the five thousand people living in the Khiva region, powerful pumps were installed to draw water from the river below. The machines were poorly maintained, and so, one by one, they started breaking down. And then there's the problem of clogged pipes. In order to maintain the same volume of water at the receiving end, operating pressures have to be raised, which stresses the pumps even more and causes pipes to burst. It all costs money, huge sums of money. The system needs to be entirely redesigned, new canals dug, and funding secured. But who's going to cough up the money in a country where water, despite being scarce, is free? Every summer evening in Central Asia, billions of gallons of water are wasted when people sprinkle their yards hoping to cool the air a bit. Countries have, it's true, begun to diversify the crops they grow and cut cotton production, but it's a transition that won't happen overnight. And if a country upstream were to decide to hoard all the water for itself, the result would be war, no doubt about it.

Reassured by the proximity of the *granitsa*—the Kyrgyz border—I walk with a light step, free from the gnawing anxiety that overwhelms me when faced with bureaucratic red tape. It's something I'm allergic to.

I rediscover the landscape. The two mountain chains I noticed far off to the north and south have, little by little, drawn nearer to one another. The immense Fergana Valley narrows into a verdant corridor. My altimeter, which had been off duty after I crossed over the

Kamchik Pass, is back in action. Beneath my feet are the foothills of the high mountains I'll be scaling in the coming weeks. Their peaks look incredibly daunting. Grapes grow over the hillsides here. Higher up, winter ice and summer fire have killed off all life, the wind has chiseled the land down to bare rock. In the irrigated orchards, the last apricots are dropping to the ground and the quince trees are bedecked with large fruit. Here and there in the glens, pumpjacks—large, steel-gray birds pecking away at the ground in slow motion—draw petroleum from the ground, which, for lack of a pipeline, the country is unable to export.

I'm almost to Qoʻrgʻontepa when a car screeches to a halt alongside me. Its two passengers question me, acting surprised and amazed, then literally abduct me, telling me that they'd like to offer me a place to stay in the kolkhoz where they work, just a stone's throw away. A short man with a white goatee and a large dagger at his hip has me sit down in the shade of a mulberry tree and brings me bread and fruit. We're in front of a charming little wooden house. A man seated at a table on the terrace is busy consulting large ledgers and punching keys on a calculator. When I arrived, he couldn't have offered me a stingier greeting. I didn't dare bother a man seemingly so absorbed, and nowadays, numbers are sacred. My two hosts disappear. They reappear an hour later, just as I'm getting ready to take off again, along with a young man who has a good-natured, submissive face. "Our friend Demir is going to put you up," the two compadres tell me. And in a flash, either from something they said or a glance one of them threw, I decipher the scenario that has just played out. After inviting me, they reached the wood house where the kolkhoz's manager—the man with the calculator—told them that under no circumstances could a foreigner stay here. Perhaps he was afraid that I might stick my nose in his account books, thinking, like in the good old days of the Soviets, that every foreigner is a potential—and therefore probable—spy? Not wanting to lose face, the two companions had to run from one farmer to the next until they managed to find someone willing to put me up. Who should I thank: them or

Demir? The kolkhoz owner, happy at how things turned out, now comes over and holds out a hand. I pretend not to notice: I wouldn't want him to have to shake hands with a possible (or rather probable) spy, for it might be held against him when he's up for a promotion!

Demir Ashurov has, to be sure, a face that borders on the angelic. In any case, it's how I imagine a cherub must look! He closely resembles Mouloudji—a French singer who, when I was a child, moved me to tears with his song about a poppy flower and a bleeding heart.* My designated host drags me through the muddy back-alleys of the village where the kolkhoz employees live; he pulls his cow, I pull Ulysses. The strong smell of manure emanates from every yard. Demir lives with his wife and three children in a house composed of two small buildings. The kitchen is located in the smaller one; the living room is in the other, and that's where he has me sit down on a cushion. He proudly tells me that he built this half of the dwelling himself. This is where they live, eat, and sleep. The only furniture is a wood crate, atop which sits a television whose picture is more black than white; it's quite frankly impossible to tell what's on. While we drink tea and his wife readies the meal, he explains that they're quite busy on the farm right now. They've cut the *bug'day*, the wheat; they've burned the stubble and are now planting corn, *kukurus*, to be harvested in the fall. Demir owns a cow, which supplies them with milk for their children. The kolkhoz authorized him to farm fifteen *sotix* of land, the little wall-enclosed plot just outside his doorstep. I'd say it covers a little over five hundred square feet. And he's not paid in cash, either, but in foodstuffs, which are the same crops he works hard growing on the large estate. The calculator-wielding owner's accounts must be in good shape, seeing that the system functions more like a form of serfdom than an actual business, even a post-Soviet one. Fortunately for him, so to speak, Demir was involved in an

---

* TN: Parisian-born singer Marcel André Mouloudji. The song in question is called "Comme un p'tit coquelicot" (Like a Little Poppy), released in 1951, with lyrics by Raymond Asso and music by Claude Valéry.

accident, so he receives a monthly pension of three thousand so'm hard cash (about $4.25), with which he can buy a small number of manufactured goods—provided he keeps close track of his expenses, of course.

His wife arrives with a platter of *plov*. She sets it on a small fabric tablecloth spread out on the floor, and the entire family sits down around it on cushions. Two children have to share a spoon since there are only five of them. The household's entire collection of dishware seems to consist of five cups and three bowls. I pretend that I've just eaten and only sample the *plov*, seeing how the children look like they want to polish it off. I then head off to the farm tool storeroom where I sleep on a blanket. In the morning, as I'm bidding the family farewell, Demir's wife brings me a round of flatbread she cooked for me the day before. I hand the children a few banknotes. I offer money to Demir and his wife, but they both categorically refuse. They face the problems of the poor and I those of the rich: since leaving Samarkand, I've only managed to spend the equivalent of about $150, primarily in the two or three tourist hotels I stayed in. The rest of the time, when I slept on a *karavot* in restaurants or with locals, no one would take my money. The sum I have left is large for them—22,000 so'm—but ridiculously small for me—28 euros (approximately $25), and I have to get rid of it all before the Kyrgyz *granitsa*.

At a *choyxona* in Xonobod, for my last Uzbek evening, I let loose and eat like a horse. Raphael, the young waiter, and Iorken, the owner, are polite in an un-Westernly way, and practically turn taking care of me into a competition. When they hear that I find the evening air a bit chilly, they bring out so many of those famous wool *kurpacha* blankets that my *karavot* feels like a feather bed. In the morning, Iorken tells me that he won't accept any of my money. I finally manage to convince Raphael to take a wad of bills, probably more than he earns in a month. Tomorrow, I'll no longer need Uzbek so'm, but Kyrgyz som.

I finally reach the border a day ahead of my visa's expiration date, feeling bitterly disappointed that from Samarkand to here, I never once came upon the slightest trace of the old Silk Road. Religious monuments aside, Central Asian countries wash away all memory of it. In Turkmenistan, razed by one of Genghis Khan's sons, the shining city of Merv has been a ghost town ever since. In Uzbekistan, the glory of Samarkand sprang from a war fought by Tamerlane, not from wealth generated by trade. The reason for this is that anything related to commerce is by and large neglected. "Attention is given to the glory of sovereigns, not to the material life of populations."* We all know this, all we have to do is think back to our history books: battles, heroic deeds, treason, treaties—the lives of our forebears have seemingly been reduced to military events and political decisions. And the city of the "lame devil" itself was in ruins when modern architects saved Registan Square and practically rebuilt the Bibi-Khanym Mosque. Lenin and Stalin were bulldozing mosques and replacing them with movie theatres only yesterday; today, those men's statues are being taken down and replaced with supermarkets. Tides quickly turn. No sooner have shovels been put away than pickaxes are brought out.

What will I find in Kyrgyzstan, whose border I'll be crossing in only a few minutes? I've been told over and over that I'll face a host of difficulties, that I'll be asked to produce a thousand documents, that Russian soldiers are greedy and thick-headed. So I'm taut as a bowstring. But I sail through customs without a hitch. The agents wearily motion me to keep moving and not bother them, so I have to insist just to get them to stamp my passport! I'm no fool: without the stamp, they won't let me in! The Kyrgyz military is just as relaxed, and in ten minutes the formalities are over and I'm resetting my watch, turning it back an hour. But that doesn't mean that the administrative red tape is over. Before I can settle into my hotel, I have to pony up and join the "OVIR," the Office of Visas and

---

* Luce Boulnois, *op. cit.*

Registration, the organization in charge of visitors from abroad. It's a legal requirement in all former Soviet republics: foreigners have to pay the cops who keep an eye on them.

When I leave the territory, I'll have to present a form that can only be obtained 435 miles away in Bishkek, the capital city. Since there's no way I'm about to make such a detour, I try phoning the French consulate. In vain, since it's the weekend. Tomorrow's Monday, but I'll be in the mountains and won't have any way to get in touch with them. I email René Cagnat, the Honorary Consul I met in Paris, who's a leading expert on Central Asia.* I'll keep my fingers crossed that, by dint of his knowledge of the country and its bureaucratic labyrinth, I'll somehow get my hands on the precious exit permit.

Jalal-Abad, the first Kyrgyz city I come to along my route, is a hive of activity beneath a sun whose rays, moderated by the elevation, feel more like a caress than a sting. My first steps in this country are blessed with wonderful encounters. In the shade of an arbor, a merry group of *aksakals* is busy cooking *plov*. They call me over. Customers gathered out in front of a *chaikhana* to watch me and my cart go by invite me to join them for a cup of green tea. Everyone says how I don't look my age. But in fact it's they who look older than theirs. Privations when times are tough, dreary work and weather, too much vodka: by fifty-five, they're already old men. In Central Asia, elders are respected, fed, and don't have to work if they don't want to, for their children take care of them. The Kyrgyz, both young and old, wear strange pointed hats—the *kalpak*, made of white felt with a brown reverse—and soft, lavish riding boots, as thin as socks and shined up like a second skin, which they protect by slipping on clogs. Here, language and laughter reign supreme. A young girl passes by, her hair so blond that it seems to capture and refract the sun, her eyes like green algae: Russians are more numerous than in Uzbekistan. I

---

* René Cagnat, *La Rumeur des steppes* (Paris: Payot, Collection "Petite Bibliothèque Payot/Voyageurs," 2001).

understand now why someone wanted me to have a dagger: any man without one is naked.

In the city where I take a day off, I stuff myself with sweets trying to regain weight. I discover *samski caprik*, a sugar crust pastry filled with raisins and candied raspberries; *pryanik*, another pastry, rolled in melted sugar; and finally, *rulik*, a cake made with two kinds of chocolate and garnished with strawberries and cream—excellent, though somewhat tough on the stomach. The woman working the hotel reception desk, strapped in a brilliantly colored silk dress, has a hearty laugh when I give her my last name. Here "olivier" is a kind of salad. I'd like to know more, but she's too busy guffawing: she finds my surname a source of endless hilarity.

In the morning, having learned that I was here, Cass and Ross are determined to see me. They're headed to Pakistan on a tandem bicycle. She's Australian and he's English. They have the confident, simple demeanor of great athletes, with bodies that communicate as much as their voices. They came here last year and resided near a lake with a family they photographed. Rather than send the snapshots in the mail, they decided to deliver them in person. The pair camps, although they occasionally check into hotels to recharge their electronic devices. Cass has a digital camera and takes pictures of anyone who asks. She shows them the photos she took on the screen, lets the subjects admire themselves, then erases the images so the camera's memory doesn't fill up. Those I photograph, on the other hand, have to wait a long time—and in some cases a very long time—before being able to gaze at themselves.

On my way out of Jalal-Abad, as I mentally size up the summits to the east, I soon realize that my calves are about to be called into action. The road climbs sharply between mud walls on which tobacco leaves have been hung to dry. Out on the terraces, carpets of apricots are shriveling up, storing up sunlight that they will once again surrender when winter sets in. When the fruit is dry, it's known as *kuraga* in Russian and *turshak* in Kyrgyz. Another form of energy is being stored up for winter: squares of manure have been laid out to dry on the sidewalks.

I encounter my first horsemen. Nonchalant, with *kalpak* caps and brightly colored shirts, they move along at the slow pace of their animals. Here, time is *not* money. The road forgoes asphalt: it turns into a road of dirt and stone as it clambers up the hills. I hope that Ulysses will be up to the challenge! Despite the altitude, it's hot out. My watch reads 1,000 meters (3,280 feet) and 97°F. Over the slopes, thousands of hectares of sunflowers are slowly wagging their hairy, flavescent halos in magnificent unison. I start up the mountain. I won't head down again for several hundred miles, at which point I'll be in China—if, that is, I manage to get those blasted papers from Bishkek!

IV

SOLTANAD

Khorosho! Khorosho! (Good! Good!). Farmers, their noses in the air, look like they want to drink in the first few raindrops to fall since the start of this broiling summer. But their happiness is short-lived. Winds higher up soon drive away the clouds. Along the road, women are filling buckets with small ladles from the trickle of murky, foul-smelling water flowing in the creek bed. Here, as on the plain, one man's sewer is another man's waterhole.

Someone placed a wolf carcass beside the road at the entrance to the village of Mikhaylovka. Stones have been placed around it to keep drivers at bay. The animal was killed by a bullet to the side. The carcass is being exposed in all probability "to set an example," in the same way that people back home once nailed owls to barn doors. Live wolves—and owls—don't care one bit about the dead bodies of others of their kind. The practice only serves to reinforce humankind's own fears. And children—after being haunted by the carcass for a few nights—are then primed to become wolf-killers themselves as soon as they can handle a rifle. Ever since I set out from Jalal-Abad, people have been warning me that there are wolf packs at higher elevations. I should, at the very least, they tell me, carry a dagger, like everyone else. But I'm armed with optimism and recklessness, and I'm by no means afraid of wolves at this time of the year. I fear them, at any rate, less than I do men.

I obstinately march on toward the summit on a road hewn into the rock, dotted with boulders that force us—Ulysses and me—to

tack back and forth over terrain that's obviously more suited to journeys on horseback than on foot. But who actually walks here? Even
the poorest of men has an animal to ride. As I'm struggling to climb
out of a narrow valley hemmed in by a forest of oak trees, the sound
of two horses' hooves makes me turn around. Ishenbek and his sidekick Abdenbay are heading back up to their summer encampment
in the mountains. They both have that distinctive skin tone caused
by excessive sun and vodka. Without so much as slowing his steed,
Ishenbek asks where I'm going.

"You're crossing the *Pereval*? Tonight, you'll sleep at my house.
Here, catch!"

And he tosses me a rope, tying his end of it to the pommel of his
saddle. I fasten mine to Ulysses's tow bar and, all of a sudden, I'm
happily trotting behind his horse's ass, no longer having to work so
hard, conversing with these horsemen who raise foals and spend each
summer up in the hills, only heading back down toward Jalal-Abad
after the first snowfalls.

The encampment is composed of several yurts. My hosts lead me
to the largest one. The village elder offers me the place of honor—
the one that's usually his—far to the back, directly across from the
door, and he sits down beside me, on the men's side. The women and
children are to our left, the men to our right. Outside the yurt, the
foals are tethered to a stake lest they nurse too much from their mothers; the mares' milk is used to make fermented *kumis*, Kyrgyzstan's
national beverage. They let me try a few sips. It's a bit sour and only
slightly alcoholic. I promptly ask if I can lie down. Running behind
the horses for part of the climb wore me out.

In the morning, I'm worried; I didn't stock up on supplies and now
I risk running out of food. There's no guarantee that I'll run into
nomads higher up, and I've already gone through most of the packets
of noodles I had bought. The valley is now very green and narrow;
much of it is occupied by a stream, hemmed in by high cliffs. At
a bend in the road, I come upon a tent city. One of the tents, the

largest, is marked UNHCR (United Nations High Commissioner for Refugees). Inside, there are two or three tables. It's a restaurant and I'm served a sumptuous noodle soup. Zainoura, a young Kyrgyz woman with a Mongolian face who's knee-high to a grasshopper, tells me that she saw Cass and Ross yesterday. The two touring cyclists, now a day ahead of me, must be having a hard time powering their heavily loaded tandem over the mountains! But they were tremendously fortunate. Yesterday, they witnessed what Zainoura calls an *ulak*, but which is better known in Central Asia as a *buzkashi*: a rancher threw a party in celebration of a birth. The birth of a baby boy, of course. For a girl, there'd be no point in whooping it up. In the *ulak*, a group of horsemen fight to gain control of the remains of a lamb whose head has been cut off. Whoever succeeds in dragging the dead animal to the center of a circle wins. Aside from that, anything goes. The riders, whips in their mouths, prod their horses into the fray, nudging them with their legs. Man and beast are one. It's an unimaginably violent sport. Another *ulak* is planned in less than a month, for the national holiday. But I'll be in China then . . . or so I hope.

I return to the climb, which now grows very steep. The road, hewn into the rock, overlooks great chasms. Are the small white spots down below lambs or boulders? Both, apparently. Sheer drop-offs, torrential mountain streams, summits covered in snow or cloaked in clouds: my head starts spinning at the sight of such wild beauty. It's not very hot out, but I'm sweating profusely, breaking Ulysses free from one stone, only to have him butt up against another. I move forward at a snail's pace. Two eagles glide on the wind, as if in slow motion. There's an occasional muddy rockslide to ford. A truck, agile as a goat, catches up to me, then zooms past. Its right wheels skim the precipice in places. The driver knows that his vehicle has just enough room to get by. A short distance on, several crumpled carcasses at the bottom of the ravines remind me that it's a game at which not everyone wins. The truck's dump bed is full of workers both young and old who, as I'm about to find out, are looking for work in Kazarman.

They tell me to climb up into the bed along with them, but when I refuse, they wave making joyful, provocative farewell gestures. Bye-bye! They should have shown a little humility: a half hour later, I'm back alongside the truck, which is spewing oil. The driver and his sidekick are stretched out on their backs beneath the engine. The passengers, sitting on the short grass, are bored to tears and, given the elevation, those in shirtsleeves are shivering. They'd like to chat, but I'm soaked in sweat and, afraid of catching cold, I keep right on climbing. The truck passes me up nearly an hour later, as I'm approaching the summit. But a little farther on, it breaks down yet again. That's the last I see of it.

Flocks, trunk-deep in flowers, wander freely over the slopes. The mountain is dressed in three colors: knolls brown from the sun; verdant valleys, some babbling with mountain streams, which are nearly dry in this season; and, overhead, in negligees of vaporous clouds, mountain peaks that, from time to time, show off their virginal snows and glaciers, glinting cruelly in the sunlight.

When I get to the top of the Pereval, it's 2:30. If I've understood properly, the word designates both the mountain and the pass. The panorama before me is fabulous. I find myself once again wondering about the profound and unspoken joy we feel when looking out over a vast landscape. It's a silent and strong jubilation, like a drawn-out orgasm. Is this the same irrepressible joy that the so-called "greats" of this world experience when they look out at the masses? That would explain why they so virulently defend their high rank. For a half hour, strapped in my vest and shivering as the strong wind whips the low grasses, I let the sweat I worked up during the climb evaporate while munching on dried fruit. I love mountains, their power, their diversity, and their destructive nature, too. This is the world as it once was, still pristine despite the winds, rains, and men; wild as at the birth of these billion-year-old rocks. While Kamchik Pass is barren and sterile, this mountain is not. Here, grasses and flowers grow, and life holds on in every stem. To the east, I see an endless succession of summits. The Tian Shan and Pamir mountain ranges are squabbling with one another over which of the two is the highest in the world, and they scrape the sky to frighten off any men who might entertain the idea of climbing them.

These visions are still vivid in my mind's eye as, over the next two days, I race down all the way to Kazarman. I was told that I would find a hotel in the little mining town, which produces each year a ton and a half of gold. I have every intention of lounging around for an entire day and scrubbing off all the dirt picked up in the mountains. In a small village last night, the only site I could find to plant my tent was near a pile of manure. I feel as though I carried the stench with me out on the road. Sadly, the woman running the tiny hotel dashes my hopes with a single word: "Full."

"There's no other hotel?"

"No other!"

An icy drizzle has begun to fall. I just stand there with my arms dangling by my sides, Ulysses's tow bar in the mud. What am I supposed to do? Where am I to go? That's the moment my guardian angel decides to send me a stand-in. A young woman comes over. She runs a store nearby. Soltanad is dressed like a Russian—or an American, rather—with a tight-fitting T-shirt, blue jeans, and a baseball cap; but her face is distinctly Kyrgyz: she has lavish charcoal hair, delicate bronze skin, and eyes that are slightly slanted. Her voice is strong, but it has a slight catch in it. She speaks refined English with obvious pleasure and is so talkative it makes my head spin. A half hour later, having wolfed down a large bowl of noodles she cooked for me, I'm sound asleep on a thick wool mat in her parents' small apartment, which she shares with her brother Daka and two female cousins. Then, led by my guide to the public bathhouse, I soak in a steaming bathtub, while my clothes spin round in her washing machine. Conversing with Soltanad is easy: ask her a question and she talks on and on to no end. A brilliant student, she took first place in a national competition and won a year-long stay in the United States. Her father and mother work in Jalal-Abad: he's an engineer, she's a teacher. They're both originally from Kazarman. Her father was one of twelve children and her mother one of ten. All of the kids, or just about, went on to live and marry here. I can't walk ten steps in the city without Soltanad stopping to introduce me to an aunt or uncle. Through the various marriages, she has a good forty of them here, as well as hosts of cousins. It'd be easy to think, at times, that everyone in the city belonged to her clan.

Her parents come back to Kazarman to see the family and flee the pressure cooker that Jalal-Abad turns into in the summer. Soltanad stays here during the hot months along with her younger brother and runs a tiny shop selling beverages, candy, and cakes. But her core business consists of buying empty vodka bottles from local kids who pick them up after they're tossed away here and there by drunkards. The kids immediately reinvest their earnings in candy, which the young woman serves up while Daka carefully examines the bottles they've brought, making sure there are no chips in them. Once bagged, they're transported to Bishkek by . . . yes, an uncle—one who owns a truck.

Another uncle, a teacher at the city's middle school, puts me up for the night. Rain has begun to fall over the city, so I spend my entire rest day either sleeping or in conversation at my young friends' shop.

Soltanad is twenty-one and is studying in Bishkek. I ask her all the questions I've been wanting to ask about Kyrgyz society, but couldn't. She's happy to respond. Having lived in the United States helps her view her country and its inhabitants calmly, and with an outside perspective. She and her brother are the only people I meet in Kazarman who don't have metal teeth. When she tells me about the city's one industry, a Canadian-run gold mine, I burst out laughing: "The mine produces very little. But the largest lode isn't in the nearby mountains anyway. It's in the cemetery!"

Yes, the Kyrgyz love gold teeth and young people often let their cavities run their course—especially those affecting their incisors—so that they can flash a golden smile as soon as possible. It isn't unusual to offer a gram or two of the precious metal as a birthday gift so that someone special can have a beautiful, shiny new tooth. Soltanad remembers how she once found four teeth in a drawer. Her mother told her that they belonged to her grandmother. My assumption was wrong: apparently, the dead stop by the dentist's office before going to the cemetery!

Though Muslim, the Kyrgyz are monogamous and, to Soltanad's knowledge, men don't have official mistresses here, as I saw with Ashur in Uzbekistan. In Bishkek, she knows a few uninhibited women who are sexually involved with their boyfriends, but the vast majority marry as virgins. It's in their best interest too, for, although the boys like to play the field first, they have every expectation that their wives will be pure on their wedding night. It's customary for the husband to report back to the gathered family the following day and vouch for his bride's virginity. Otherwise, watch out: the poor woman will be treated like a servant and humiliated by her in-laws on every possible occasion.

With laughing eyes, ruby red lips even without makeup, and high cheekbones, Soltanad's radiant beauty is like balm for the soul. And while most Kyrgyz women prefer to hide their charms beneath ample garments, Soltanad took to wearing close-fitting clothes in the United States. I ask if she has a suitor. She does: a Uyghur student she met at the University. But though her parents know who this boy is, they have no idea Soltanad has taken a liking to him. She wouldn't dare speak about him to her father, who intends on having her marry a Kyrgyz man. Unlike the Uzbeks, the Kyrgyz don't force their children to marry in birth order. Despite her varnish of Western culture, Soltanad will most likely give in to her father's wishes in choosing a spouse, just as Zarina did. Parental authority remains unchallenged in Central Asia. But at the very top of the social pyramid are male elders. Whether Kyrgyz, Uzbek, or Turkmen, every man dreams of old age. It's a kind of paradise that can be enjoyed here below. *Aksakals* hold all the rights. Their every counsel is considered a command, their every whim is indulged without hesitation. Soltanad mentions, for instance, an old man who got the urge to live it up in Bishkek, the faraway capital. To cover the cost of his little spree, including his travel and hotel, the whole clan chipped in, everyone giving whatever they had without batting an eyelid.

Soltanad's uncle, who put me up for a night, warned me in no uncertain terms against continuing along the road heading east toward Naryn, as I was planning to do. So I take a road going south. I camp near the open-pit gold mine. In former times, the mountain dwellers of Central Asia placed lambskins at the bottom of rushing streams, which trapped flecks of gold. Some claim the practice gave rise to the myth of the Golden Fleece.

Some nomads invite me to join them for breakfast—milk and cheese—and they offer me a loaf of bread. Except for larger towns, there are no bakeries here. Women bake bread just before mealtime. They keep the dough in a pan: it's prepared every three or four days from flour, baking soda, salt, and liquid yogurt called, just like in Turkey, *ayran*. I meet Utbek, a young Kyrgyz man, and his sister, and they walk with me for a short, three-hour stretch. They're on their way to spend the weekend at their family's encampment, walking twelve miles on the outward journey and an equal distance on the return, to the school where they're boarders during the week. Before bidding me farewell, they point out for me their tent settlement down in a valley. Farther along, a farmer shearing his sheep invites me to quaff two glasses of *kumis*, which he draws from a wineskin made from the hide of an entire sheep, sewn shut where the head and front legs were. An old woman offers me a large bowl of yogurt. She seems very poor and when I insist, she takes my banknote.

I like this contact with nomads, their rough simplicity, their hospitality. The fact that their yurts close with just a simple curtain symbolizes this. Any traveler can come in and is welcome. People are less hospitable beyond the steppe. In residential villages like Kosh-Dobo, where I set foot this evening, residents who are away have secured their doors with large Russian padlocks. Mothers call their children back and sweep them inside the moment they catch sight of me. I'm sent from one door to the next; there's a government bureaucracy feel to the experience. I head off angrily and knock on the door of Manas, the village headman. He's not home. It's his father, Nacir, an old *aksakal*, who cracks open the door, then closes it in my face. His granddaughter Guljane, however, objects. She admonishes her grandpa and offers me a cup of tea, then sets about preparing the meal while I tell her about my journey through her country. After listening in, the old man has a change of heart: he runs out into the village and returns with all his retiree friends so that they can have a look at the phenomenon and admire his generosity!

Guljane sets a bed up for me in a large, empty room. Manas is there in the morning and gives me a warm welcome. He's a tall, muscular fellow; atop his skull he wears the inescapable *kalpak*. He's both the mayor of this village and the manager of an administrative district called, in Russian, a "*rayon.*" Which prompts me to nickname him "*chef de rayon*"—meaning "floorwalker" in French. Poor humor, yes, but today, I need a little cheering up! We share a large bowl of *jarma*, which is a kind of savory cold soup made from milk, flour, and yogurt. Manas offers me a black felt *kalpak* with white designs and a pom-pom but refuses the threadbare hat I offer him in exchange. It's true that with my headgear on his head, he'd probably feel as ridiculous as I do with his *kalpak*! But my hat keeps my head warm in these icy mountains so I tuck it back in my pack. Father and daughter seem close to one another, and my guess is that she told him how her grandfather was ready to turn me away last night. Their gift of the *kalpak* is quite possibly meant to make up for the offense.

Manas guides me through the village to help me find the right road. We walk past the school where he's also a teacher. His wife, who's not home right now, teaches English. The Kosh-Dobo school has nearly eight hundred students out of a total population of 3,500 inhabitants, which sums up rather well this country's extraordinary demographic vitality. My host bears the most famous name in all Kyrgyzstan: Manas is the national hero created by the Manischis, bards who once traveled from tribe to tribe, telling the tales of Manas's exploits. It's said that, if put end to end, the heroic deeds of

Manas would fill an entire encyclopedia, such that his story has been nicknamed "The Iliad of the Steppes." Uzbekistan, for its part, chose as its champion Tamerlane, absolved of his crimes for the occasion. Kyrgyz's Manas is more likeable, for the armies he massacres with the help of his son Semetei and his grandson Seitek, exist only in the imagination of the Manischis, who, even today, recite his exploits from one yurt to the next throughout the long winter. Some purists point out, and rightly so, that Manas is not specifically Kyrgyz, for his story is told throughout Central Asia. But only here did people adopt him as their own.

For, historically speaking, borders are a recent invention in this region. The only limit to the nomads' domain was the reach of their sword. And if today we speak of "Kyrgyzstan" to refer to certain historical facts, it's to provide a geographical reference point only. Furthermore, given that the shadow of the Soviets hovered over these countries for nearly a century, the international community is only slowly gaining an awareness of them again. How many Europeans can successfully locate Kyrgyzstan on a map of the world? And yet events that took place here forever changed the history of the West.

The history of Kyrgyzstan is linked to that of its powerful neighbor, China. China, from the very first Silk Road caravans, first tried to assert its influence through diplomacy, most notably through marriage diplomacy. There's no counting all the Chinese princesses who, known for their high culture and beauty, were married off to "barbarian" chieftains. When Marco Polo finally managed to leave the court of the Great Khan, it was because he offered to accompany a princess to be "given" in marriage to Arghun, a western king. By the time the young woman finally arrived at his court, her "husband" was already dead. But no matter, the princess would wed his son. Another princess exiled by destiny in this way, and who is very dear to the heart of the Chinese, is Liu Xijun. A Wusun chieftain, whose subjects raised horses as nomads somewhere between modern Kazakhstan and Kyrgyzstan, wanted a Chinese fiancée, so he sent a thousand horses as an engagement present. The young Liu Xijun would, in poignant poetry, sing of her distress as an émigrée, and of her longing for the comforts of a sedentary life:

> *The round tent is my palace*
> *Its walls are of felt*
> *Dried meat is my only dish*
> *My drink is mare's milk*
> *Endlessly, I dream of my homeland*
> *My heart is aching . . .*

In the face of such homesickness, it should come as no surprise to hear how another Chinese princess, according to legend, is said to have risked her own life by carrying silk worms with her in her chignon: she held onto the hope that, in the bitter cold of exile, she might one day find comfort in the marvelous fabric's soothing touch, and not be stuck wearing rough wool garments only.

Having conquered Xinjiang,[†] the Tang Empire's hunger for power knew no bounds and its armies traveled all the way to Bukhara. But its ambitions would eventually result in a most terrible loss. For over two thousand years, the Chinese had managed to safeguard the secret of silk-making. Chinese control of the art lasted until the eighth century. Anyone attempting to export silk moths or their eggs faced the death penalty. An unfortunate war taking place a short distance beyond the modern-day border of Kyrgyzstan, however, would soon undo of all of these precautions. The country's north was indeed the site of the famous battle that, in 751 CE, changed the face of Central Asia. At Talas, Imperial troops suffered their most humiliating defeat. Several thousand Chinese soldiers were taken prisoner and deported, first to Samarkand, then to Baghdad. And

---

* In Michèle Pirazzoli-T'serstevens, *La Chine des Hans: histoire et civilisation* (Paris: Presses universitaires de France, 1982). TN: This version of the "Lament of Hsi-Chün" is translated from the Chinese by Arthur Waley in *A Hundred and Seventy Chinese Poems* (New York: Alfred A. Knopf, 1919), p. 75.
† Also written Sinkiang.

those prisoners were the ones who would reveal to the West what had been, until then, three of the world's best-kept secrets: how to make silk, porcelain, and especially paper. This latter invention had the greatest impact on the West, since, by replacing parchment, it changed how knowledge and technical know-how was transmitted. On the heels of that revolution would come yet another, that of the printing press. And it was the West, the last region to inherit these technologies, that would develop them the most; China, on the other hand, where they had been invented, would soon stagnate in ruinous conservatism, and close itself off to the outside world.

Some historians believe that Kyrgyzstan was also the site of the Stone Tower. The Greek geographer Ptolemy mentions it in the second century. According to him, it was at the foot of this famous tower that businessmen from China and Persia exchanged merchandise before returning home. It's not hard to imagine the fabulous market that was held for centuries at the foot of the structure. And yet today we're unable to pinpoint its precise location. Some place it in Kyrgyzstan; others claim that there were two, one of which was in China; and there are those who believe that it was in the city of Tashkurgan. But no one has yet presented irrefutable proof locating it in any of these places.

After Kosh-Dobo, on the road that day, I walk with Mohamad. His boots are worn, but he keeps up a fast pace. That's because he's used to it: an irrigation specialist, he works five miles from Kosh-Dobo and walks both ways every day. Then Lorlan accompanies me for a stretch. The kid might be eight or nine—he's not sure of his age. He disappears inside a huge fur-lined coat a thousand times too big for him and which covers his pony's croup like Manas's cape. His boots must be at least size ten, but they keep his little feet warm, and when you're on horseback, what difference does the size of your shoes really make? Since his legs are too short to reach the stirrups, though they're raised as high as they'll go, he has wedged his feet into the straps they're attached to. Consumed by curiosity, he rides alongside me for a good half hour, remaining a few yards away. When I motion him to come nearer, he balks. I show him my camera and he comes over, beaming a sunny smile; then, as soon as I've snapped his picture, he gallops off and disappears into the distance. A half hour later, he's back with two cousins, young centaurs like him, and they beg me to take another photo. Wanting to look his best, he has taken off his large coat, which now lies across his saddle.

In the village of Osoaviakhim, Baket is overjoyed. He's celebrating the birth of his son and has invited twenty or so people. But a surprise guest—me—becomes the highlight of the party. The child is in his grandmother's arms, all trussed up like a Sunday roast. A bracelet has been put on his wrist made of tiny glass pearls, each decorated with a black dot. They are *göz manchok*, literally, "eye beads."* If someone casts an evil spell on the wearer, the pearls rupture and the curse is warded off. Both adults and children wear these amulets, either as bracelets, necklaces, or anklets. Between the moment I arrived and midnight, we sit down to eat three separate times. Between meals, we nibble on dried fruit while sipping tea or vodka and making countless toasts. Slightly tipsy, Baket plays a kind of three-stringed guitar for us, the *komuz*. Exhausted, I ask permission to head off to sleep. He suggests that I spend the night in the immense and sumptuous yurt set up behind his house. My host rents it for ceremonies, marriages, and parties. Of the several kinds of yurt, this is the largest; it can accommodate up to fifteen people year-round. The tent is superbly decorated with those famous *shyrdak* and *tushtuk* rugs made in Kyrgyzstan, which display brightly colored wool designs on a felt, neutral background. Baket gives me a lesson in the different parts of the yurt, in particular the *tunduk*, a wood circle located at the top of the tent where two rows of three shafts cross. The *tunduk* appears on the Kyrgyz national flag. It symbolizes unity, since men come together beneath it in the yurt, where it secures the wood beams supporting the roof, known as the *ook*. The smallest yurts have fifty

---

* TN: A talisman. In Turkey, it is known as the *göz boncuğu*.

ook beams; this one, the largest, has one hundred and ten. During the day, the *tunduk*'s peephole is left open to let in air and light. At night, a piece of felt is drawn over it with ropes in order to block it up and hold in the heat. That's no luxury: at this elevation, the temperature drops below freezing every night, even in the summer. But with all the *kurpacha* quilts my host brings me, I fall into a deep sleep as though I were in a nest. In the morning, Baket points out to me that the *kalpak* Manas gave me is meant for winter weather, that it's too hot; despite all my refusals, he gives me a brand-new, lightweight one for the summer.

I'm thrilled to be in Kyrgyzstan. A lover of westerns, I find something of that special atmosphere in this country: the landscapes, the horses, as well as the horsemen with their gaudy shirts and nonchalant attitudes. It's all here—except that *kalpak*s replace Stetsons! In town, out in front of the post office, four or five horses are patiently waiting for their owners' return; there are some back of the building where Soltanad lives, too. I come across a few men trounced by vodka who are being bravely carried back to their yurts by their trusty steeds.

In the mountains, I walk alone, but from time to time a rider suddenly gallops over to me from the steppe, emerging from behind a hill or out of a valley, and asks for . . . a cigarette. It's apparently a way of meeting people and, although I don't smoke, I've purchased two packs so that I can meet the demand.

Atop a mountain pass, I find myself nose to nose with a young boy whose name is also Manas. He gets down from his jet-black mare and talks to me about what's currently on his mind: one of his animals has gone missing. He's out looking for it. He tells me that it might take him a day or all week. Having smoked his cigarette, he gets back on his horse and spurs it down the near-vertical slope where, in the high grasses, he quickly disappears, heading nowhere. An immense flock of sheep flanked by four or five riders takes the mountain pass by storm, then makes its way back down the gentle slope heading north. From afar, the black backs of this multitude resemble an undulating blanket as it slowly slips over the mountainside.

Total silence except for the wind. Tracking the flight of an eagle, I discover a kind of horizontal plateau, a surprising sight in this craggy landscape. Beyond it, bathed in blue light, rise snow-capped peaks. A galloping horseman plunges into the valley in my direction, trampling large blooms of periwinkle and weaving back and forth between blue-blossomed shrubs. The road to Baetov is simply magical. I traverse little villages nestled in flower-filled valleys. I walk beside torrential mountain streams on paths so narrow even Ulysses has to squeeze past. Above us, jagged peaks reach for the sky. A red-stone cirque blocks my way: it's a vertical, bare wall of rock, with no visible gaps. But at the far end, I discover a narrow passageway. I have to portage my gear this time, and it takes me three round trips to get up a precipitous path, strewn with large stones that break loose beneath my boots and tumble down the slope, taking large, loud leaps before they smash into the grass with a final thud, a few hundred feet below. On the first trip, I haul up my backpack, then the duffel bag in which I stow my camping gear, and finally Ulysses, all folded up. Fooled by some false flats, I make the mistake of reloading my cart too soon. There's another steep climb and, arch as I might while tugging at the tow bar, I can go no farther. Three young shepherds stop and ask me a few questions, then decide to give us a push to the top. One of them has a pair of binoculars around his neck. They, too, are trying to locate a lost animal. The only food they have with them is a liter of milk, tucked in the youngest one's jacket.

The village of Baetov—the name means "the queen of the water"—boasts a telephone line and post office. It's Friday and the French consulate in Bishkek should be open. I urgently need that document, without which I won't be able to leave Kyrgyz territory when I go through customs at Torugart Pass. No one really knows why, but it's the least advisable place to cross over into China. The border is closed there from September to May due to snow, as well as on the weekend. No matter how insignificant the festival on either side of the border, the customs officers close up shop. Not long ago, they closed everything down, saying that it was raining too hard. Just like that, without warning! And even when they can be found manning their stations, I've been told that officers on both sides quibble with tourists there more than anywhere else. Untold numbers have had to turn around after making the difficult 435-mile journey from Bishkek, convinced that they have all the necessary papers. And some several times! Still, stubborn as a mule, that's where I want to cross. Because it's the spot nearest the ancient Silk Road, and everyone knows how exacting I am with respect to the route I've decided to take! In the early seventh century, one of the most famous Chinese travelers, the monk Xuanzang, crossed the Pamir Mountains near here, at Kok-Art. It's the pass Marco Polo is said to have taken as well—although some claim that he would have crossed by way of Afghanistan. In any case, this is the most natural path one would take when leaving the Fergana Valley.

It turns out that there's just as much red tape on either side of the border. But on the Chinese side, the women who helped me plan my trip back in Paris did all the work. So all I have left to do is get that damned paper from Bishkek without actually traveling there to fetch it, which would be an absurdity. The phone call I make to the French consulate gives me an idea of the trials this country's citizens must endure when dealing with the administrators who govern them. Yes, the consulate I call is French, but Gulsheva Karabasheva, whom I get on the line, though brought up with Soviet bureaucracy, is now well-versed in French rules and regulations to boot. Which means that I'm dealing with state-of-the-art red tape! She speaks French, but her dry tone of voice makes me think of an old English governess.

"I sent you an email last week and . . ."

"I didn't receive anything."

"It was addressed to René Cagnat, the consul and . . ."

"Honorary Consul only. And he didn't forward it to me."

"How can I get the document?"

"You have to apply for it at the Ministry of Foreign Affairs, and the turnaround time is two weeks. There are laws in this country. You have to follow them."

I agree completely, but first you have to know what they are. I found out about this official paper entirely by chance. Her voice is so sharp and ice-cold that I feel my ears freezing over.

"Is there any way I can get it without traveling to Bishkek, and in a shorter time frame? If it's a question of money, I'm ready . . ."

"You have to travel to Bishkek. We'll submit the application for you."

"But I'm 400 miles away, I'm traveling on foot and . . ."

"Please, sir. If you're unwilling to do your part . . ."

Then, to completely demoralize me, the shrew fires a Parthian shot:

"Don't even try getting through without the form. Our own ambassador was turned back when he didn't have it. Even as a diplomat, it took him three days to get it! *Voilà . . . Au revoir, monsieur!*"

And Gulsheva, in typical bureaucrat fashion, simply hangs up.

My only option is to appeal to my dear miracle workers in Paris. The women dial up their contacts in Bishkek and promise to have the document faxed to me, in quintriplicate, in the small town near the border.

You see, Gulsheva, it wasn't so difficult after all!

V

TOKON

After Baetov, the winding road passes a series of mountain massifs that I hope to see the other side of in three days. Around 10:00 a.m., at an elevation of 2,200 meters (7,220 feet), the ground is covered in a kind of sparse, low-growing heather. Bronze in color and quite fragrant, it dresses the mountain in velvet. Stopping to lunch on bread and cheese after reaching 2,700 meters (8,850 feet), I sit on the wayside, my feet dangling over the edge. It's a fabulous view, a balcony overlooking infinity. The snowy summits I glimpse in the distance and that merge with the sky, are they forty, fifty, or sixty miles away? There's no gauging a horizon so vast. Never have I breathed air this pure; never have I contemplated such immensity. In the foreground, a thousand feet below, large swaths of stubby grass are traversed by freely-roaming herds. Clouds driven by the wind cast shadows that glide swiftly over the ground, and in which my imagination gets lost: one after the other, I distinguish an imp with a long beard, a fox, Manas galloping by on his horse, the Grand Vizier Iznogoud,* and the outline of Africa. A bloody-walled canyon gashes the steppe as though a blade had just sliced into its flesh. Farther on, the corrugated metal roofs of Baetov, which I left behind before dawn, shine like fragments of a broken mirror. Behind them, an immense wall of

---

* TN: Iznogoud (note the play on the English words "is no good"), is a comic character created in the 1960s by the French writer-illustrator duo René Goscinny and Jean Tabary.

chalky mountains sculpts a large cirque, beyond which, at the edge of infinity, high summits of black rock and white snow sit on the horizon. A cool wind sweeps over the mountains. Lambs and greedy goats, oblivious to all this grandiose beauty, pass by me as if I weren't there. Far below, two children are playing in the carcass of a truck that must have missed the bend at the location where I'm sitting and plunged five hundred feet down into the abyss.

In the evening, dead-tired, having climbed more than one thousand meters (3,280 feet) over the course of the day, I reach Tokon's yurt. It lies at the bottom of a valley like a large white beast against a backdrop of green, overlooked by the trail above. Smoke rises from a pipe jutting through the roof. In the foreground, two women are seated in the grass who, with their backs to me, appear to be in quiet conversation. To the north, a horseman is galloping off to round up a few mares that wandered too far from the encampment. The sun is dropping behind the peaks; it paints them blood-red, then transforms them into Chinese shadow puppets. A bucolic and majestic landscape, one of rock and awe, where time stands still and fortunate passers-by like me breathe an air of eternity. As I stand before this vision of enduring beauty, I'm reminded of those paintings known as "Persian miniatures," which so successfully depict *immobility*, and which attempt, with innocence and naïveté, to marry the immemorial with the ordinary, while joyfully capturing the immutability of ephemeral things.

My watch's altimeter reads 3,400 meters (11,155 feet) and, as soon as the sun is hidden, the air grows cool. It would be no fun sleeping outside tonight. I tear down the slope, propelled by Ulysses who owes it to me, given that I've been heaving and tugging him all morning. I greet the two women who, caught by surprise, react with some alarm as soon as they hear me coming up from behind. But straightaway grandmother and granddaughter beam me a smile. Their jute bags are full of dried cow dung for the hearth. Without the least discussion of the matter, I'm invited to spend the night. I place the grandmother's heavy bag on Ulysses, and we trudge over to the yurt. The horseman I had spotted off in the distance gallops over, hops off his pony, and takes the girl's bag. It's her younger brother.

Tokon is waiting for us near his felt house. He's my age and stands taller than most Kyrgyz men I've seen so far. His face is burned from high-altitude sunshine and his pointed eyes are such a luminous shade of blue that they appear lit from within. He spends all summer here with his wife and grandchildren, his flock of sheep, and several cows and mares. The boy tosses the bags into a corner and now comes back and stands next to his grandfather. About twelve years old, wearing the leather cap of Russian tank crews, which can be adjusted with a string, he sports a fur-lined sleeveless vest over a red sweater. His pony followed him over without his having to call out. He attaches his mount to a stake close by but leaps back on the animal at regular intervals to gallop out onto the prairie where he tries to restore order to the anarchy of flocks grazing over the surrounding hillsides. His sister, barely any older than he is, is the true homemaker, for their old and weary grandmother tends to minor chores only. It's this little girl who milks the cows and mares with her grandfather, who counts the sheep as they're brought into a cave serving as their overnight shelter, and who makes bread on the stove: an old, cow-dung-fired tin drum. We sit down on little benches around a circular table near the roaring stove in the middle of the yurt, which maintains a pleasant temperature, even though outside, cold air is settling over the mountain. The meal couldn't be simpler: a loaf of flat, round *naan*, which Tokon breaks and distributes to those gathered, the largest piece going to the guest of honor. We dip these chunks back and forth in cream and rancid butter in two bowls on the table. After the meal, Tokon and I share a cup of *kumis*.

Darkness has fallen. A kerosene hurricane lamp lights the room. The girl asks us to take the table outside; she then unfolds five large fleece-lined mats and sets them one next to the other, followed by five large wool blankets, and we all lie down with our shoes off, though fully clothed. The beds are warm, but the blankets short: to keep my feet from freezing, I sleep curled up in a ball.

The tea we have for breakfast is salted, and we add *malaka* (milk) to it. It's the first time since Istanbul that I'm served something other than pure tea. Tokon's wife readied a large bag of *kurut*—or *kurtob*—for me. They're balls of cheese the size of marbles, molded in the fist. As for butter or cream, though, I have a terrible time convincing her that I simply can't take them with me, for they'd spill in my pack.

At this altitude, the landscape inspires dreams. There's a biting, sunny chill in the air that's perfect for walking. The preceding days' long climbs have toned my muscles and I almost instantly recovered from yesterday's fatigue, the way conditioned athletes do. The grassy hills are inhabited by marmots and they whistle as I go by, then plunge into their burrows. I also see curious field mice who wait at the edge of their hole until I'm right nearby before going in for shelter, and even some *lagomys*: small, little hare-like pikas that impishly leap about. Early in the morning, just as it's starting to get light out and the herds have begun stir, impatient to head off to the hills, numerous columns of smoke rising straight up into the cloudless sky allow me to pinpoint the location of all the nomad camps nestled in the valleys. Around 11:00, I head down into an immense dale, evenly carpeted in low grass. I spot a village tucked away at the far end. It will take me two hours to get there.

It's a beautiful day and nature here is so delightful that I'm of a mind to take my time. I finally walk at a leisurely pace, rediscovering the subtle joys of progressing slowly, and strong bursts of endorphins soon have me on a hiker's high. Contributing to this is the fact that, even without my asking, the generous Kyrgyz authorities granted me a three-month visa. But since paradise is not of this world, I still face one problem: I'm hungry. Given how much I've exerted myself, my body's crying out in hunger—Tokon's little pieces of bread dipped in cream were simply not enough to restore all my strength. Besides, wanting to be sure everyone got their fair share, I handed some of the pieces he gave me to his grandchildren. I've finished all my remaining food, including the freeze-dried *poulet basquaise*—a rather pompous name for a mixture that didn't have the least bit of chicken, tomatoes, or peppers in it, and which was the last of the reserves I had brought with me from Paris. But still, this morning, despite my hunger, I'm happy.

There's no grocery in the village of Ar-beyit. A young Kyrgyz man, Urumat, offers to cook something up for me . . . then immediately gives the job to his sisters while he basks in the cold noon sun and questions me about my journey.

In the evening, caught off guard in a storm, soaked and freezing, I go for cover in a house near the Kulak Pass ("ear" in Kyrgyz).

"Two weeks ago, four Frenchmen passed this way on bicycle," my host tells me, and he slides his index finger across his throat.

I gasp, with a start: "Someone slit their throats?!"

He's probably still laughing. Among the Kyrgyz, it's a gesture meaning that the person in question is stuffed to the gills.

Inquisitive men come parading through his house. The face of one of them is ravaged, scarred, and misshapen. They tell me that he's the farrier and was kicked by a horse, a mishap that turned his head to mush. Four men, wearing military camouflage and armed with rifles, approach on horseback, on their way back from the mountains. They're looking for a runaway but refuse to say any more. One of them spends a long time sharpening his knife while we sip tea.

I can't seem to warm up and spend part of the night shivering in my "extreme weather" down bag, guaranteed for temperatures as low as 10ºF. On the other side of Kulak Pass, I come face to face with the immense valley that will lead me all the way to Torugart. But for the time being, my goal is to reach Tash Rabat. I've been dreaming of the place for several weeks now. It will no doubt be the only structure I'll come across on my route this year with a direct connection to the Silk Road. I did see the ruins of two caravansaries over the past few days, but, being constructed of packed earth, there was almost nothing left. In Turkish, *taş* means "stone." In these regions, where walls are made of felt, stone buildings are rare, and place names underscore that fact. *Tashkent* is the "stone capital."

The road to Tash Rabat traverses a valley carved by a torrent through ruby-colored rocks. It's a place of stark beauty. Caravans headed into this valley on their way to China. Today, the route to China bypasses the mountain and this old road has become a dead-end. My first glimpse of the edifice takes my breath away. The caravansary is located smack dab in the middle of a wild, barren cirque. Several yurts have been set up nearby by nomads who, for a few dollars, offer tourists the experience of living like shepherds.

Tash Rabat, which dates from the tenth century, is considered one of the greatest buildings of that period in all of Central Asia. The square structure, each side of which measures approximately 150 feet, is made of black basalt. This large, thirty-room building is entirely covered, which, though uncommon, is hardly surprising, given that snow covers the ground here for over six months each year, starting in October. There's some controversy with respect to the building's origins. Discovered by archeologists in the early 1980s, the spot was cleared of a layer of mud brought by landslides in which it was buried. It's said that it was a temple before being turned into a caravansary, then finally into a fort prior to its abandonment. The guide is the daughter of a nearby farmer. She has phonetically memorized a short speech in English and spouts it in one breath—if someone interrupts her, she has to start all over from the beginning. Her explanations are, at times, a bit hard to swallow. She shows me a small room dug into the ground, covered with a large stone pierced with a hole. It's through the hole, she says, that food was delivered to the prisoners, for this was a jail. But at the other end of the building, there are two other pits, but no bored stone. That's easy to explain, the charming child tells me, without batting an eyelid: there are two prisons, one for men and the other for women. As if there were so many women in tenth century caravans that a prison had to be built just for them! An underground passage supposedly leads all the way to Kashgar, sixty miles away as the crow flies, but no one has ever explored it beyond the first few feet. As for the room where merchandise was unloaded, she refers to it as the "kitchens." Each chamber was topped with a stone dome. Some of the collapsed domes, most likely the result of earthquakes, have been rebuilt. The entire structure cuts a fine figure in its severe mountain dress. While I can certainly accept that it was originally a temple, I doubt that it was built by Nestorians. In fact, the largest square-shaped room, which is two stories high and topped with a dome, has in its center a hearth that, if anything, resembles a Zoroastrian temple. This must be the spot where Zoroastrian priests kept the eternal fire burning.

At the end of my tour, I'm back at the valley's entrance; here, Muhamad Nurpeisov and his wife Aygul open their small house and neighboring yurt to tourists passing through. They're helped by one of their ten children, Gulina, who also takes care of the couple's littlest ones, Indira and Alina, two joyful and devious little girls. Alina, the younger of the two, spends hour upon hour strumming her guitar for us and singing nursery rhymes in a somber, monotone voice, her face devoid of any emotion. Indira has a mischievous look and high cheekbones so ruddy it looks like she's wearing makeup. I meet two young Frenchmen here, kicking off an incredible, out-of-the-ordinary, three-week vacation. For next to nothing, they're going to buy two riding horses and a packhorse and head off to visit southern Kyrgyzstan as nomads would, transporting their food and canvas tents with them.

I make the most of my day off by washing and mending my clothes, especially my pants, which, as they do every year, started turning into tatters about nine hundred miles into the journey. I then hail a cab and ask to be driven twenty-five miles away, by way of the Naryn Road, to the small village of At-Bashi ("horsehead" in Kyrgyz). At the post office, I phone Paris and have the much-discussed documents—so dear to Gulsheva—faxed to me from Bishkek. The man at the counter pays no attention to the computer but instead calculates my expenses on his abacus. The bill is much higher than all the cash I have left in som, the national currency. So I can't pay the postman, but he's very gracious and doesn't raise his voice, as I feared he might. He simply tells me that he can't take dollars and sends me off to the bank. But the bank doesn't exchange foreign currencies either. So my driver takes me to the bazaar. No matter how small, Central Asian bazaars are places where there's always a way to work things out, for Asians have a real sense of business and are incredibly resourceful. Here, on a square surrounded by high walls, horses and sheep are for sale, and the inescapable brazier sizzling with *shash-lik* makes my mouth water. Several men express their willingness to handle the transaction, but when I take out a fifty-dollar bill, they freeze: no one has enough cash to exchange such a colossal sum! Soon, in concentric circles, the entire bazaar is busy at work trying to resolve the issue. Finally, two horse traders pool their fortunes to purchase my banknote. I can then settle up with both the postman and the taxi driver, and I have what I need to leisurely wind down my journey in Kyrgyzstan.

On July 8, at 5:30 in the morning, I'm all packed up and ready to go. But Muhamad and Aygul would never let me slip away without first having me drink a sacrosanct morning *chay*. By the time the samovar's finally steaming, an hour has gone by. I'm chomping at the bit. I've been apprehensive about this day for weeks, and with good reason. On both sides of the Pamirs, which I have to cross, I'll face numerous challenges. Here, just like anywhere else in the world, travelers have to go through customs at the border. But in addition to these—forty miles in advance of it on the Kyrgyz side and sixty miles beyond it on the Chinese side—there are police checkpoints. And in the no-man's-land in between, it's forbidden to travel by bicycle, let alone on foot. In short, if I can't convince the authorities on both sides, they'll force me to travel one hundred miles in a vehicle. I've been mulling this over since the end of my last journey, eight months ago. So I've decided to approach the problem in two ways, a different way for each country. On the Kyrgyz side, I'll try persuasion. The contacts I've had with the handful of police officers and soldiers I've come across in this country have been good, so I think

I can convince the men at the Korgon-Tash checkpoint, whom I'll meet today, to let me walk.

As for the Chinese, I've been warned not to take anything for granted. Back in Paris, I tried to reach the Chinese Embassy several times and was ignored. A letter I sent to the ambassador went unacknowledged. When I phoned, I never managed to get past the switchboard. So I decided to tackle the problem inside-out. Last January, six months before setting out from Samarkand, I made a special trip to Beijing to meet with Pierre Morel, the French ambassador to China. He's a tall, elegant man with slightly rounded shoulders, who sports a bowtie. He gave me a warm reception and was optimistic. "What an amazing undertaking! We'll try to convince the Chinese authorities to let you walk from the border all the way to the outpost in Tuopa. They couldn't possibly refuse." Unfortunately, a few weeks later, the Chinese Foreign Affairs Minister replied *meiyou* (no). So I adopted a more "political" approach. An old friend of mine, a journalist I worked with in television many years ago, François Loncle, is now the president of the Commission of Foreign Affairs in the French National Assembly.* I asked him to intercede on my behalf. Eager to help, he even persuaded Raymond Forni—president of the National Assembly—to do the same.† And they both wrote to their Chinese counterparts. Although I never received news of the final outcome of their efforts, I hope that they did the job and that the Chinese border guards have received their instructions. Furthermore, carefully folded and kept in a plastic bag in my pack, I have a letter from Pierre Morel, translated into Chinese, which asks border authorities to grant my request.‡ So all hope is not lost: I'll just have to get these soldiers' stone-cold hearts to soften up a bit.

---

* TN: François Loncle served in this position from 2000 to 2002; he was also a member of the National Assembly representing France's Eure department from 1997 to 2017.

† TN: Raymond Forni was vice-president of the National Assembly from 1998 to 2000 and president from 2000 to 2002; he passed away in 2008.

‡ These documents can be found in the appendix.

So, as I step out of Muhamad and Aygul's little house, full up on tea, I'm feeling reasonably optimistic. The little girls are still sleeping; Gulina's sick, she has been in bed since yesterday evening. It looks like rain, the temperature's mild. The valley that will lead me to the border is wide and beautiful. The river's running low, but there's a little whitewater where it splashes over the stones. The endless prairies, blanketed in low grasses, have turned golden brown in the light of the rising sun. Walking soothes me. The herds of cattle and horses, responding to some mysterious call, slowly move downstream, their long shadows seemingly reluctant to follow them. The road climbs up a gentle slope, the air grows brisker. Ulysses, unflinching as always, bounces over the rocky path.

At noon, I reach the village of Ak-Beyit, near a mountain pass at an elevation of 3,200 meters (10,500 feet). Some young people have gone to check their traps and show me a half-dozen marmots they've captured and killed. Some parts of the animals are for eating, while others, they explain, are kept for their medicinal virtues. They invite me to join them for lunch, but I'm too impatient, and share only in a cup of tea. I'm near Korgon-Tash now and I want to know, once and for all: will they, or won't they, let me walk?

At 3:00 p.m., I arrive in sight of the border checkpoint: a series of large, white, two-story buildings, surprising at these altitudes where one-story houses are the norm. They're surrounded by barbed wire and two large barriers block the road. I go up to them resolutely, telling myself over and over: "Be diplomatic! Be diplomatic! Smile!" My heart's pounding at over a hundred beats per minute, and it has nothing to do with walking or the elevation. As I approach the four or five Kyrgyz soldiers who've already spotted me coming, I force myself to put on a friendly face and I shake each one's hand. At this very moment, there's no more affable fellow than I in all of Central Asia! Even before they ask for my passport, I take out the little papers that summarize, in Russian, my long walk from Istanbul, and thrust them under the nose of the one who seems to be in charge. The effect is exactly as I hoped. He reads them aloud and his colleagues, giving

me a collective thumbs up, express their admiration for my achievement. While answering their questions on the route that I took to get
to Kyrgyzstan, I take out my passport and hand it to the headman
who barely glances at it, not wanting to miss a word of my story.
But the trickiest part remains: to persuade them to let me walk from
here to the border. I'm on the verge of broaching the subject when a
car, approaching from the Chinese side, comes to a halt. The Kyrgyz
driver who gets out is furious and insults the customs officers. I'm
suddenly forgotten. In the car are two tourists—a Spanish woman
and a Japanese man—who tell me that there was a problem at the
border post and that they were forced to turn around. Not a good
sign! Their guide, who works for a travel agency in Bishkek, is in such
a rage that he looks like he's about to start throwing punches at the
soldiers. It's the perfect moment. One customs agent—a kind-look-
ing, portly fellow with a mustache, who, in my eyes, seems incapable
of doing any harm—has remained outside the fray. I wave at him
vaguely as though we were in this together—a gesture that could
easily pass as a farewell—then skedaddle, flashing him a broad grin.
If they intercept me, I can always plead that it was in good faith!

I head off without looking back, on the alert, my ears wide open:
yes, I can still hear their loud voices. A good sign. And, in an additional stroke of luck, two trucks pull up, which keeps the customs
agents busy. I get away as quickly I can. I finally feel beyond their
grasp when I hear the sound of an approaching vehicle. It draws
up alongside me and stops. In the cabin is the man with the mustache . . . he opens the door. I'm busted! He finally noticed that I'd
snuck away, and now he's going to take me back to the border *manu
militari*! . . . But no, that's not it: he shrugs his shoulders and tells
me to hop in. It's not an order, it's an invitation. People are the same
everywhere I go: they grasp *in theory* that I walk, but they keep trying
to get me into their cars! I extend my warmest expression of thanks.
The man assures me that there are wolves, that the area is dangerous. I risk getting eaten, he says, clacking his jaw. I laugh and begin

once again kowtowing over and over in thanks. The truck drives off. Whew, that was close!

Once again, the setting is absolutely marvelous. To my left, barren hills beneath a peak that probably tops out at over 5,000 meters (16,400 feet), directly above Lake Ozero Chatyr-Kul, nudge the road due south. The sky has cleared up and a white sun seems to set fire to the vast steppe, over which the stony road dashes straight off into infinity. I glance at my altimeter: 3,300 meters (10,800 feet).

As evening falls, the wind picks up. It brings cold temperatures and big black clouds and, once again, it's threatening rain. As I start wondering where I might be able to camp, I discover, in terraced rows on a hillside, a succession of small, buried bunkers made of thick slabs of concrete into which have been cut loopholes. They're small forts from the days when the USSR and China were at each other's throats, and even actively going at each other along the Siberian border. I look them over and, like a king, I take my pick: I'll settle into . . . the one that hasn't been used as a latrine. I light some pieces of dried cow dung and they start giving off so much smoke that I have to step out, but before long, they become a comfortable and non-asphyxiating source of heat, and I cook my last serving of noodles. Let it rain all it wants tonight: I'll be safe from both water and wolves.

It's my next to last day in Kyrgyzstan, and the road keeps rising. I know that I'm heading toward another pass at an elevation of over 3,500 meters (11,400 feet). It's cool out. My eyes are on the ground in front of me and, as I walk, I obsess once again over what tomorrow might bring: will I or will I not get through? A bus that stops after having passed me by stirs me from my reverie. A large throng armed with cameras and camcorders snorts and chirps in a tongue I recognize to be Italian. What a joy to see how astonished they are! Just who is this fellow—clearly a Westerner—walking through this desert steppe? Dying for a fresh bit of news to report back to their friends, they rush over, gather information, express their surprise, exclaim their admiration, take photographs and movies, and speak with their hands, overjoyed at this little break from their rigid time-table, which has left no room for the unexpected. Needless to say, they're also happy to be finally able to move their rear ends, which have been glued to their coach's bucket seats since they left Bishkek at dawn. When I tell them that I started out in Venice, in honor of Marco Polo, and that my first book is already being translated into Italian, the chirping doubles in volume. Before they head off again, they ask me if there's anything I might need.

"Why yes, I'm hungry. Could I buy some food from you?"

A woman quickly rises to the challenge and takes up a collection. She comes back after conducting a veritable food hold-up. Later on, I even find that one of the sandwiches has a bite taken out of it, some-one's solid jaw having left its mark!

Around 3:00 p.m., the road turns sharply east and the spectacle that pops out at me from behind a hill is so breathtaking that I let go of Ulysses and, my knees giving out beneath me, I drop to the ground and sit down. There—seated in the grass and soul free—I observe the scene: the road leads, straight as an arrow as before, over grasses scorched by frosty nights and sunny days. Gusts of wind send choppy waves over the fields. A large lake shimmers to my left and several birds fly over it, too far away, though, for me to identify them. But that's not what has me choked up. My eyes are drawn to the immense black wall far off in the distance, topped by yet another, equally colossal white one: I've just reached the Pamir Mountains! Its peaks are so high, so stunning, and seem so menacing, that it's immediately clear to me that the first travelers who dared venture toward this barrier of cloud, rock, and snow, did so with fear in their hearts.

At these heights, travelers of yore had to leave behind their Bactrian camels and rely on yaks instead. The shaggy, slow-mov-ing, and feebleminded animals were more sure-footed and therefore better able to advance over ice without slipping, an event that could mean losing or ruining the precious bundles. But yaks couldn't carry as much, so as soon as they had put the mountains behind them, the merchants transferred everything back to camels, their preferred animals. At the trading post, one camel was worth eight yaks, nine horses, and forty-five sheep!

We're not far from Mongolia where barter was, moreover, the only medium of exchange, with surprising equivalences—and I'll let you judge for yourself: for the Mongolians, a steer was worth five sheep, a horse equaled two sheep, a woman was worth five horses, and a rifle cost two women.

Thick curtains of rain sweep over the plain like squalls at sea. Two sloppily-dressed Russian soldiers are inspecting a double row of elec-trified barbed wire. I'm about to run out of water. I try to stop a car, but they're few and far between, and the vehicles that do pass have been hired by tourists who think I'm trying to hitch a ride and don't want to be bothered by a shaved-headed fellow in tattered clothes, looking like nothing but trouble. A taxi finally stops: out pops a little Italian man, round and squat, video camera in hand, and he begins inscribing circles around me, asking me a thousand questions while still screaming at his wife, an attractive brunette wearing a hat who can't be bothered to move from her seat in back of the cab.

"*Ah, dees is wonderrrful, wonderrrful! Notes, take-a notes!*"

"*Dere's no point-a, since eet's all recorrrded!*" is her sensible reply.

The Kyrgyz giant who chauffeured them here takes a jerrycan of water from the trunk and fills one of my bottles as his passenger continues to film and prance about like a goat with indigestion from having munched on a few too many coffee beans.

I camp about six miles from the Kyrgyz border. I learned from a guidebook that there's a three- or four-mile band of no-man's-land between the two countries, and then an archway constructed by the Chinese, which marks the edge of their territory.

Although I covered over twenty-five miles today, I have trouble sleeping. It's very cold out. Several critters prowl around my tent. One of them runs into my mess kit I had set on a stone and knocks it to the ground. The sound causes a stampede. I try to catch a glimpse through the mosquito netting, shining my headlamp into the moonless night. An animal springs from the beam of light and disappears into the night, but I'm certain it was a wolf. Although I only became afraid after seeing the animal, the feeling is by no means less intense, and I peer out into the darkness for a long time. That's one of the drawbacks of traveling alone: vulnerability, for there's no one to comfort and reassure you! A little later, as the sun is coming up, a foal wanders over this time to sniff around my encampment. I shout, and it gallops away. My hands and feet are numb. The roof of my tent is so stiff that I'm afraid the canvas will split if I fold it, so I go for a run out on the plain to warm myself up and to give the rising sun a chance to melt the frost.

As soon as I have Ulysses back on the trail, I start obsessing about what's going to happen next. Will I or won't I get through? The Chinese make wealthy Westerners arrange for a Chinese travel agency to be waiting for them on the other side of the border. Forced trade. If there's no one there to pick you up, too bad, they'll send you back. Did the CITS—the official Chinese travel agency—get the message from Paris? Mr. Wang Wan Ping, the agency's manager for Xinjiang, was kindly willing to put me on the list of his tourists, despite my not being one of his better customers! He calls me "The Walking Man." Will he plead my case, given his familiarity with my adventure? I feel so isolated and vulnerable right now due to my inability to manage these connections and all the customs paperwork, that just to think that people in Ürümqi and Paris have me on their minds me lifts my spirits.

But before I start worrying too much about the Chinese border, I first have to get through Kyrgyz customs. When I get there, the office is closed. I rush over to the first customs agent. He motions me to relax: "In a bit." To cope with the wait and my anxiousness, I decide to strike up a conversation with a teenager who's also waiting, along with two of his friends. The kid looks at me condescendingly, says nothing, then turns his back to me. Yes, there are assholes in every country and of every age, and such behavior is significant to me solely for its statistical value.

When the office finally opens, the document they're interested in seeing after my passport is a fax from the Chinese stating that they're waiting for me this very day. I explain, to no avail, that I've been on the road since June 22 and don't have anything like that: they couldn't give a hoot, that's my problem. Then they ask me for that much-mentioned laissez-passer that had caused me so much worry. And of course, they want the original. After fighting with them for twenty-five minutes—by the clock—they point me to the right door, the one leading to China. True to form, when they ask everyone to get into a car, I pretend not to notice. I grab Ulysses's tow bar and make for the arch. My odds are one in a thousand. And today's not my day: a soldier who doesn't look like he's joking around blocks the road with his machine gun and points me to the vehicles. They can't be avoided if you want to cross the no-man's-land between the two border checkpoints. I ask the couple apparently in charge of the disdainful teens whether they'd be willing to let me ride with them in their travel agency's vehicle. In a stuck-up voice, the man brushes me off with the most asinine reply imaginable, one he considers unanswerable:

"Impossible! We are diplomaaats!" he says, as though his mouth were full of petits fours.

"On vacation," I impertinently point out.

"Yes, but *diplomaaats*."

Come, come! His "we" strikes me as odd. As if the offspring of diplomats, whether full of themselves like these three or not, were born with diplomatic passports in their mouths! I don't insist: I find such plenipotentiary nonsense perfectly unbearable.

In the end, it's some kind Italian tourists—this place is decidedly teeming with them!—who invite Ulysses and me to hop into their minibus for the four-mile journey.

Torugart Pass is surreal. Imagine a great archway, some fifty feet high and painted pink, that suddenly appears out of nowhere in a rocky,

ice-covered landscape at an altitude of 3,700 meters (12,000 feet). Two
metal gates block the way and two Chinese sentries, machine guns in
hand, frozen at attention like bronze statues, quickly quell any vague
notions of forcing one's way through. We watch as thirty "candidates"
or so walk past, having arrived in vehicles belonging to Kyrgyz travel
agencies, which then remain there until their drivers are certain that
their customers have made it through. Clear evidence that, even under
the aegis of professional agencies, crossing is never a sure thing. We all
get to know one another, we chat. Everyone takes a seat, here or there,
including the diplomats, who deign to plop their noble derrières down
on the same grass as the Italians and me, since no one, alas, bothered
to roll out a diplomatic lawn for them! They look bored beyond belief.
But like us, they keep a close watch on what's happening on the other
side of the archway. There's a parking lot there and a small structure
with a flagpole in front of it waving the red, star-studded Chinese flag.
That's where the cars will come to pick us up, regardless of our rank.

Around 11:00, the first four-wheel-drive vehicle pulls into the
parking lot. A young woman dressed all in white and sporting a golf
cap walks to the archway and my name is the first one called. Mr.
Wang Wan Ping didn't forget me! Thank you, Mr. Wang Wan Ping!
I joyfully grab Ulysses and head in the woman's direction, but one
of the sentries waves for me to stay put. He says something to the
young woman, which sounds more like a bark, and without a word,
she turns around and steps into the customs office. She comes back
out ten minutes later without so much as throwing me a glance and
gets back in her car. Is she about to drive off? No, the vehicle remains
where it is. The chauffeur sets about cleaning the windshield. Come
on now! So we're back to waiting. For how long? Isn't it incredible,
though, how much anxiety they're putting us through? We're like
high-school seniors about to find out whether or not we made the
grade and get to graduate!

At 12:00 sharp, the young woman steps back out of her car and
motions me to come her way. As I walk beneath the archway, I turn
around and bid my diplomats a wry, retaliatory goodbye.

The young woman introduces herself as Rosa. She's not Chinese—Han, that is—but Uyghur—meaning Turco-Mongol. She has a pleasant smile and tells me that we'll soon be on our way, but that there's a final formality to take care of. We go back into the office. I have the ambassador's letter at the ready, but the only soldier present, upon seeing me, issues some kind of brief command.

"You'll have to wait outside, you're not allowed in the building," Rosa tells me.

She comes back out not long after. The driver loads Ulysses into his four-by-four. What am I to do? Rosa tells me that walking is out of the question, that the customs officer refused to even glance at Pierre Morel's letter, but that there's another border checkpoint approximately six miles on. I grudgingly climb back into the vehicle, disappointed and furious, but do I really have a choice? Without a telephone handy, I can't call Wang Wan Ping who might be able to intercede once again on my behalf. So I pin my hopes on the next Chinese border station. Perhaps they'll be more flexible there than here.

While Rosa presents the customs papers to the two agents who meet us out on the porch at the next border checkpoint, I quickly slip the ambassador's letter under their noses. One of them reads it aloud. They laugh, while pointing to the car. There's nothing I can do. My nose glued to the window, I watch the remaining fifty-six miles go by. I'm not missing much. Is it a case of sour grapes? On the Kyrgyz side, I found the landscape fascinating, whereas on the Chinese side it's a bleak, rocky valley devoid of all vegetation. Now and then, the four-by-four climbs embankments covered in mud or stones that have been deposited by rivers of melting snow, and which no one has cleared away. It isn't easy, but I get the driver to stop for a moment when I spot a Kyrgyz couple heading down through the valley. The man is leading a mule, while tethered behind it stride two Bactrian camels. On the first, apart from packages, is a woman tightly clutching a young child in her arms; a second child is snuggled up behind her, hanging onto her coat. The other camel, attached to the first's tail, is weighed down with several enormous bundles. An elderly couple relocating with their grandchildren. Have they, too, been turned back at the border? I'll never know. The driver's nervous and tells me to hurry up and get back in the car. If someone reported him for stopping, the Chinese military would likely take disciplinary action against him.

Tuopa, the true border checkpoint, is sixty miles beyond the archway at Torugart. Officials don't seem to care to know whether we're bringing money or objects into China. All they're interested in are books and cassette tapes. The regime is more concerned about ideas than arms. And as far as that goes—I'm sure you'll agree—they darn well should be! We all know how revolutions are born. A young woman who, for professional reasons, was carrying photos on a CD with her, tells me later on that the customs officer, since he had no way to view them, simply broke the disc into pieces.

I tell Rosa that she can drop me off here, that I want to continue on foot since it's no longer a military zone. The chauffeur panics. He wants to drive me all the way to Kashgar, like all the other tourists he regularly comes to pick up at Torugart. I make it clear to him that that's out of the question. He dashes off to phone Wang Wan Ping who instructs him—it's the least he can do—to let the Walking Man walk! Rosa, before heading off, warns me of "political demonstrations." I play the idiot and try to get her to explain a little more, but to no avail. Given that she's Uyghur, she undoubtedly knows all about the troubles facing the entire province: an independence movement has emerged in opposition to the policy of systematic and ruthless colonization being pursued by Beijing. Uyghurs, who made up ninety percent of the population in 1955, today make up barely fifty percent.* They're ethnic Mongols and are Muslim, unlike the Eastern—or Han—Chinese. There are rumors that pro-independence

---

* TN: According to a report published in 2018, Uyghurs constitute 8 million people out of a population of 19 million, or 42.1%. "Xinjiang Territory Profile," *BBC News*, 12 October 2018, https://www.bbc.com/news/world-asia-pacific-16860974.

militants have asked for assistance from the Afghan Taliban, and that has the Chinese police very nervous. I avoid letting kindhearted Rosa in on this, but if I do encounter pro-independence Uyghurs, I'll be delighted to have them tell me about their movement.

The vehicle now gone, I glance up at the summits we've just left behind. It's 3:00 p.m. So here I am in China! Goodbye bread, hello rice. Well, that reminds me that I finished my last reserves as well as those that the Italians gave me. In a Chinese restaurant near the customs office, they point me back out the door without explanation. It must not be mealtime. Two or three other attempts yield the same result. It would seem that, not only have I changed countries, but I've also kissed common courtesy goodbye.

After a quick descent that took us all the way to Tuopa, the road follows a valley sandwiched between forested slopes. It's hot out, but that's to be expected, for we just lost over 1,200 meters (4,000 feet). The road is blacktopped, which should make Ulysses happy after having bounced along for weeks on Kyrgyzstan's rough roads. Less than an hour into my walk, I encounter a curious crew. Two men are circling some kind of motorized cultivator to which an elaborate trailer has been hitched. I can guess the device's purpose from its iron claws and the clumps of wool: I've happened upon a Chinese carding machine! We are, after all, in sheep shearing season. The machine is smoking like a chimney: it has run out of water. Having just refilled my bottles, I empty two of them into the radiator and, in a flash, the machine starts right back up! Seeing that I bailed them out, the two men invite me, with a series of gestures, to their house for tea. I accept, so I attach Ulysses behind the carding machine and sit down on its narrow floorboard. Then off we go on the most incredible carriage around! And to my great delight, the diplomats—you know, those disdainful ambassadors—pass us up in a car that's a true reflection of who they are. They must be patting one another on the back for having refused to make room for an oddball such as myself!

The carders live two and a half miles away in the first houses of a village that doesn't appear on my map and whose name I can't make out. Having had tea and having refilled my bottles, I get back underway. I plan on making Kashgar, forty miles from here, by tomorrow evening.

I take my time discovering this new country, the sixth since leaving Istanbul. I did the calculations last night: I'm about to travel 930 miles in China this year and 1,870 the next. The distance from China's western border to Xi'an, the Imperial City, accounts for over a third of the entire Silk Road.

I'm poignantly aware of the fact that I didn't do myself any favors by giving up on the idea of learning Chinese. In prior years, so that I could communicate a trifle with the people I met, I studied Turkish before crossing the Anatolian Plateau. I took a few courses in Farsi, the Persian language, so that I could read the alphabet—and therefore road signs—and I committed several phrases to memory. But in Iran, even in the tiniest village, I always came across some university student who, with dreams of emigrating in his head, was resolutely learning English. For Russian, spoken in the three countries I just traversed, things were easier. I had taken lessons many years ago before going on a trip to Moscow, where I had been invited by my friend Sergei, who's extremely proficient in French. I could still recall the Cyrillic alphabet and a smattering of words. I took several more lessons with a high school teacher, then increased my vocabulary while on the road. A pocket dictionary helped me fill in all the words I was missing in a language that I would really like to speak because—I have no idea why—I find Russian words to be very inspirational, and eye-catching. One might scoff, saying that I never mastered even one of the many declensions, but to me, that's entirely irrelevant. I've been happy with a practical competency, as I've sought only to understand and to be understood. It goes without saying that the two phrases I used most were "*ya ne znayu*" (I don't know) and "*ya ne ponimayu*" (I don't understand)!

As for Chinese, I initially toyed with giving it a try. But it would have required a great deal of something a retiree like me has precious little of: time. The first obstacle lies in the fact that Chinese has four tones. I haven't the slightest ear for music and have never been able to differentiate between *mā* (mother), *mǎ* (horse), *má* (hemp), and *mà* (to scold). The second obstacle is that you have to learn hundreds upon hundreds of ideograms. My memory is a sieve crowded with millions of memories and all it retains are strong emotions and a few select images, I don't really know how or why. The prospect of having to memorize umpteen hundred of these strange figures had me worried enough already, but when I was told that the term "longevity" can be conveyed by a hundred different ideograms, I cried uncle! The third complication seemed to me to be the most important: "Which language do you want to learn?" people asked me. "Mandarin, Cantonese, Shanghainese, or one of the hundred or more other dialects spoken by fifty-six minority groups?" And the soupçon of resolve I still held onto was shattered when I came to the following realization: nearly half of my journey across China was going to be among the Uyghurs. They are, of course, Chinese nationals, but they speak a Turkic language, unrelated to Chinese, both in terms of writing and speaking. And the Turks themselves told me that they can't understand their own distant cousins! Only numbers still bear some resemblance in the two languages. In Xinjiang, the region I'm now entering, half the population is Uyghur and the other half Han. So, screw it, I gave up on both Chinese and Uyghur! I bought a little dictionary but it's not of much help. It's in English, but offers Chinese words that I can't read, let alone pronounce.

I hope to meet interesting people nevertheless, people with whom the language of the heart—and that of the hands—play leading roles. As for everything else, my day-to-day needs are simple, and I've committed a few words and phrases to memory so that I can eat, sleep, and find my way.

On this, the very first day, that's easy: to get to Kashgar, there's but one road. I mentioned earlier how I had discovered that, after passing beneath the Torugart archway, courteousness had remained behind at the border; but the world around me has changed as well: there are no more slow-moving horses and riders sporting bright-colored shirts, but motorcycles and backfiring tractors. Kerosene lamps are gone, replaced by electricity everywhere, which, sadly, is used primarily to generate noise. Whether from open windows or from loudspeakers installed high atop pylons, people are yelling, singing, reciting, pontificating. The faces are no longer the same either: I was expecting, after the Kyrgyz with their slightly slanted eyes, that those of the inhabitants here would be slanted even more. But it's quite the opposite: I feel that I've taken a step backwards. Most of these men and women look like they could be cousins of the Anatolian Turks I met two years ago.

The houses are all built on the same model: they're single-story structures with yards enclosed by high mud or brick walls. Since each one takes up a lot of space and opens out onto the road, the first village I traverse is in fact one continuous street without a single intersection. I walk for nearly six miles past walls and closed doors on either side. After Kyrgyzstan's wide-open spaces, welcome to the Great Corridor of China.

I look for a place to camp. I locate a spot in the middle of a mud-brick factory. The men dig a hole in the ground, mix the soil with water and straw, then pack it into a wooden mold. The brick is left in the sun for several weeks, if not several months. Stirring the noodle soup I bought in Tuopa, feeling rather glum, I get to thinking that I had better brace myself for a long, solitary journey. I've learned that distances are something I can handle. As for total solitude, I'll soon find out.

VI
KASHGAR: CITY OF MERCHANTS

Ever since they forced me to climb into a vehicle, I've been walking with a grudge against Chinese soldiers. On my road to Kashgar, they're making their situation worse by standing in my way again, only this time, by forcing me to go a greater distance . . . on foot! For, on the direct route, troops are conducting maneuvers. At a fork in the road, a soldier brandishing two small flags in order to divert cars stops me. There's no getting through. I try to get some information from him: for how long will the road be closed? But there's more humanity in the eyes of a cobra than in his. He motions me to get a move on in the direction he's pointing, or else. The prank winds up costing me an extra nine miles, which, in the large scheme of things, is small potatoes.

A short distance before the city limits, police officers are once again barring all traffic, even preventing pedestrians from walking on the shoulder. A convoy of three hundred trucks or so transporting soldiers, cannons, and rocket launchers is headed downtown. It's very hot out on the wide avenue leading to Kashgar. Once the convoy has passed, pedestrians are allowed to circulate. We number in the hundreds, all walking single file along the narrow service lane. I make one or two attempts, and others with me, to reach the pavement, but we're pushed back, since here come some sixty Japanese four-wheel-drive vehicles with tinted windows: the military's top brass is on its way to the base. Given how carefully the avenue was cleared,

91

I observe how the powerful and dreaded "People's Army" as it calls itself has set things straight: army on the avenue, people in the gutter. And today's only a rehearsal. Imagine what it will be like for the parade tomorrow!

With respect to Silk Road history, Kashgar is one of Central Asia's shining pearls. Not only does it fire the imagination of adventurers and merchants alike, it was also at the focal point of what might be called the first cold war between the British Empire at the height of its power and Czarist Russia. Situated at the westernmost edge of Xinjiang—China's largest province, three times as big as France—it's home to a mere sixteen million inhabitants. It was invaded in the first century by a Chinese general, Ban Chao, who ruled over the region for more than thirty years. This "man with an iron fist" went to war on account of a horse: when he asked permission to enter a certain Central Asian city with his troops, the city's rulers, who were vassals of the Mongols, agreed, but on condition that he first sacrifice his horse. He refused to give up his steed, and instead sacrificed a few of his soldiers in the war that ensued.

Xinjiang was free from Chinese domination until the seventh century, and Kashgar was a key player in Silk Road trade. Travelers coming from what is today Kyrgyzstan, Afghanistan, and Pakistan, had no choice but to pass through this oasis before skirting around the immense Taklamakan Desert, by either the northern or the southern route. This is still true today.

In the seventh century, the emperors of the Tang Dynasty reclaimed a foothold in the region to ensure the security of convoys en route to Central Asia, and, once their troops had begun marching, they had them press on as far as Bukhara. The Arabs, in their thirst for conquest in the early eighth century, got as far as the Kashgar Oasis. But neither group ever managed to establish permanent settlements across the Pamirs, which stood as a formidable obstacle, a natural Great Wall that kept the two worlds apart. After the Battle of Talas, the Chinese would never again attempt to colonize Central Asia. The Arabs, who made incursions this far in 713, saw that the site was impossible to secure and consequently withdrew. But at the end of the fourteenth century, the Timurids sacked Kashgar, allowing Islam to conquer the region and forcing out Buddhists, Nestorians, and Zoroastrians until only it remained. The temples of other faiths that weren't so lucky as to have disappeared beneath the sands— where, hidden from view, they would survive for centuries—were ruthlessly destroyed, their paintings scratched out, and their statues pounded to pieces.

At the outset of the twentieth century, Kashgar was at the center of an undeclared war between the Russians and the English, each coveting Xinjiang, situated at the fringe of both empires. China had been weakened and was unable to defend what was then called Chinese Turkestan. The Russian and English consulates in Kashgar, veritable spies' nests, operated from behind the scenes, hatching artful schemes. This secret battle, which the English nicknamed "the Great Game," would first end in a draw; but China would ultimately walk away with the prize.

Entranced by the city's romanticism and hoping to catch a nostalgic whiff of "the Great Game" and the good old days, I stay at the Chini Bagh Hotel, which today stands more or less on the former site of the British Consulate. Just a few steps from here, tourists can also sleep in the sumptuous suites of its former Russian rival, now also a hotel.

Although the manna from heaven brought by the caravans has, little by little, ceased to fall, Kashgar still remains a city of merchants. And the Sunday market is one of the most fabulous Silk Road events I've seen to date. For the full experience, it's imperative to get up early, before daybreak. I hail a donkey cab and we plunge into the old city's narrow streets. There's an unbelievable crowd rushing to get there, transporting their merchandise on every vehicle known to man, jostling one another as they hurry along: donkey carts and handcarts, motorized and pedal-operated tricycles, bicycles, motorcycles, cars, trucks, and wheelbarrows. All that's missing are the camels. You can never reach your spot soon enough, for missing out on a potential deal

is out of the question. So the men force their way through, yelling
"Posh! Posh!" which might translate as "Room! Make room!" These
calls, isolated at first, multiply until they become a murmur, then,
the nearer you get, a steady background drone. Every Saturday and
Sunday, sixty thousand people squeeze into this place, and that's not
counting all the tourists who come to Kashgar for the sole purpose of
witnessing this fabulous market. Country dwellers sometimes walk
for several days in order to sell their goods here, and they're not about
to arrive late and find there's no room left to set up shop!

The spectacle is so strange, so colorful, that my camera fires away
nonstop: a man taking a horse for a test ride charges around in the
middle of the crowd, the turquoise eyes of a little girl serving customers in a restaurant, a woman cloaked in a heavy brown cloth with
an array of religious caps on her head that she's hawking, and on
and on. I don't know which way to point the lens; then, in a trice, I
stop. No photo could ever convey the mercantile effervescence, the
swarming mass of humanity, the swirl of colors, sounds, and smells
that spreads little by little until it carries you away. It's impossible not
to be swept off your feet by the wave that crashing over you, pushing you, dragging you, and raising you up; until, suddenly, you find
yourself part of the jumble, whether you like it or not. But in fact,
you do like it, since you know full well that this is *life*, and you even
catch yourself turning a critical eye on the markets of the West: those
civilized places, overburdened with dignity, codes, and petty conven-
tions. Maybe it's because you have the feeling that, here, *community*
is a word that still means something. People play the game—in this
case, they play the merchants—but deep down inside everyone feels
equal to everyone else, no one takes social status seriously the way
people do where we come from. Therein lies the magic of the Orient
that has so fascinated travelers from the West. How could one ever
capture on film the thousand odors wafting up from these acres of
perspiration, from the suint of the sheep, from the burned grease of
the *shashlik* on sulfured charcoal, from the animal excrement, from
the fruits and vegetables spoiling in a corner; or those subtler smells

floating in the air above the spice vendors stalls? You could visit the market with your eyes closed, your nose would have no trouble at all guiding you to the ripe fruit stalls, or the leather vendors!

In one street, perhaps thirty cobblers—their shoeless customers chatting away with them on little stools—are banging their hammers on small anvils, or making their sewing machines from a bygone era cackle clickety-clack. A bit farther, knife sharpeners force us to cover our ears as they make their iron blades screech on grindstones operated by pulling intermittently on a string spooled around the axle. One clever fellow has connected his grindstone to his bike's crankset, which rests on a stand, and he races along, dripping in sweat, going nowhere. The donkeys, by the hundreds, let out pathetic brays, broken by the sounds of impatient horns, for time—*Posh, Posh!*—which everywhere else stands still, is here transformed into money. The din in the street where audiovisual equipment is sold is unbearable, each salesman having adjusted the volume of his TVs or hi-fi systems to the only level people care for here: one so loud it pierces the eardrums. But the most consistent sound of all is the hubbub of the throng itself. How many languages are being spoken here? The most exotic tongues are those of tourists, who, in their universal uniforms, can't be missed: pants or Bermuda shorts with lots of pockets, hats jammed down over pale faces, cameras or camcorders slung across their chests, eager to store up all these images and dazzling colors—for the journey will only fully crystallize in the illustrated accounts they give of them later on.

There are not many Han Chinese at the Kashgar market. But every single Central Asian ethnic group is represented. Local Uyghurs wear Western dress. But the others—Kyrgyz, Kazakhs, Mongols, Tajiks, Uzbeks, and Afghans—are often in traditional garb. Large numbers of Pakistanis, wearing long shirts atop pants of identical cloth, have come either to buy or to sell.

I put my camera away some time ago now and simply wander about, following the crowd, letting the hustle and bustle, this veritable bath of emotion, soak in through all my pores and senses. It's too strong, too vast, too meaningful. There's no way to remain behind the lens. You have to dive deep into the crowd and embrace it; you have to melt into it. Famished, I drop several times into food stalls where patrons quickly and silently consume servings of *laghman*, then dive right back into the market's madness. Here, everything is sold, everything can be bought. In keeping with Asian tradition, each zone has its specialty; whether for knives, candy, hats, shoes, or clothing, each boasts a succession of fifty stores, all selling the same products. Prices are never posted. It all depends on how good the merchant is at selling and how good the buyer is at haggling. In the cameras and optics section, three Japanese soldiers are loudly negotiating the sale of a pair of heavy binoculars. Over there, vendors sell nothing but dried fruit; over here, all they sell are collars for mules and donkeys, cobbled together from worn-out motorcycle tires. That works since the road wore down their outer edge only, whereas the donkey will abrade but the sidewalls. In a short, blind alley, in front of canvasses on which all illnesses known to man have been painted with écorché-like realism, doctors and apothecaries have laid out their vials: their dried herbs, toads, scorpions, and snakes. Squatting down with one eye fixated on the images, patrons try to reassure themselves that their particular malady isn't among the lineup of horrors. A stone's throw away is the street where debris, garbage, waste, and scrap materials are reborn for the umpteenth time. Pieces of scrap metal, rusted spare parts, old jugs, pieces of leather and plastic, chipped bottles and vases, wires, piles of oily rags: it's all for sale right here. Stunning, surreal images. One fellow, standing on his own two feet, is fervently negotiating the purchase of a single boot, while another squeezes past him, old and legless, clinging to the neck of a mule: "*Posh! Posh!*"

But here is the most fascinating activity yet: a crowd, which I estimate to consist of around 250 or 300 women, are walking about in silence as they hold out in front of them, on one arm or in two hands, a garment, dress, skirt, or corsage they want to sell. The throng is so thick that the women wouldn't dare display their goods on the ground as is done elsewhere, for it would only be trampled upon. Each woman is at once a seller and a buyer. Tired of the pretty dress purchased here or elsewhere, they seek to get rid of it at the best price so they can buy a new one. And so, no sooner have they pocketed the money from a sale, than off they go, trying to figure out how they're going to spend it. Prices are communicated in a whisper. Hands caress the silk or wool. The eyes speak louder than words. Money goes round and round.

Is there anything that *can't* be found among the thousand-and-one objects for sale in Kashgar's market, which was and still is the largest along the former and current Silk Road? Everything, in incredible quantities, is on display: ropes, plastic bags, lottery tickets. An old man is setting sparrow traps, gluing corn kernels to them. Another man wanders through crowd, holding up a melon and large knife, selling slices upon request. A few kids with large platters on their heads are hawking sugar and honey cakes. A bearded man, a Kyrgyz *kalpak* on his head and holding a goat on a leash, is quibbling over the price of a spade.

Sun and fatigue finally drive me away. And yet I'm used to walking twenty if not twenty-five miles a day! But all the shuffling and emotion have exhausted me more than if I had climbed to the top of a mountain pass along Kyrgyzstan's byways.

Off Nuo'er Beixi Street, a little gateway gives access to a park located beyond the Idkah Mosque at the heart of the city. It's a place of restorative silence. Reeling from the crowd and its frenzy, here, I rest for a while.

Not far from a boilermaker who, aided by his assistant, is hammering red-hot copper into the shape of a bowl, sits a small Uyghur restaurant overflowing with customers. Outside, four men work nonstop cutting quarters of meat into small pieces and threading them onto skewers. Inside, people press up against one another, jamming onto benches. Don't bother waiting for a clean glass, just grab your neighbor's as soon as he gets up to leave, wash it with scalding tea and toss the liquid onto the ground. The television's blaring, and everyone's yelling to hear one another or to place an order with the overburdened servers, who then dash off like hares. Atop roaring charcoal fires, pyramids of kebabs spatter droplets of grease, which flare up, giving off a bland odor. Green tea is served by the liter, in large aluminum kettles.

The backstreets of the blacksmiths' quarter, located around the mosque, lure me in like flypaper. I stop in my tracks, transfixed on the sidewalk or riveted in the middle of the street, fascinated by the spectacle. From time immemorial, people have been making hundreds of objects here, out of iron, cloth, copper, gold and precious stones, glass, or wood. From axes to traditional hats, from jewelry to bread: everything here is made in little cabana-sized stalls overflowing with merchandise. The artisans and their helpers, focused and filthy, work outside on the sidewalk. Wood turners, seamstresses, bakers, blacksmiths, hatters, knifemakers, tinsmiths, goldsmiths, silversmiths, and mechanics can be found mixed in with restaurants, bookstores, dentists, cobblers, and bric-a-brac sellers. It's a veritable university for artisans. There are no books and notes are taken with the eyes. At a barbershop where I have my chin and head shaved in preparation for my journey into the desert, the master leans over me, and, in the background, three apprentices look on with great seriousness and focus, awed by how confidently he flicks his razor. Fortunately for me, I can only carry with me the indispensable, otherwise I'd buy a hundred beautifully made but perfectly unnecessary knick-knacks. In 1997, in this very bazaar here in Kashgar, I stopped dead in my tracks at the sight of an old craftsman tapping the last nails into the soles of a fine pair of riding boots. The materials were so beautiful, the man's gestures so admirable, that I purchased the boots. I've never used them; I don't even ride horses! I simply wanted to keep alive the memory of that moment—so commonplace here, but so rare in the West—of fleeting communion between hand and eye. Back home, whenever I chance upon those boots, the image of the old man leaning over his work in that shadowy shop pops into my mind with photographic precision.

Far from Beijing, where the last of the old neighborhoods are in the process of being leveled; isolated at the end of the last century by a series of despotic warlords; walled off when the Pamir and Tian Shan borders were closed in the aftermath of the Soviet and Chinese Revolutions—Kashgar's small streets, stalls, mercantile traditions, and bazaar have been marvelously preserved. Here, I breathe in a little of the ambiance that must have existed in the days of the Silk Road, back when it so entranced travelers. And I doubt that I'll find a more authentic atmosphere anywhere else. Kashgar is, beyond a doubt, the only city between Istanbul and Xi'an to so firmly assert its personality. What a pity that I wound up having to stay in a luxury hotel! If only I had been fortunate enough to have been invited in by one of its inhabitants. I would have believed, if only for an instant, that I had traveled back in time.

Government agencies are more "modern." I wish to visit the museum bearing the fancy name of the "Silk Road Cultural Relic Show." I finally find it, but . . .

"It's 11:00," the guard tells me. "It's closed."

"But your brochure says that you're open until noon. That's okay, though, I'll stop back at 2:00, since the guidebook says that . . ."

"Ah! We're closed this afternoon. Today only."

"Tomorrow then . . ."

"That won't work either, I've lost the key."

So I'll be leaving the city without ever having seen its "relics," but I couldn't care less, since the Sunday market was everything I could have possibly hoped for.

I prepare the next chapter of my journey while resting up for four days. An unprecedented indulgence. A nasty cold sore that appeared on my lip—a warning sign of excessive stress and fatigue brought on by crossing the border at Torugart—has gone down a bit. I eat like a horse six times a day. The kebab-makers on Nuo'er Beixi Street recognize me and take to greeting me. It's probably not often that Westerners venture into this greasy spoon! The owner charges me the Uyghur rate, and I order the same thing each time: noodles with two helpings of meat. A group of French travelers led by Emmanuel Lincot, tour guide and eminent expert in Chinese painting, is in town. I entrust them with some of my notes and rolls of film, which they agree to take back to Paris for me. We dine together. I rather enjoy speaking French again for the first time since leaving Samarkand. And it will likely be the last time until I arrive in Turfan, the end of this year's stage, beyond the Taklamakan, nine hundred miles from beautiful Kashgar.

VII

DESERT RAIN

I don't have much time to play the tourist, but before leaving Kashgar—and for want of a museum—I'd like to pay a visit to the Fragrant Concubine. Her Uyghur name is Iparxan, but the Chinese know her as Xiang Fei. Her destiny was both extraordinary and tragic. In the mid-eighteenth century, her husband, a Uyghur leader, fomented—then led—a revolt against the emperor. He was defeated and executed; his wife was taken to Beijing as a prisoner, but before long, she was the Emperor's favorite. Her secret? A natural body scent with aphrodisiacal properties that worked on men in general, and on the Emperor in particular. The sovereign's mother considered it unconscionable that a prisoner should have ensnared the emperor's heart, so she decided to put an end to it. She forced the young woman to commit suicide. That's how Iparxan's tomb wound up in the very beautiful mausoleum consisting of a dome and four minarets that had been originally constructed at the end of the seventeenth century for her grandfather. It took 120 people three years to carry her coffin on a palanquin all the way to Kashgar.

I leave the city after four days off on August 14. Before me lies the sinister Taklamakan Desert. It's immense, just imagine: 116,000 square miles, one-half the size of France! It has a tragic reputation—its Uyghur name means "the place from which one never returns." Ancient texts, including those of Marco Polo, speak of demons that called out to travelers to lead them astray. The region's geography and history do not contradict the legend. The many mountain torrents flowing down from the Tian Shan and the Himalayas and irrigating the oases grew scarce. Without water, the inhabitants had no choice but to abandon these dead cities. By the twelfth century, entire oases had vanished. It's said that three hundred cities and villages lie buried beneath the sand. Locals claim that in the nineteenth century, 360 cities were swallowed up by the Taklamakan *in a single day.* Excavations have managed to uncover several sites, revealing archeological treasures, much of which headed to museums in the West, stolen by European or American "prowlers."

It's very hot here in the summer. In the winter, the temperature can vary between 104ºF by day and -4ºF by night. Rarely have travelers tried to penetrate this ocean of dunes. Caravans, like modern highways, avoided it, passing either to the north by way or Turfan, or to the south by way of Hotan. I've chosen the northern route. Both of them head out of Kashgar and meet up again in Yumen, at the Pass of the Jade Gate, which once marked the China's western boundary before it annexed Xinjiang.

My departure date is ideal for walking. During the months of June, July, and the first half of August, temperatures are too high to walk here, so I voluntarily opted to roast in the Fergana Valley instead of in the desert sands. My walking schedule was supposed to bring me here at the end of August but, as is my wont, I'm over ten days early.

I'm beyond the oasis in no time at all and, all rested up, I set a swift pace. To my left is something resembling a dirt wall: it's the foothills of the Celestial Mountains, which I'll be hugging for the entire 930 miles to Turfan. To the right, looking south, is the desert—an endless, motionless sea. It's a peculiar sight, to say the least: ordinarily, flat terrain curves downward at the horizon. Here, nothing of the sort. The ground is perfectly level all the way to the edge of the horizon, where, in a white haze, earth and sky blend into a single cottony fuzziness. The road undulates and rises imperceptibly as it nears the mountain, but most of the time it runs in a straight line and is perfectly horizontal, without landmarks, without anything at all to grab the eye. From time to time, two or three houses unexpectedly emerge from the emptiness. Adobe buildings built alongside the road, and upon which they rely: restaurants, machine shops, and beverage and melon vendors sheltered beneath makeshift tarps.

By the end of that first afternoon, the Taklamakan has sent me a message: this will be no walk in the park. A north wind has picked up, carrying fine, almost imperceptible, powdery dust that blots out the landscape and hides the sun. A sandstorm on the first day: what luck! While it does help to lower the temperature, it's by no means pleasant. My hat pulled down tight, my face protected by my kaffiyeh, and my eyes by sunglasses, I forge ahead along the road, with large trucks suddenly coming into view from time to time, as if out of dry fog.

But none of this undermines how fit I feel, and I cover thirty-one miles without really trying. The village where I stop hasn't a single hotel to offer. I ask an old Uyghur seated in front of the gate leading into his yard whether, for a little money, he would be willing to put me up for the night. He gets up without a word and comes back, handing me a loaf of *nang*, a kind of small, round bread popular among Uyghurs. Straight from the oven, they're delicious, but in no time at all, they're hard as rocks. The man motions me to go eat his offering somewhere else. The condescending, exasperated gesture of a man who has no intention of settling down with devil's spawn like me. I ceremoniously hand him back his dry bread and pass through the village without stopping, hardly interested in being humiliated a second time. I camp a mile and a half down the road in a spot that I hope is deserted. But no sooner have I set up my tent and lit a fire to heat up my soup than a band of curious youngster swoops in on me. The laughing, invasive presence of these little brats helps me forget their parents' arrogance.

Around 8:00 p.m., it starts drizzling. There's nothing surprising about that: it's in the summer that this part of Xinjiang gets its paltry rains. But at 1:00 in the morning, I'm awakened by a strong storm accompanied by violent winds. My tent's canvas must not be very well waterproofed, for before long, it's raining as much inside as out! What's more, I pitched camp in a low spot and a stream has begun to grow in it. Stark naked in the darkness and the rain, with nothing but my headlamp to light the way, I hurriedly relocate. Though I'm nearly sixty-four, I'm still a novice camper, but the elements are giving me a veritable crash course: a poorly oriented tent that swells like a parachute in the storm; a fire that stubbornly refuses to light; an unsteadied food tin that tips over in the fire, snuffing it out; a loosely attached rainfly that takes to the air and forces me into a frantic sprint to catch it—I learn through my mistakes and will soon be a pro.

In a restaurant at Qipan Shuimo, a Uyghur man who introduces himself as Imur is apparently obsessed with money and takes me for a fabulously wealthy Westerner. He babbles on and on in front of the other customers, asking how much each of my belongings cost. One by one, I refuse to tell him the price of Ulysses, then my pants, then my camera, and so on. For my watch, he changes tactics:

"I'll buy it!" he says, sure of himself.

My watch, which looks like a wrist-sized computer, is also an altimeter, a barometer, and a thermometer, and it has caused me trouble before, as it arouses people's greed. On a piece of paper, Imur writes "one hundred yuan" ($12—the watch is worth over $200). He then pleads false amounts in an attempt to learn what I really paid for it. I play along.

"Much more than that!"

"Two hundred?"

"Much more."

"Four hundred?"

I take the paper and add a zero.

"Four thousand?"

He can't believe his eyes. For him, that's a colossal sum. But I'm not done yet, and add yet another zero, then another. Everyone laughs, except Imur. I've pulled it off: my audience has no idea what my watch really cost.

People are obsessed by money here. During my first two years on the road, I was troubled by the widespread generosity I encountered. No different than anyone else, I'm very moved by the gifts people give me, but I find it hard to accept donations from people who are clearly much poorer than I am. Nearly everywhere I went in Central Asia, even in hotels and restaurants, people refused to take my money no matter how much I insisted. For kids, I had little pins and candy to hand out, but for adults I had nothing, since my choice of locomotion prohibited my bringing presents for those met along the way.

In China, the problem is the other way around. Starting in Tuopa, I began noticing that, in restaurants, the arrival of a Westerner was seen as a windfall that should be milked for all it's worth. In the first restaurant where I stopped after crossing the border, the owner wrote the price of the meal on a piece of paper: "TEN YUAN." That was, I find out later on, twice the usual price. Three or four customers got involved, saying something to him that soon became obvious; he took the little paper back and wrote: "TWENTY YUAN." Formerly in China, government agencies advocated a special tax on foreigners, which was promoted and broadly implemented until the 1990s. The surcharge ranged from two to five times the price locals paid. For several years now, however, the government has *officially* forbidden making "big-noses" pay more. But the message hasn't gotten through. In hotels for foreigners, prices displayed apply to them only, and employees divide it by two, three, or four for Chinese guests. In restaurants, the price is typically twice the usual rate. Small street traders are the only ones who don't practice this form of ostracism, which is more annoying as a matter of principle than for the amounts in question.

Historically, Silk Road merchants were also taxed, especially during the road's heyday. Local chieftains demanded tribute from passing convoys. If they failed to get what they wanted, they plundered the caravans. Travelers paid; they had the means since they reaped colossal profits from their business, which sometimes amounted to 1,000 percent! In the first century CE, Pliny the Elder wrote: "One half of these almost innumerable tribes live by the pursuits of commerce, the other half by rapine: take them all in all, they are the richest nations in the world, seeing that such vast wealth flows in upon them from both the Roman and the Parthian Empires."* Heading west, the merchants transported bolts of silk cloth, of course, but also furs, ceramics, bronze weapons, cinnamon, and rhubarb (not as a vegetable, but for medicinal purposes). On the return trip, they carried gold, precious stones, glass, ivory, perfume, coral, saffron, spices, and cosmetics. They transported exotic animals, which the imperial court in Xi'an greatly desired: parakeets, peacocks, falcons, gazelles, and especially the ostrich, or "camel-bird," which so fascinated the emperor and his subjects. Quite often, tagging along with the convoys were persons in some sense "imported" from the West: dwarves, acrobats, and jugglers.

As a result of being seen as a money purse, while at the same time unable to talk to people, I feel as if the very nature of my journey has changed. Now that I've all but given up on having locals spontaneously welcome me into their homes, I'm no longer out on a "walk," but on a "hike." Walking, camping, eating, sleeping, then walking yet again; this is what my journey has become. In Central Asia, I walked among friends. Here I hike among providers. But I have to be careful not to overgeneralize. And I persuade myself that more wonderful encounters lie ahead.

Here's a case in point: a postal truck stops. I recognize the driver. Yesterday evening, my water bottles were empty, so I asked him for some water. All he had in his jar was tea, but he gave me half of it. These jars, known as *guan*, are curious objects among the Han Chinese. Nary a soul heads off to work without one. They put a few

---

* Pliny the Elder, *The Natural History*. Volume 6, chapter 32, line 68. Translated by John Bostock (London: Taylor and Francis, 1855).

tea leaves in it in the morning, then as the level drops, they add fresh water. In the evening, it's nothing but clear water, but no matter. In every restaurant, there are always thermos bottles full of hot water for *guan*. You don't have to be a customer: anyone can enter, take some, then head back out. Often, so as not to be bothered by the jar or to avoid burning their fingers, the Chinese hold it in one hand, or hang it from the end of a lanyard. Most often, *guan* are simply upcycled instant coffee jars. But some are quite elaborate little thermoses encased in leather or steel sheaths. Upset that he wasn't much help to me last night, this morning, the driver has purchased a bottle of spring water, and he presents it to me as a gift. Meanwhile, I had fortunately solved my problem, for the quarter liter he gives me won't last long: I go through four times that every hour! The charming man must have told his colleagues about me since, from that point on, all of the *China Post* truck drivers honk their horns twice and wave as they go by.

This morning, I also get to know Sepulla and his motorcycle. He's Uyghur with a mop of hair that's tousled by the wind from the ride, since no one wears helmets here. He hasn't shaved in a long time but sports a very elegant black shirt. He looks to me a bit like a Calabrian peasant (although I've never met a peasant from Calabria). He comes to a stop next to me, greets me, then does a walk around Ulysses. Like all my cart's admirers, he touches it, caresses it, and squeezes its tires, wanting to check their air pressure.

"The right one's low," he remarks, his thumb pushing into the rubber.

He goes back to his motorbike, takes out a pump that's carefully lashed on with a cord, but, unfortunately, the Chinese nozzle refuses to unite with the Russian valve. Sepulla wastes no time. He starts his bike back up and, using sign language, indicates that in a short while the tire will be flat, but that we have enough time if I hop on behind him so that we can get to the village before it's too late. So off we go with Ulysses racing along behind us at over thirty miles per hour! I keep an eye on the state of the tire, fearing that, if it has too little pressure, the hub might begin to slice into the rubber. While the mechanic is busy fixing the wheel, I invite Sepulla to lunch, but he doesn't have the time and putters off. So I sit down all alone for a serving of *saï*—noodles cooked with sweet peppers, eggplant, and chilis—and watch as a crowd forms around Ulysses, offering definitive personal assessments of my traveling companion, now a veritable celebrity.

As I leave the village behind, the purple flowers of the tamarisk shrubs are bursting forth like Bastille Day fireworks, leaving long, colorful trails in the night sky. The mountain has also arrayed itself in strange-colored rocks; some white, others burnt-bread brown, bottle-green, fig-green, and red . . . all spreading east like an immense artist's palette, the hues of which change almost imperceptibly as the sun journeys across the sky. The road sometimes rises, allowing me to catch a glimpse of the Taklamakan Desert's first dunes off to the south. In a very remote corner of this realm of death live golden-leaved Euphrates poplars. To reach water, their roots plunge to depths up to fifty feet. It's said that they need one hundred years to grow, one hundred years to die, and that the trunks remain standing yet another century before they finally fall over. And their wood is so hard that it takes three more centuries to turn to dust and mix with the sand.

As the days go by, I find that I truly enjoy camping and especially the active solitude that it requires: setting up my tent after first checking which way the wind's blowing; securing the rain fly by wedging it under large stones in the event of a sudden storm; looking for wood and making a fire for dinner—there's always plenty to do! One nice thing is that here, there's no time lost doing dishes. Water is far too precious to devote even a drop of it to tasks like that, or for washing up. An old bourgeois reflex, however, still has me swiping some to brush my teeth. Only after I've done all that, and taken a few notes, do I give myself over to my evening in the desert and watch the spectacle of nightfall. Night first comes quietly, as if in slow motion. To the south, the horizon grows increasingly less distinct, while to the west, the peaks are surrounded by a reddening halo. With the back of my head resting on the sand, I savor a slice of sweet melon and observe, mesmerized, how the sun first resists, then is suddenly devoured by the mountain's incandescent teeth. Though completely swallowed up, it still sends out a few rays, which set the sky on fire and ignite the clouds. Time hovers in mid-air. With sleep staring me in the face, the first star gives the signal, then a thousand others light up. In that instant, I taste the relative coolness that descends upon the sands, following afternoon temperatures that climbed to 104°F. My muscles finally relaxed, my energy spent, flattened, and worn away by a full day of hard work, I slip into my tent, let lassitude wash over me and, on the hard ground, fall into a deep slumber. How ironic when I think of all the endless hours of insomnia I normally endure lying on a comfortable mattress in my quiet house in Normandy!

Although I get caught up the poetry of the desert at dusk, the next morning, even before the sun is reborn in the east, I spring from my tent and throw myself wholeheartedly into the day's struggle: I have to reach the tiny dot I've marked on my map before night sets in, and I have to do so undeterred by the heat, the melting pavement, and the vastness of this place, which, early in the day, feels hostile. Only when I'm back on the road does the desert grow friendlier, coming to life in its own special way, with discreet strokes, noticed only by the initiated. Here, a tuft of camel grass, miraculously spared by the inferno, may be shriveled, but lives on. Over there, a small hillock, wart-like in this infinite space, throws a meager shadow onto the sand. Beaches of pebbles—what surge of water could have brought them here?—stretch in places over the yellow sand. In the far reaches, the cruel light loses its brilliance, and merges with the horizon where it kisses a cloud.

One morning, while water boils in the only pan I brought with me, I head back over to my tent looking for a packet of noodles, which is what I eat for breakfast every day, and spot an enormous spider crawling over my sleeping bag. It's a beautiful, slightly translucent shade of green. Since the terrors of the Karakum in Turkmenistan, my fear of these crawling, stinging creatures has only worsened. In a flash, I grab the bag and fling it onto the sand. But though I conduct a thorough search, picking the bag up and turning it over, the critter's nowhere to be found. Carefully, while reprimanding myself for such an irrational fit of spinelessness, I crawl back into my tent and do a systematic search. It isn't in my boots. Nor it is in my food bag or backpack, which I empty out onto the ground, methodically inspecting any possible corners in which it might lurk. Last of all, I turn over my hat, the only object not yet explored. Nothing there either. Where could it possibly be? I painstakingly poke around my empty tent once again, but don't see it. It must have gone back into its hole. Eager—as usual—to cover as much distance in the morning before being overwhelmed by the heat, I have a quick breakfast, stow my gear, pack it onto Ulysses, and am on my way. I happily forget about my tormenter all day long, but as I'm setting up my tent that evening, the thought of the spider pops back into my head. I'm not sure why, but I still have some lingering suspicions. I open my canvas shelter's zipper and take a cautious look around: nothing. I climb in, still on my guard, and examine every corner. Nothing. Then it dawns on me to look up. There it is! Clinging to the fabric by its humongous legs, motionless, but still very much alive! Without pausing too long to consider how it managed to survive in the rolled-up canvas, I scurry out of the tent, grab one of my sandals, and strike the roof so hard the critter falls to the ground. The instant it lands, with a ferocity magnified by fear, I crush it until nothing remains but a ball of mush. I regain my composure but am far from proud of my actions. What harm did this little araneid do to me? It's perhaps not even the least bit dangerous. But a lot of good it does for me to feel regret and remorse now: the dreaded thing is dead! Just when I had finally found life in the desert.

I'm drawn to villages. The beauty of their names is not lost on me, though I don't know what they mean: Qipan Shuimo, Xike'erkule, Wudaoban, and on and on. Sofy translated a few of them for me later on: Sanchakou, for example, is "Mouth of the Three Forks." And the one with such a nice ring to it, Sanjianfang, means "Prison Number Three." Unfortunately, the reality of these towns fails to convey the poetry of their names. A few buildings stand alongside the road, all of them devoted to commerce. Beneath a canopy, two or three tables have been set up; a lamb's carcass hangs from a beam and meat is sliced from it upon request: it's a restaurant. I'm sometimes greeted with a smile, more often with a kind of curious indifference. There's no denying that the cold reception I detect is often the result of extreme timidity: proof of this is that the customers don't budge or say a word until the manager, male or female, shows some interest in my strange wagon. Then they feel that they can come over and touch Ulysses before going about their business. Central Asians have a lively and affectionate appetite for foreigners: what has become of that? Where are all the amazing encounters I had in Turkey, Iran, and Uzbekistan? I've fallen into a new world. And I do mean "fallen," like down a well.

A fellow arrives just as I'm finishing my lunch. Someone must have gone to get him, for he comes straight over to me. With his beard, the cap of a religious man on his head, and a burning look in his eyes, I know all about characters like him, having run into hundreds of them. This one cuts to the chase:

"Are you Muslim?"

He has a rather unfriendly face, but I feel obliged to reply.

"*Meiyou*" (no).

"Where are you from?"

I take out my little notes. He reads them aloud. Other guests have drawn near; they listen to him, then look at me, intrigued, without a hint of bad intent. But the bearded man begins haranguing the group. What he's saying needs no translation. For him, I'm a liar. There's no way I could have walked so far from the Chinese border. This ignoramus probably hasn't the slightest idea where Samarkand even is! But oh! If I were Muslim, I probably would have been able to do it. But lacking Allah's help, how could anyone walk so far? He snatches the map that I had spread out on my table and points to Wudaoban, nineteen miles away.

"And you say you're going to go there on foot?" He mimics driving a truck. "You're hitchhiking!"

I get up, go over to him, point to my flat stomach and his pot belly; then, mimicking a brisk walk, I suggest:

"Come along with me! It will help you get back in shape!"

The onlookers laugh. He sits down with the rest of them and starts up a conversation in which he's the star, blatantly paying no attention to me.

Starting out this morning, I promised myself that I'd make Wudaoban by evening, which amounts to twenty-eight miles over the course of the day. A tiring distance, but perhaps there's a hotel in the village and, you never know, a little water?

The road's blocked. Here's one of those nasty surprises that crop up and put the kibosh on all your plans, made so carefully in the euphoria of a new day. They decided to resurface the road. In the meantime, bulldozers have cleared a path through the stones at the foot of the mountain. Trucks are stirring up dust and I can hardly breathe. I'm running low on water. Ulysses jounces over the sharp-edged stones. Still no village. With nightfall closing in, I resign myself to pitching my tent near the roadway, halfway up a hill. With trucks roaring all night long in first gear over the denuded terrain, I can hardly sleep. In the morning, I crest the mountain only to discover Wudaoban just a short distance downhill, and that the "village" consists of only two houses: a restaurant for me and a "garage" for Ulysses. I've just had breakfast, but, feeling a bit despondent, I order a bowl of noodles and ask for water. They point me to a metal drum under the canopy. The mechanic must also be getting his from it, for iridescent patches of oil float on the surface of this tempting H_2O. But beggars can't be choosers, so I fill up my bottles anyway!

During this seemingly endless detour, Ulysses bounces off a stone in a low area. One of my water bags, which must have been poorly attached, falls off without my noticing. A driver who just went past me spots it. Despite the bumpy road and the trailer he's pulling, he manages a U-turn, catches up to me, and hands it back. I thank him profusely and offer him money, but he turns it down. Losing that five-liter bag would have amounted to a serious handicap! A little later, a motor coach and then a car packed with an entire family offer to give me a ride since, they tell me, bad weather's heading my way. And here it is now! Just as I reach the paved road, a sandstorm blows in. The wind's so strong it has picked up little pebbles and blasts me with them. I have to protect myself by going down into the ditch, which is rather deep where I happen to be. As the storm gains strength, a driver, leaning into the wind, brings me a watermelon and, without waiting for me to thank him—words that would be swallowed up by the noise of the wind—he runs off to take refuge in the cab of his truck. The cloud of sand rises high into the sky, blotting out the sun; night-like darkness falls over the desert. Visibility drops to zero, and cars, unable to see the road, come to a halt. The howl of the wind is insane. Rain begins to fall all of a sudden in a heavy, icy downpour. It rolls off the roadway and pours into the ditch, so I have to get out. Pressing, snuggling up against Ulysses beneath the oilcloth that ordinarily protects my bags, I wait for the raindrops' din on my shelter to let up. In the howling wind, I hear the laughter of Taklamakan's devils.

Ten minutes later, the rain has washed the sky clean. A searing sun reappears and dries everything up in no time flat. If it weren't for the puddles reflecting the sky, one might actually doubt that anything even happened. As soon as the rain lets up, the driver heads off. Too late to share the melon with him. I cut a large slice of melon for myself and it's a good thing, too, since, a short while later, it silently slips off Ulysses, onto which I had secured it. My heavens, I'm losing all my "property" today. I am certainly not as adept as the Chinese, who lash the most unbelievable loads of cargo onto their trucks.

Well in advance of Sanchakou, smoke from the mine lets me know where the village is. Large yellow machines carry stones to the ovens. The ashes fall back on the village, blanketing it in gray dust. A dozen houses line the road on the desert side. On the other is the mountain, which abruptly ends at the edge of the road. From a distance, it looks like a huge monster that has buried its head in the sand, and whose body, spiked with a thousand sharp-edged scales, is crouched over the ground. The water I'm given is drawn from plastic tanks filled somewhere else, since the wells here are salty. Two police officers seated at an inn where I've ordered a restorative noodle dish call me over. One of them, weasel-eyed and whose upper lip is graced with a thin mustache, points to my clothes and holds his nose. I know, I'm stinking the place up! But I have no choice, I'll have to wait till I get to Aksu before I can wash my threads. No, you won't, the shorter cop tells me. He comes back five minutes later along with a woman who, for one dollar, pushes me into a room where I can change, then takes my dirty clothes and dips them into a frothy washtub. It's so hot out and the air so dry that, by the time I finished my plate of noodles, she's back with my laundry. She wasn't able to restore my shirt to perfect whiteness, but it's so impregnated with grime that it would be unrealistic to expect she could. The red dust, mixed with my sweat, has more or less permanently dyed the fabric. I head back out, clean as a whistle. Unfortunately, the very next day, sweat and another sandstorm effectively spoil this praiseworthy attempt at presentability. But what would be the point of that anyway? I sometimes think that the filthiness I've gotten used to makes it easier for me to slip into the crowd and the landscape unnoticed. Most of the people I meet are covered in a crust of grime much like mine.

In Shajingzi, it's a great joy to see trees. The pleasure I feel is connected with thoughts of my house in Normandy, which is surrounded by forest. What a delight a tree is! And how inebriating it is to see so many of them. I'm fortunate to live near an abundance of nature. But although there are trees here, there's no hotel, not even a "*dortoir*" (dormitory). That's the French word I use to refer to the kinds of places I've stayed in several times intended for truck drivers or peasants from distant villages who've come to "the big city" to sell their wares. Hotels like those we think of in the West are found in mid- or large-sized cities only. In Chinese, these dorms are called *luguan*. They're ridiculously cheap, for me anyway: less than a dollar a night! The basic design is always the same: a large courtyard in which twenty trucks or so can easily fit. The entrance is closed by iron gates, which are padlocked at night. The site is enclosed by high walls, and backed up against them are twenty or so rooms— little cubes measuring seven feet to a side—each with a single window for light. The furniture in each consists entirely of three single beds, which, in reality, are nothing more than wooden crates turned upside down. The owners aren't bankrupting themselves laundering the matting, pillows, and blankets, either, and they evidently only sweep the floors when there's so much dirt that the doors won't close. Nothing keeps them from opening, though, since almost all the locks are broken. In the courtyard, which doubles as a truck repair shop, the oily mud never completely dries, and it sticks to the soles of people's shoes. Still, I'd rather sleep in a *luguan* than camp out in the desert. I insulate myself from the place's grime by laying my sleeping bag out on the bed, then slipping into my sleep sack on top of it.

Luguan, with respect to their design, are distant cousins to Central Asia's caravansaries. I wonder . . . what were hostels, or *kung kuan*, like in the days of the Silk Road? No doubt just as dirty. *Kung kuan* were first reserved for the emperor's ambassadors and messengers. Pilgrims and traders were only allowed in if there was extra room. In Chinese society, the latter were lower on the social ladder than peasants, higher only than women. That says something, doesn't it? Servants constituted the proletariat in what was an extremely hierarchical society.

Another storm looks to be brewing. As I leave the village, I come upon an abandoned house. I decide to hunker down inside for the night. I drop Ulysses off in the first room that I come to, which has

no door or window but, with a roof in good condition, should provide cover from the thick clouds piling up. I inspect the rooms that
open out onto the courtyard and discover an entire family of squat-
ters. Their truck broke down; it's parked out back where two men
are trying to fix it. They have a woman and three teens with them.
They're all the more thrilled to share their shelter with me since none
of them has ever seen a Westerner. They make up for lost time: one
after the other throughout the evening, they come over to spy on me,
laughing, watching my every move, and commenting each with great
excitement. Before lying down, I realize that they've never seen someone brush their teeth—their toothless smiles are evidence of this. For
them, it's such an extraordinary spectacle that all six of them, called
over by the youngest, line up in front of me as I begin brushing.
Bothered by this intrusion into my open-air bathroom, I turn my
back to them, but then they run around to the other side, and line up
once again: they clearly don't want me to deprive them of this one-
of-a-kind show! So, I resign myself to them being there. But then it's
time for me to spit the paste out, and I really don't want to do that in
their direction. So I turn around. But once again, they make another
comical mad dash and watch, gaping in wonder, as I rinse my mouth.
In the morning, likely to thank me for the gala evening, the woman
comes over to invite me for breakfast. But I ate much earlier and am
ready to get going. I get back underway after taking their picture in
front of the abandoned house. Unfortunately, they didn't know how
to write their address, so I won't be able to send them the shot.

VIII

ENDLESS COUNTRYSIDE

The road I'm walking down is flat, uniform, unremarkable. With steep mountainsides to the north and limitless desert to the south, I understand Teilhard de Chardin who wrote: "Xinjiang is quite likely the most isolated region on the planet."* As for me, unable to speak the region's languages, the isolation I feel is profound personal loneliness. Well, since I cannot speak with others, I speak to myself. And I try to settle a question I've often been asked but which I find so hard to answer: What is it I've come looking for here in this desert and high up in the Pamirs? It's an experience that brings me great joys and memorable encounters, of course, but fear and suffering as well. For wisdom, yes. But what kind? That ancestral serenity we associate with ascetics who "retire" from the world? I am, after all, a "retiree"! I'm not so sure about that, at least in terms of my personal destiny. Slowly, walking along now at a snail's pace, with the help of daydreams and solitude, the answer emerges, little by little. It may be unconventional, but it's mine, one shaped by the passing landscapes, the reflections I've had and the people I've met. There's no denying that I seek to free myself from the madness that seems to be infecting Western societies. Our world moves too quickly, as if it had lost its mind. It is therefore urgent that we slow down. But I don't want to flee, let alone to stop moving forward. I want to attempt to live at

* *Lettres de voyage 1923–1939* (Paris: B. Grasset, Collection "Les cahiers rouges," 1956).

117

the rhythm of thought. And walking slams the brakes on this race to the death—a race we mistakenly call life—and which has taken over our so-called "civilized" societies. Which, as far as I can tell, have ceased to exist, except in the distorted mirror that television holds up to them.

Before pondering where I'm headed, though, in Samarkand, I began reflecting in short bursts the reasons why I left. And above all, what I most urgently need to know: where I'm from. I left primarily because I had a thirst for adventure that I had repressed in the course of an all-too-reasonable life. Education, work, family, children. I was, like so many others, bound on every side by these sweet chains—elastic, yes, but tenacious. I needed to detach from my habits, my routine, the reassuring comfort of my life, the get-togethers with friends, the nightly news, the birthdays, and the house I had yet to pay off. To break free from all of that, to stretch the umbilical cord, just as my children, in adolescence, separated themselves from me without it affecting one bit our love for one another. That's reason number one. Next, Danièle, my wife for such a long time, had always longed to travel. I'd venture to say that I set out to carry through with her dreams of seeing the world—dreams cut short by death. I needed to let go, to cast off all the faded finery, to lay myself bare. For travel prepares us for that final departure as well, the one when the great scythe cuts us loose for good. Dying? Yes, and why not? It's something everyone eventually does, and in that respect, at least, I have no desire to be any different! But first, in one last great hurrah, I want to start all over. "Age," or so we say, our chins trembling slightly, precedes "old age," then decrepitude and death. They're coming for me. But before I sign up for that increasingly popular club of "old" men, I wanted to give myself one more youthful shot in the arm. To prove to others—and myself as well—that I was still full of life.

In setting the goal of traveling the entire length of the immense Silk Road, I was pursuing two objectives. The first was to find out whether muscle is ageless and whether flesh, weak though it may be, will obey a strong mind. Whether willpower is all it takes to fulfill one's wildest dreams. I also wanted to go the distance slowly, thumbing my nose at urgency. But isn't there danger in delay, considering that death is nearer now than ever before, that time is flying by? Let Time wait! But once again and above all, I refuse to let anyone make me sit out the game. I want to exercise my right to exist, aware now as I am of the pitfalls that go along with that right.

In Western countries, "old folks" are made to "retire." They're left by the wayside. Not out of respect for their age, as is the case here in the East, but for the sake of efficiency. "Youthism" pushes them aside. The triumph of adolescents, of young people, did almost as much damage in the West as the Cultural Revolution did here, when sorcerers' apprentices with little red books in their hands had the power to decide whether their fellow human beings would live or die. Advertisers realized early on that the youngest among us are also the easiest to influence. The results of this can be seen every day: young people in all their finery—but wearing "brand names" only—foot the bill for a party at which, without realizing it, they're mere spectators. Back home, I'm nothing but an "old fart," here *"aksakals"* are venerated: I reject both labels, for each one goes too far. Let's treat one another according the plans we make, according to what we bring to life. As for myself, I'm placing my bets on the future, even if that means I'll have to break through a few barriers. Go back into my tent or withdraw into a cave? Nothing doing! Wisdom, for me, must involve commitment. That is to say, a course of action. Still, every so often, we have to go on a little solitary retreat and swallow a spoonful of solitude so that we can get back to the world better than we were before.

Establishing the Seuil Association* was a dream come true, one that has kept me going ever since. I want to show our "efficient" world just how absurd a system is that simultaneously pushes seniors aside and excludes young people.

---

* An overview of the Seuil Association can be found in the appendix. TN: Pron. [sœj] (like "soy").

No, for me, wisdom won't be found high atop the icy Pamir Mountains or in East Asia's burning deserts. My wisdom is in the wholehearted, active lives of those who seek to make the world a better place. Retirees are supposed to ease off and get some rest? Who's kidding who! For those who want that, I have nothing to say, but what about everyone else? Are we simply to scrap all that they've learned since childhood, all their professional know-how, all the experience they've gained in dealing with other people and with life itself? I'm not ready to withdraw; on the contrary, I want to sink my teeth into life by making sure I get my share of it, my *full* share. My wisdom—yes, that's it, I've put my finger on it—is to be "unwise"!

It's August 25 and I'm closely monitoring the kilometer markers. I've determined that when I reach the fifteenth, I'll have traveled 2,000 kilometers since leaving Samarkand (1,240 miles). The moment it comes into view, I let go of Ulysses, take a running start, and leap over it. I then take an apple out of my pack, peel it religiously, and bite into it, a little at a time. I top off this mini celebration with a few pieces of dried fruit and a long draft of warm water. Only 1,000 kilometers to go! But the toughest part is behind me now. Or so I hope.

The next day, my body lets me know that it has exceeded the limits of what it can endure. A whopping bout of turista first creeps up on me like a forward scout, then the entire army launches an all-out assault: severe pain in my left foot, thigh, and hip, and I start losing a staggering amount of weight. My recovery times increase dramatically, and, when I set out each morning, I'm still somewhat tired from the previous day. If I want to make it to the end, I'm going to have to slow down. There's no question that I've been pushing myself too hard. I had planned to cover the three hundred miles or so from Kashgar to Aksu in eighteen days: I did it in twelve without the slightest break. I'm fortunately not even nineteen miles from Aksu, and this evening I'll experience the joys of warm water and a razor blade.

That's the dream I'm caught up in—one in which wonderfully sudsy water and the rich fragrance of bodywash mix with immaculately white clothes—when someone calls out to me. Back to reality. Two cops, near their car parked off the road, motion me over. My first police check since entering the country, or a hold up? I raise my guard. Quite wrongly, though, for these two good men only want to share a large watermelon with me!

The road into Aksu is dreadful. Dirty, crowded with tractors and trucks spewing acrid diesel fumes; but what's most unbearable about it is the noise. You get the impression drivers had conspired to constantly lay on their horns. Architecturally, the city is of no interest whatsoever. As in most large Chinese cities, the old houses have been demolished to make way for Soviet-style block buildings, which, though still new, are already dreary.

This is where, in September 1931, the two different crawler-tractor caravans of the *Croisière Jaune* (Yellow Journey) met up. The caravan coming from the west had covered much more ground than the one from Beijing. The latter group first had to deal with a breakdown when the rubber of their vehicle's tracks fell to pieces. Chinese authorities had then blocked it for four months in Ürümqi. Warlords, meanwhile—no doubt manipulated by players in the "Great Game"—were slicing each other's throats throughout the region.

The city's weather is like autumn in Normandy: cool, almost chilly, with a stubborn mist that makes the sidewalks shimmer, but which is too light to wash off the countless gobs of spit left by both Chinese and Uyghur alike—one point the two groups have in common. The hotel I stay in is a splendid example of Chinese bureaucracy. As I'm about to go out the door, I'm graciously invited to help myself to one of the umbrellas reserved for guests. I gladly accept, but then the employee asks for fifty yuan ($7).

"That's a lot just to borrow an umbrella."

The young woman doesn't understand. For the next ten minutes, they try to hunt down an interpreter, who finally arrives. I'm in no hurry. I repeat what I said.

"There's no charge for borrowing it, sir. The fifty yuan is the security deposit."

"But I just left two hundred yuan as a security deposit with the reception desk!"

"That's a different till."

Faced with such an obvious point, I do as she asks and walk out. I've only gone a couple hundred yards when another employee, out of breath, catches up to me.

"You forgot your receipt!"

This is a marvelous country, where time and manpower are not appreciated in terms of money! The matter kept three people busy for twenty minutes.

In the evening, my skin adequately scrubbed, I dine in a restaurant where they suggest I try the fish. Not thinking, I accept: when they bring it out to my table, I realize that I'm going to have to eat it with chopsticks! I've gotten better at it since my first attempts, when part of the meal invariably wound up in my lap, but I fear that, this time, I might not be up to the task. I've made great strides, though, and the dish is so tasty that the next day I order it again! The owner, his wife, and his employee, delighted to see me a second time, make repeated "welcome" and "bon appétit" bows. As I'm finishing my plate, a young woman enters and goes over to have a word with the owner before coming my way:

"I'm an English interpreter and the chef sent me to you."

"He asked you to come speak with me? Well, that's a nice gesture and I thank him . . ."

"No, that's not it. He wants me to inform you that the fish is larger than yesterday, so it will cost twice as much."

Then off she goes, mission accomplished. The fish isn't any larger, but the owner, fine fisherman that he is, nicely reeled in the big one—the big-nose, that is!

One day of rest was all I needed. I must confess in good faith that, when I claimed that any healthy person could accomplish my journey, further clarification is needed. Since setting out from Istanbul three years ago, I have indeed aged, but thanks to walking, I've toughened up. The three hundred miles just traveled in twelve days are proof that my endurance has improved considerably over these past three years on the road. My fitness is such that, in the span of twenty-four hours, I've regained all my strength and overcome my pains. Upon leaving Aksu, I travel twenty-seven miles as though walking on air, without the least bit of fatigue. Just outside the city, an enchanting sight stopped me dead in my tracks near a grove of poplar trees reflecting in the stagnant water of their irrigation pond. Between the branches, the proud peaks of the Celestial Mountains were doing their best to live up to their name. A mesmerizing spectacle, the 7,000-meter (23,000-foot) summits seemed nearby in the pure morning air, just as the sun was peeking over the horizon, setting the eternal snows on fire and making the glaciers sparkle.

On the road, hundreds of young people were pedaling to school in slow motion, held back by impassioned conversation, or perhaps still immersed in dreams. . . .

One young girl, upon seeing me, panicked and bolted, dragging her bag into the ditch beside the pond, where she tripped and fell into the water. I went over to help her, but that got her screaming all the more. Another little girl hopped off her bike to lend her a hand and comfort her. "Don't worry, the big-nose is not going to eat you!" For some Chinese, Westerners are still "foreign devils." And the fact that there are children, like this girl, who shudder at my sight, is proof, if any were needed, that there is still, in this country, a deeply rooted culture of fear or even hatred of those who are different—*laowai* (foreigners).

In Aksu, a Chinese teen boy, accompanied by two friends and his father, aped me from behind, trying to make them laugh. He started walking behind me, as close as possible, while imitating my every move. I finally noticed him and stopped in front of a store window:

he did the same. I turned my head his way hoping to laugh along with him, but he turned his. His friends and father burst out laughing. I'd had enough. I decided to teach him a lesson. I continued down the sidewalk, picking up the pace: he followed in my footsteps. Then, abruptly stopping, I turned around and yelled "Aaaahhhh!" The flash of fear in his eyes and the terror written all over his face as he leaped to the side before running pitifully back to his friends and father stuck with me the rest of the day. I was the only one laughing. All four of them were afraid. Then, in a flash, their disrespect turned to hatred. I smiled, motioning them to come over and talk. They went down the first street to the left, never looking back. I doubt that Uyghurs would deliberately ridicule a foreigner like that. They are, it's true, less hospitable than their brethren in faith on the other side of the Pamirs, but they have their reasons. For fifty years, they were forbidden to speak to foreigners. Taboos like that are not easy to overcome.

As the day wears on, I catch up to a long line of donkey carts. The last one belongs to Tohti. He and I strike up a conversation using hand signals and my little papers, which his son reads to him. He's a shriveled-up little man in his forties, strapped in a shapeless vest too small for him, and his weasel-like face peers out from beneath an apple-green cap. He's missing two incisors. This is one more fellow who's not going to believe that I'm sixty-three years old, for, as everyone knows, by that age, people no longer have teeth. He invites me into his house for tea. Since arriving in China, it's the first time I've been invited like that, and I'm tickled pink. A Uyghur farmer, Tohti lives in a house nestled inside a small courtyard at the center of his village. Beneath a canopy, he has parked one of those minuscule tractors that put out a lot of noise and pollution. He parks his little cart and donkey and invites me into his house, a rather vast single room approximately twenty feet square, with dirt floors and bare cement walls. My host points out that he built the place himself and that he planted the young poplar trees that hold up its flat roof. Two small windows let in a little daylight. Half the room is occupied by a large wooden platform covered with a gray-felt carpet. Surrounding the platform, a piece of red fabric with geometric designs has been tacked on to decorate the wall, reaching a few feet up. The rest of the room's space is taken up by its meager furnishings: a pile of blankets, a small chest in which the family's winter belongings are stored, and a treadle sewing machine. Without access to electricity, they use kerosene lamps for lighting. This is where Tohti and his wife live, eat, and sleep along with their three children, age twelve to sixteen. The oldest daughter, Akiz, injured her left foot, and it has more than doubled in volume from a nasty infection. A yellow canker, as big as a two-euro coin, is bordered by red flesh, and the wound is oozing pus. She sponges it with a dirty rag that has probably served that purpose for several days now. She remains silent, but deep pain is written all over her ashen face.

"You should take her to the doctor."

Rubbing his thumb and index finger together, Tohti indicates that he can't afford to. In the meantime, the youngest daughter and her mother have prepared tea, which they serve on a small, low table atop the platform. The wound is so nasty that I can't get my mind off it. I try to show them that they have to boil water, wash the wound, throw the rag out, and use a new one. I sense that they're not particularly interested. Tired of fighting, I ask how much it costs to take someone to the doctor. "Twenty yuan," Tohti tells me, suddenly more attentive. I then do something stupid. Since I don't have enough cash in my pants pocket, from the inside pocket of my shirt, I take out a wad of banknotes. I pull out fifty yuan and hand the money to her father. He tucks it in a pocket. I doubt he'll use it to take her to the doctor. The entire family surrounds me. Tohti puts on a solemn expression.

"You will dine with us and sleep here."

He looks at me differently now. He gives his son an order. The boy comes back a little later and hands his father a knife in a leather sheath. I pretend not to have noticed. Is he harboring bad intentions? Since I can't be sure, I have to act quickly. The sight of the wad of money, though not all that thick, has got the man crazy with greed. If I don't want to be robbed, or have a taste of his dagger, then I had better leave—and fast. I bid them a quick farewell and dash off through the village's dusty streets piled with garbage to make my way back to the National Road. I look behind me several times to be sure that I'm not being followed. This is once again proof that, although traveling solo helps me meet people, there's always a chance that I might run into a few bad apples. It would have been nice, though, to sleep with a roof over my head.

All night long, with the wind twisting the canvas every which way, water streams off the roof and into the tent. I finally fall asleep in the wee hours of the morning, just as the storm is beginning to ease up. Crawling out of my tent, I notice that the rain is cold but light. A little shepherd in shirtsleeves, chilled to the bone, has taken shelter behind a tree, and is protecting his head with a plastic bag. An hour later, it's his sheep who decide to head home, and he follows them. I put my jacket on. I was afraid of burning up in the Taklamakan, and here I am shivering! In the rain squalls that have the nearby poplars twisting and turning, I think I hear the devils Marco Polo mentioned snigger.

Since there's no way to build a fire, I get going again on an empty stomach. There's a village just over a mile away. If I'm to believe my map, it's the last one I'll see before a long, eighty-seven mile stretch of desert. My morale is once again bright blue. At 10:00 a.m., I have a spicy late breakfast while a convoy of thirty-some jeeps parades by, sponsored by a Malaysian oil company. The lead vehicles are flanked by four motorcycles, and a police car in back leads a truck carrying parts. A large sticker on the jeeps reads "Team Adventurers." The "adventurers" are doing their best to look the part: gray outfits with dozens of pockets, and the obligatory dark glasses and gloves. You couldn't find a more adventuresome-looking bunch in all Asia! But I suspect that the oil company has them booked in four- and five-star hotels.

On the outskirts of the village, a fork in the road presents a choice: I can reach Kuqa to the left, by way of the mountains, or to the right by way of the desert. I opt for the desert, where I cross paths with a cyclist—I've met maverick velocipedists like this every year. This one's a true adventurer, even without the multi-pocketed suit and dark sunglasses! Wouter Bussemaker—a thirty-two-year-old Dutchman with a blond head of hair and very blue eyes behind horn-rimmed glasses—is a computer scientist. He left it all behind and hopped on his bike in search of adventure. He was just in Pakistan. He seems to be in good physical shape and expects to reach Beijing before October's out. It looks like he, too, occasionally rides double stages, for his lower lip is swollen with large cold sores—a sign of fatigue, insufficient hydration, and too much sun. It's interesting to note that the more channels of communication open up and modernize the world over, the more travelers there are in search of slowness and archaism. It's a sign, no doubt, of a growing need to rebel against and resist what we like to call a "productive" world, one in which speed is virtue number one.

The route I've chosen is truly desert-like. I've left the Celestial Mountains behind and here, in this level terrain where sand has little by little replaced gravel or red soil, nothing grows. Wherever I turn, I see only infinite flatness. I could almost convince myself that I'm out at sea. I feel happier walking along right now than I have at any point since my journey began. My body feels so good that I stop thinking about it. I advance as in a dream and formulate plans for the future. Ulysses follows along effortlessly. I bought enough food to last four days and filled all my bottles, and I can always ask truck drivers for more water should I need it. Numerous vehicles stop, offering, of course, to take me on board: is it because I'm radiating the pleasure I feel inside? When I refuse, the drivers feel obligated to give me something: a melon, a *momo* (one of those steamed breads stuffed with vegetables or meat), a bottle of water, a large cluster of grapes. There are days when both people and the desert are at their best.

To my great surprise, I discover a group of three dwellings that doesn't figure on my map, nineteen miles from the nearest settlement. Two of the houses facing the road are occupied—as seems to be the rule—by a restaurant and a postage-stamp sized garage/tire-repair shop. Behind them is a long building composed of a series of small rooms, each equipped with a door and window, which makes me think that it must be a *luguan*. Even though the afternoon is half over, I take advantage of this godsend and order a meal from a sleepy young Chinese fellow, who drags his feet but finally starts cooking. Out on a large parking lot in front of the house, three pretty girls are chatting beneath a canvas canopy, seated on a *karavot*. Two of them are in short skirts, which I'm not used to seeing here; the third has on yoga pants and a T-shirt—surprising outfits for young Uyghur women in this corner of the desert! No doubt the spouses of the drivers of the three trucks parked in the lot.

As I wolf down my very spicy mutton stew with sides of potatoes, eggplant, and peppers, I notice two more young women passing by. They, too, are easy on the eyes, and they head over to a wire in the sun to hang their undergarments out to dry. Employees? The workers I typically see are never quite as attractive or dolled up; they never wear makeup and are always busier than these women appear to be, who look rather like they're on vacation. My final doubts are swept away when, from a room in the building to the rear, a truck driver steps out in the company of a sixth woman. I've finally understood— it took me a rather long time, you're thinking!—that I'm in a bordello. Communist China has its whorehouses, too; this one happens to be out in the middle of nowhere. Roles are distributed in a way that mirrors the society Beijing would like to establish in Xinjiang: the men, visibly the bookkeepers, are Chinese Han; the women are Uyghur. It's the same province-wide, with few exceptions. Chinese settlers have taken the secondary and service jobs and have left the Uyghurs to till the soil—or, in this case, the beds. As for the Han Chinese immigrants, they tend the till.

In a hamlet, I pitch my tent on a threshing floor that was used in the most recent harvest. As always, a few dawdling youths come over to watch. A man with yellow teeth and a mustache sporting a Mao cap is next to arrive, alerted by word-of-mouth. He's a local farmer and is very interested in my gear. He seems delighted. He's so happy that he sits down on a stone and starts singing. He has a superb baritone voice and the youths and I, squatting down, form a circle around him. Judging from the children's expressions as well as his, these are sad songs. His voice is pure; in my mind's eye, I imagine him in a Russian choir, and for a half hour I'm no longer the sole object of curiosity. Unfortunately, it doesn't last long. Word has spread that I enjoyed the performance. Someone from the village comes to get me. A dozen people have gathered together. One by one, the men step forward and sing while the women listen on. No one applauds. They then ask a young boy with a nasally voice to sing—which he does, at the top of his lungs, practically blowing out his vocal cords. But everyone seems to think it's great, so I do too, and I nod to show my satisfaction.

A short distance in advance of Xinhe, I meet a kind old man. Amur Tümür (which is Tamerlane's name, spelled "Amir Timur" in Samarkand) is eighty-one years old and in great shape. He passed me up on his bike and has been waiting for me in front of his house. As we drink tea, his daughter climbs up a ladder and picks two beautiful clusters of midnight-blue grapes for us. Amur would like me to stay for a day or two. Unfortunately, if I'm unable to obtain a one-month extension of my visa in Kucha, I won't have a day to spare if I want to reach Turfan before the one I was issued in Paris expires. I have to proceed as if the worst-case scenario were, in fact, the most probable!

At the bazaar, I taste some dumplings people call *karu* here. But above all, I try the *rhudus*, which are small, dough-coated meatballs cooked in a potato bouillon and flavored with onions and garlic. Garlic is found in every dish and on every restaurant table. Both the Chinese and the Uyghurs are convinced that it's a top-notch disinfectant, something the French also firmly believed in the past. The entire Mediterranean Basin has celebrated garlic from time immemorial, singing its praises for its medicinal, prophylactic, aphrodisiacal, and magical powers—"*bon ail contre mauvais œil*"—"good garlic to ward off the evil eye." In fact, it originally came to us from the vast Kyrgyz steppe, having circumnavigated the Caspian Sea. So it's hardly surprising that it's still consumed in such great quantities here in this region.

Locals eat *naan* bread from the city of Kuqa, flat galettes as big as Ulysses's wheels. People also bake little bagel-shaped breads with a very dense crumb called *girde naan*.

The landscape changes very little. It's summer, so here in the oases as elsewhere, the harvest is in full swing. The wheat has been cut and threshed by hand. Large tarps lie on the bare ground covered with red chili peppers spread out to dry, transforming the landscape into a crimson patchwork. And in the background rise those familiar gray mountains, visible once more.

One evening, having pitched my tent near a village, the idle youths who come to witness the campsite ceremony offer me a few ears of corn. What am I supposed to do with them? They laugh at my ignorance and light a large wood fire in a pit, then cook the corn on a bed of embers. It's a welcome change from my usual menu of instant noodle soup. Delighted to have taught a big-nose something, the young people sit conversing among themselves for a long time near my tent.

The way into Kuqa is quite entertaining. The road, built on an embankment, looks as though it sits on top of the flat, earthen rooftops of the outer neighborhoods below it. Crisscrossing the city is a profusion of donkey- and horse-drawn carts; they're light and comfortable, mounted atop four bicycle wheels. They're covered with a kind of frilly bed canopy—a whimsical sunshade. The donkeys and horses are decorated with a multitude of red and blue wool pompoms. There are also many *san lun che* (meaning, word for word, "car with three tires," or tricycle) equipped with a fabric hood. Some passengers hide behind a small curtain, so that they can travel incognito.

For the tourist, Kuqa's interest lies not in the city itself, but in its outskirts. A prosperous Buddhist civilization flourished here before Islam erased it from the map. Outside the city, the ruins of four ancient cities bear witness to this past. The nearest one—close enough such that I can explore it during the day off I grant myself— is called Qiuci. It's the old regional capital, about two miles west, formerly called Yancheng. When Xuan Zhang, the traveling monk whose tomb I'll try to see when I get to Xi'an, visited it in the seventh century, when it was called Yiluolu. He noted that two one-hundred-foot-tall statues of the Buddha stood at the western entrance, and that there were a great many monasteries. The three other cities— Subashi, Wushka, and Tonggusibashi—are beyond my reach. As are the region's numerous caves, the most famous of which are located at Kizil. Nicknamed (among other things) the "Caves of a Thousand Buddhas," it took nearly half a millennium to carve out and decorate them. In the days of the Silk Road, they rivaled the caves of Dunhuang in the quality of their paintings and sculptures. Experts have detected no Chinese influence, for when they were built, the Han people had not yet seized this territory. The German von Le Coq and his partner Grünwedel carried the most beautiful pieces back to Berlin with them. At the dawn of the twentieth century, German "prowlers," along with their English, Swedish, French, and American counterparts, returned home with statues, paintings, and inscriptions, and they stirred up such a craze for orientalism that the men decided to bring the caves back to life. Or at least remind people that they once existed. When the two German orientalists carried out their excavations, the region was still very wild. Le Coq tells of a twelve-year-old girl married to a sixty-year-old man who decided to flee. She was eaten by wolves and all that was ever found were her boots with—and it's a gruesome detail—her legs still in them. Suffice it to say that, back in those days, the area wasn't quite ready to host tourists.

Although I can't visit the Caves of a Thousand Buddhas, during my day off in Kuqa, I muse on what the Silk Road, so renowned today, might have once been like here. Opened by the Han Dynasty two thousand years ago, then cautiously shut down by the Ming emperors in the fourteenth century, it has recently begun to open back up. But there's no comparing today's road with the way it once was. In the seventh century, Xi'an, the imperial capital, was likely Rome's equal as the largest city in the world—six miles by five— with two million inhabitants. Five thousand foreigners lived there: Turks, Indians, Koreans, Japanese, Mongols, Arabs, Armenians, and Malays. Religious freedom was such that Nestorians, Zoroastrians, Buddhists, Manicheans, and Jews could freely build their temples there.* Nestorians were Christian. At the Council of Ephesus in 431 CE, they rejected the unity of Christ's divine and human persons: for them, though messiah, he was a man, not a god. The council ruled against them and they had to flee. Heading east, they erected sanctuaries all along the Silk Road. The Manicheans, persecuted by these same Christians in the Balkans, also found safe refuge in the east, first in Samarkand, then in China. They practiced a religion born in Persia that pitted light (the spirit) against darkness (the flesh). Von Le Coq would later discover a very rare fresco representing Manes near Turfan. Manes, known also by the name Mani, claimed to be the final Messiah, an idea disputed by Zoroastrians. He was challenged to a verbal sparring match, lost, and was crucified.

I am, moreover, struck by the fact—and I think about this several times along the way, each time I see a temple or mosque—that religions traveled the Silk Road in one direction only. Buddhism and Confucianism never reached the West; by contrast, during certain periods, other religions were allowed to blossom in China. The reason is that the two chief religions practiced from the Atlantic Ocean to the summits of the Pamirs—that is to say, Islam and

---

* Judy Bonavia, *Introduction à la route de la Soie : de Xi'an à Kashgar, sur les traces des grandes caravanes* (Geneva: Éditions Olizane, 1995).

Christianity—allowed no competitors and blocked them from coming in, sometimes quite violently. The clearest example of this is, in fact, Zoroastrianism's attempt to reach France by way of the Cathar religion, which resulted in the Albigensian Crusade. "Kill them all, God will know His own!" cried Simon de Montfort, after Orthodox Christians captured the city of Béziers in 1209, when asked whether women and children should be spared. The reason religions from Persia and the Mediterranean migrated to China is because their faithful had been tyrannized and persecuted throughout Central Asia, or in the West. Know-how, silk, gunpowder, the compass, and paper, it turned out, were far easier to export out of China and into Europe than were creeds.

What has become of the Silk Road today? It's true that goods are once again starting to flow, though not on the backs of camels, but in trucks. That, however, is where similarities end. There's no such thing as freedom of religion in Afghanistan and Iran, and it's limited in every country where Islam predominates. Political freedom is such a rare commodity that, from Beijing to Istanbul, the only meager traces of it are found in Turkey. Elsewhere, it's entirely unheard of. And the fierce crackdown in Tiananmen Square, as well as the zeal with which censors go after books and cassette tapes, are proof that in China, it's still a long way off.

After two thousand years, all these countries are still unstable. The most recent revolution to date, that of Iran, as well as the 180-degree change in political direction in the ex-Soviet republics, testify to this. The facade of peace that currently prevails exists only in the shadow of army kepis, more-or-less-politicized police forces, and assault rifles. Civil war is raging in Afghanistan and Tajikistan. In other words, the road I'm traveling is really only just barely open and is extremely fragile. My fear is that, in the years ahead, it could become one of the most unstable and turbulent places on the planet.

On display behind protective glass at the Hotel Qiuci are a few more or less authentic valuables that only rich, Western tourists can purchase. Mixed in with the Buddhas, swatches of silk, and gold coins are . . . rolls of toilet paper. The value of things, as everybody knows, is a function of their rarity. Thus, from the famous syllogism whereby everything rare is expensive, and cheap horses are rare, we're forced to conclude that expensive horses come cheap. What, for curiosity's sake, does one of these rolls of TP cost? I inquire and find out that they're worth eight yuan: the price of two platters of noodles.

I head to the Immigration Police to try to extend my visa. I'm kindly shown the door as they explain to me that a request must be made no more than one week prior to the expiration date of the initial one. In other words, if my request is turned down, I won't have enough time to complete my journey! Yet another absurd syllogism! And so, I had better plan on winding things up before September's out, when the visa I obtained in Paris expires. I'm booked on a September 28 flight. If I want two or three days to tour Turfan and two in Ürümqi, I'll have to reach the oasis no later than September 23.

That same evening, I realize that, in order to meet that deadline, I'll have to keep up the feverish pace that I've been traveling at since I left Kashgar. In fact, this is no longer a "walk," but a "race against the bureaucrats"!

Outside the post office, I meet Mohamatjan Qurban, a public letter-writer. Seated on a stool four inches high, he presides over a wobbly little loose-planked table. Four or five of his colleagues are seated there with him, but at the bottom of the stairs. Of all the tables, his is in the worst condition. But he doesn't care. All Mohamatjan worries about is staying ahead of the game. And the game today, for someone who already speaks and writes Chinese, Uyghur, and Russian, is to speak English and to know how to use the Internet. That, he tells me, is the future. And at fifty years of age, the future is his passion. He sports a *tiubetek,* or *toki,* a square hat embroidered in shades of green and blue, the favorite colors of Muslims. His shirt is brown, his vest white, and its numerous pockets are filled with pens, the tools of his trade. His customer base is made up of the many who, unable to read or write themselves, come to him to decipher their letters or put them into writing. He proudly shows me the addresses of the different countries to which he has penned letters. Since correspondence to Chinese destinations is hardly exotic, the only addresses he has kept are in the ex-USSR and—only one, but of which he is very proud of—to America. It's for a regular customer whose son moved to the United States. Each month, she goes to the post office to pick up the money order he sends her, good son that he is. And before leaving, she dictates a thank-you letter to Mohamatjan.

Since he has a penchant for the Internet, maybe he could tell me where I could find a computer so that I can check my inbox? He twiddles his short mustache then lays out his conditions: it will be a give-and-take. He'll be happy to take me there, but first, I'll have to translate into English a few expressions he gives me in Russian. I write them out for him in ballpoint, then he carefully recopies them into a school notebook, making calligraphic hairline strokes with a Sergent-Major dip pen. The porcelain inkwell he dips his pen into could well be a Ming dynasty antique! When he's done, shrewd Mohamatjan walks with me to the Internet cafe, barely a hundred yards away. He watches what I do, asking questions, picking up what he can, like a schoolboy studying for his next exam.

IX

THE ACCIDENT

I left Kuqa on September 1, planning to cover a very reasonable stage of fifteen miles. By evening, while pitching my tent on the desert floor, I realize that I covered precisely twice that distance. Once again, the fear of arriving too late hounds me and pushes me along. How improbable, though, that I should be so concerned about missing *deadlines*. As though I were still caught up in the obligations of a professional life that involved adhering to strict time limits (e.g., "a thirty-line article by 7:00 p.m. sharp!"). This is no different, except that written lines are distances traveled and my deadlines are border crossings!

The next day, in Dalaoba, I'm on the verge of turning in when I hear a knock on the door (why would anyone knock when the door is bashed in?). It's a stone-drunk truck driver asking whether I really did walk all the way from Kuqa. I tell him that yes, I did. He bursts out in a Homeric laugh, then heads off to a bedroom eerily lit by neon lights, where a bit of merry-making is going on. Ten minutes later, another drunkard comes in, refusing to believe that I actually walk. He asks to see my boots. Satisfied with the inspection, he staggers back to his quarters, overcome by all the shots of rice wine he has downed. I hear the others burst out laughing at his story. A third fellow sets his foot in the doorway and leans in for a glimpse of Ulysses. He, too, remains unconvinced. Leave it to a big-nose to walk when so many truck drivers—such as he—could effortlessly carry me all the way to Turfan—and beyond to Beijing, if I so desired!

In Luntai—thank goodness!—there's a hotel. I'll be able to wash up and rest, so I make a beeline for the front door, relishing in advance the pleasure of warm water on my shaved head. In the lobby, a young and elegant Han Chinese woman is seated behind a counter. I step up and ask, as pleasantly as possible: Does she have a room available? She stops talking and looks me over, making a face in which I detect a touch of revulsion. I know that I smell, but come on, not that much! Suddenly she yells and points to the door, waving hysterically as if to sweep me from her sight. When I fail to do as she says as quickly as she'd like, she calls a young dandy over to help, probably an employee, who motions me to get going while making ready to push me out the door. I'm stunned. It's the first time I've ever seen displayed such profound loathing for a foreigner. The woman can no longer control her aversion. I've occasionally glimpsed xenophobic glances or gestures, but nothing so violent. I stand dumbfounded for a moment out on the sidewalk. The workhand locks the door behind me, fearing I might try to come back in.

Shortly thereafter, I find an especially filthy *luguan* that's happy to have me. Birds of a feather flock together, apparently. The door to my room doesn't close, but I still have my padlock with me, and I leave my things only long enough to run out for a shave of the week-old beard now covering my cheeks. The salon is so small that the barber can accommodate just one customer at a time. Everyone else waits on a bench outside. Stingy with his lighting, he practically shaves me in the dark, which likely explains the two gashes he leaves me with. But when he charges me four times what I have paid for the same service in the past, I raise my voice and give him only half. He accepts it without a fight. I'll remember Luntai as the place where I felt the most unwelcome. For, as if I hadn't had enough already, I decide to go to the public bath house. The fat lady running the establishment asks me for a one-hundred-yuan deposit (about $15) before letting me in, then refuses to tell me the price. She has every intention of pulling the same trick as the barber. The people of Luntai are decidedly inhospitable! Unwilling to play the sucker, I change my mind and clean myself up as best as I can in a sink. Haggling, as practiced in the souks of the Orient and Maghreb, is admirable because it has rules. Gullible fellows are, in fact, looked down upon, and when seller and buyer successfully strike a deal, they shake hands with civility, each party thereby praising the respect that the other has required of him. There's nothing like that here.

Yengisar is a very somber town. And for good reason: all its residents are in the coal-peddling business. Every yard is piled high with the black stuff. Workers load and unload trucks using shovels, or their bare hands when they're handling large chunks straight from the mine. In this dark world, Shen is covered in white: he's a miller. I need to phone Paris to reconfirm the date of my return flight, so I decide to ask this powder-covered fellow: Is there a telephone booth around here? Rather than reply, he gently grabs me by the arm and points out his small shop, which is full of purring machinery. With his round head and honest laugh, his high forehead made even higher by a receding hairline, he has a trustworthy look, so I let him kidnap me. He helps a customer finish loading bags of flour onto a donkey cart then leads me to the backyard, and into his tiny dwelling. His wife, Han like him, barely had time to even notice me, but she already has water warming up for tea. Then their boy returns in no time with all their neighbors. There's a half-dozen of them between fifteen and twenty-five years old, and they obviously adore Shen, his loud laugh and little house, the door of which is always open. It's a community of friends and he's at its very heart. Ever since I started walking in this country, no Chinese Han has been as friendly to—or simply taken as much interest in—the big-nose that I am. I've been nothing but a curiosity, a phenomenon. Shen asks me to tell my story, he reads my little papers, gently admonishing a boy who speaks hesitant English in an attempt to get him to hurry up with his translations. Then he borrows my notebook and fills an entire page with ideograms that, as I find out later, express his admiration for what I'm doing. We drink tea while munching on dried fruit and grapes.

"You'll stay here and sleep at my house!" decrees the miller.

Everyone laughs, especially his wife: where does he plan on putting me? Shen agrees to accept payment from me if I phone Paris. He promises, then fails to keep his promise. It takes every insistent bone in my body and that of his wife to get him to allow me to pay for the charges, which aren't much since all I get is an answering machine. With the seven-hour time difference, it's too early in the day, and offices haven't opened yet in Paris. I'm happy to find myself in such pleasant company. It's the first time since Torugart Pass that I've felt the mutual kindness and friendly warmth that I encountered throughout Central Asia.

But for me, the greatest surprise is to see Shen, a Chinese Han, socializing with his Uyghur neighbors. All around, the two ethnic groups live side by side, but this is the first time I've seen them actually spending time together. Everything stands between them: religion, history, food—and of these, food is not the least! Muslims carefully avoid Han restaurants out of the fear that the pork-eaters might defile the fare. The massive arrival of Chinese colonists, a millennium-old Han strategy for assimilating new territories, satisfies neither the old, nor the new inhabitants of this vast region called Xinjiang. Han colonists, pushed here by policymakers or self-interest, are reluctant to leave the land of their ancestors. The Uyghurs, although not all of them support armed rebellion, are not particularly happy that the best jobs go to the newcomers.

The recent discovery of large oil fields has further accelerated the phenomenon. And there's no denying that in the West, public outcry is focused primarily on Han settlement policies in Tibet, while what's going on here is largely ignored by media outlets in Europe and the United States. The situation should, however, concern us greatly, given that it's a real powder keg, one that I sense could eventually prove lethal. Attacks led by Uyghur militants, said to have trained in Afghanistan, are either officially swept under the carpet or publicly discredited by Chinese authorities, just like executions of pro-independence militants—of which there are many, although precise numbers are hard to come by.

I'm back on the road after my friend Shen and I bade one another tearful farewells. Hours have passed, and now night is falling. Since there's no *luguan* in Yengisar, I decide to camp. I ask some young people working in a field whether I can pitch my tent in a small corner of their land, well back from the road. At a loss, they call out to their father and he slowly strides over. He's Uyghur with a head of thick, curly hair; a wide, strong chin; and quite the build. He works in the orchard, surrounded by peach trees, in shiny city shoes and a blue shirt whose sleeves are rolled up over muscular arms. I restate my request.

"I am Uyghur," he says with pride. "I will not let you sleep outside my door. Come into my house!"

He lives with his wife, three sons, and one daughter, in a large house enclosed by tall, red-brick walls. The main building has four rooms, a smaller room contains the kitchen and reception area. Two other structures are under construction. Abdihil is thinking ahead and his three sons—Kayser, Mevlan, and Abdo Rayni, ranging in age from fourteen to nineteen—will have their own house next to their father's. As for Arzugueli, their graceful teen daughter, she's dressed like the devil in jeans, a blue checkered shirt, and oversized sandals. Her hair is imprisoned in a black scarf, but her father is not a strict Muslim since his spouse, Janatan, goes about bareheaded. She's preparing a *laghman*, and when there's enough for six, there's enough for seven. They give me a large bedroom and the whole family throws me a celebration, delighted as they are to be hosting a Westerner. As for myself, I can't help but notice that two men representing the two different ethnic groups have, on the same day and in the same village, welcomed me with exceptional cordiality and kindness. Wanting to be sure I'm comfortable, they give me a large, new bed whose mattress is still covered in plastic. Hot as it is, I sweat profusely all night long and get a poor night's sleep. I'm sorrier than ever that I don't speak at least one of this land's two languages. The pride Abdihil took in inviting me in is proof of his Uyghur culture, and I would've been happy to discuss it with him. His children are all in school and help out on the farm. A relaxed, fraternal, and peaceful atmosphere prevails in this household, the three sons showing the two women and their father great respect.

As always, these delightful encounters buoy my spirits and the following day I walk joyfully, my heart cheered by so much fraternity. And, after walking twenty-four miles, I have to finally force myself to stop and camp. After dark, the stars that light up in the sky are joined by other lights off to the south. There are immense oil fields in this region, with reserves said to be three times those found in America. Invisible in daytime, the blackness of night allows me to see the wells being drilled, their drilling derricks illuminated like Christmas trees, and the tall flare stacks, which throw yellow flashes of light into the shadows. The problem facing the Chinese is that these huge reserves are far removed from the country's cities along the coast, where the need for the oil produced here is greatest. And for lack of a pipeline, trains have to transport the crude in endless caterpillars of railcars on single track to Xi'an, 2,500 miles away. Each day, hundreds of tanker trucks and hundreds of payloads of drill pipe pass by here, revealing just how much effort goes into searching for and extracting oil in Xinjiang.

In the village named "Tuantchang 29" (Brigade #29), which has been renamed simply "Twenty-nine," they've erected a miniature Eiffel Tower. I continued on past the village and set up camp in the desert a hundred yards or so off the road, so as to be as far as possible from the noise of the trucks, which tend to travel at night. As has happened to me quite often, I'm awakened by a storm that's as violent as it is sudden. A flapping sound tells me that my rainfly is about to break loose, so I hurry out but only just in time to see it fly off into the night. Wearing nothing but my sandals and wristwatch, I sprint like a madman to retrieve what is mine. But not fast enough, and the wind, in a gust, carries it across the road. Without thinking twice, I dash after it, naked as a jaybird, in the headlights. I have to run hard a good hundred yards before I finally recover it, caught on a prickly bush. Wearing my rainfly like a toga, I stride back across the National Road with all the dignity of a Roman emperor.

On September 12, I reach Korla. It's the last large city before Turfan, the end of my 2001 journey, only about ten days away. It's a disturbing city. For several miles, I walk with dusty factories on either side. Further on, machine shops spew automobile carcasses and oily vomit out onto the sidewalks. The city center has been entirely reconstructed with new buildings and is, by contrast, meticulously clean. I even snap a surrealistic sight: a municipal employee mopping a freshly-tarred avenue!

The first hotel I step into turns me away: they're not allowed to put up foreigners. In the one that does give me a room, a police officer drops by to check my passport in an awkward show of courtesies.

I've decided to rest up in Korla for a half-day only. If I want to make Turfan in the timeframe I've set for myself, I'll have to average twenty-three miles per day. An astounding pace and one that I've managed to keep up since Tuopa, but it's not without risk. The slight pains in my legs are warning signs that I'm edging over the red line. But the "race against the bureaucrats" has its own rules. Why renew my visa a week before it expires since by that time I'll practically be in Turfan? In any case, there's no sizable city from here to the last oasis, and it's unlikely I'll find a foreign police office where it can be extended. So once again I find that what would be no problem at all in a car, is unmanageable because I'm on foot.

So, I leave Korla at noon and start up a small mountain on which several pagodas have been constructed, and whose almost-spidery silhouettes stand out against a Marian-blue sky. The weather is nice, despite a strong, easterly wind that forces me to tug rather hard on Ulysses's tow bar.

I walked past the last houses a good hour ago, and now the road ascends through a superb environment. It winds back and forth through trenches sculpted in the rock and over embankments. I'm happy to have left the unchanging desert behind for the time being, although I know I'll find it again farther on. I walk in high spirits. The half-day off has reinvigorated me.

As is my custom, I walk to the left of the roadway, for it discourages most of the motorists with a mind to give me a ride. But not this driver. His vehicle is new—it's a pickup. Behind the wheel is a Chinese Han man about fifty years old. He pulls over and hails me. I answer with a smile and wave him on:

"No thank you! I want to walk!"

He doesn't insist; but then, just as he's shifting out of first, a truck arrives from behind out of nowhere at full tilt. The truck driver—who knows what he's dreaming about?—fails to see him and makes no attempt to stop. The collision is incredibly violent. The pickup, launched like a rocket, sails across the road and plunges into the ravine, vanishing from my sight. The truck was going so fast that, despite the impact, it follows right behind the pickup on its momentum as though it were being towed and crosses the road. It looks to be suspended in air for an instant, then nosedives onto the pickup. Horrified, I witnessed it all, the collision and the two vehicles' descent into the ravine. A cloud of smoke and dust rises up from below. I let go of Ulysses and slide down the embankment on my rear. Nearing the two wrecks, it's a few seconds before I can see that, fortunately, the truck didn't land on the pickup's cab, only on its bed. From the force of the landing, the cab tipped forward. Two men have been ejected through the shattered windshield. I run over to the pickup and to the man who wanted to give me a ride. He's moving. I try to open the door. It's jammed. He lowers the window. As I'm helping him get out, I notice that he has a female passenger, a woman who must have been sleeping in her seat at full recline. Her eyes are open and bespeak horror. The man exits through the window and is unhurt. A miracle. I reach the door of the woman at the same time as the two men ejected from the truck. They, too, seem to be very much alive. A third man appears, his face covered in blood. The woman complains of pain in her back and is moaning. I try to prevent the men from moving her, but her husband and one of the passengers from the truck pick her up and carry her ten yards away to a mound of dirt. The man with the bloody face also seems very much alive. He's bleeding profusely, but the wound is clearly superficial. No one died—it's unbelievable. Without realizing it, I take mental notes of every detail with photographic precision: in the pickup, there are packages of new books bound with string. The man and woman are apparently neither artisans nor farmers. Intellectuals? Probably. The wounded man—the truck driver—was plucked from the shadows by the passengers. He appears to be in catalepsy. Seated cross-legged, his face and body are motionless except for his eyelids that close every now and then as if attempting to wipe away unbearable images. He's reliving the impact, trying to understand how it happened. I'll stay there for over an hour and he never once changes place or position. He's suspended in time. Several vehicles parked at the scene of the accident cause a traffic jam. People get out of their cars, but they don't even pretend to help, they just stand and look on.

The woman complains of severe pain in her back. Her husband is arguing with the two who were riding in the truck. They went back up to the road and managed to stop a passing police car. Each man gives his version. With a small English-Chinese dictionary I pull from my pack, I find the word *hospital* and show it to the driver of the pickup, while pointing to his wife. But he's so caught up in his discussion with the cops and the truck drivers that he brushes me aside and does nothing. It seems less urgent than what he's involved in. Perhaps he holds me responsible for his misfortunes, too? I show one of the cops the word *ambulance*, pointing once again to the injured woman. But they're also too busy, focused on checking the vehicles' papers. Dictionary in hand, I feel helpless, useless. I go back to the woman whose moaning has grown worse and prop her up with cushions ejected from the pickup upon impact. I climb back up the embankment and this time I hold the dictionary directly beneath the second cop's nose, pointing at the word *ambulance*, then I point

to my watch and the passing time. This is an emergency! He leaves
his colleague to handle the discussion and slides down the embankment with me. When he sees the woman's condition, he orders two
bystanders to help, and the three of them carry her to the top of the
berm, where they put her in a car, which immediately speeds off to
Korla.

What else can I do? The reckless driver is still lost in his flashback
movie, sitting still as a Buddha. The protagonists continue to argue.
I feel powerless, but above all terribly responsible. I'm filled with feelings of guilt that I can't control. Little by little, the bystanders begin
to drive off. The cops jot down a few notes regarding the collision,
and I take several snapshots of the accident. I write my name and
address on a scrap of paper and give it to the driver of the pickup. I
feel awful. If he screamed at me, I'd understand. Instead, he thanks
me warmly, shaking my hands, full of belated gratitude, no doubt
because I took care of his wife. I don't know what to say. The fact
that I'm unable speak to him in this moment makes me feel angry
and terribly helpless.

I finally decide to leave. The man comes over once again to say
goodbye in an even greater show of emotion. I have the painful feeling of fleeing, of leaving him all alone with his injured wife and
wrecked car. But I know that I can be of no help here. The police
officers shake my hand, too, then give me the thumbs up to let me
know that I did a good job. Absurd.

On the road, just like the driver of the truck, I replay the accident
over and over in my head. It's as if I can still hear the sound of the
collision, the squeal of the tires on the asphalt, the muffled thud of
the vehicles as they land in the ravine, and the loud echo it produced.
But one image bedevils me most: that of the truck suspended for an
instant in the air before nosediving into the void. If I had been walking on the right side of the road, I would have been the only casualty.
All night long, these cursed images play over and over again in my
mind and that sound—that horrible sound—haunts me to the extent
that I can't close my eyes.

The accident has proven what I already knew: the greatest danger I face on this road is being mown down by a vehicle. It's a fear that will hang over me now to the very end. There's no way I'm going to listen to the cops who always want me to walk on the right side of the road. If I have to confront death, I want to see it coming head-on. I recall hearing a French gendarme say on the radio: "On a highway, the life expectancy of a pedestrian is forty minutes." And on the Silk Road? As I slip into my tent that evening, I'm plagued by yet another saying that applies me. It was used during France's infected blood scandal: "responsible but not guilty."* I am indeed responsible for this accident by the simple fact that I was there on the side of the road. But I also find it rather hard not to feel guilty.

The wind is once again blowing up a storm. I had to fight for a half hour this morning just to take down my tent, holding it in an iron fist so that it wasn't ripped away by the squall. The road is narrow. I walk into the wind, on the berm. Ulysses topples over more than once and heads into the ditch; eventually, a weld on the tow bar cracks. In a cloudless sky, the Tian Shan are truly celestial, grandiose, and excruciatingly beautiful; a jumble of immaculate whites and bereavement blacks. The range splits like a crab's pincer: one ridge heads towards Korla, the other towards Yanqi.

As I struggle against the wind, I walk near workers filling potholes with tar. I get splashed by a trickle of black liquid, and it stains my white windbreaker. Thinking there's some on my face, too, I wipe my hand across it to check. A worker laughs and makes it clear to me that no, there's nothing there. Near a marsh, I forget all about the incident while gazing at some small wading birds I can't identify, as well as some mallards and teals splashing about.

---

* TN: In April 1991, French news media revealed that the country's National Institute of Blood Transfusion had in the mid-1980s knowingly allowed blood contaminated with HIV to be distributed to hemophiliacs.

About 3:00 p.m., the wind lets up. A minibus goes past me, then stops a hundred yards or so in front of me. Three women and a man get out. The man comes over to meet me and, the moment he's within range, he asks, speaking English with a strong French accent:

"Arh yiou Berrrnarrde Ohlivurr?"

I answer in the same tone of voice and with the same accent:

"Yes, ahj yehm."

And, in my heart of hearts, in a nod to Livingstone, I nearly add: "Ahj prreesume!"

So, he turns to his companions and says, in French this time:

"You were right, Sylvette. It's him!"

After I ask the aforementioned Sylvette how she knew it was me, she replies:

"It wasn't hard," she explains. "I bought your book, *Vers Samarcande*, because we were planning to travel this way. I was so interested that I went back and bought the first volume, *Longue marche*, which I'm reading in the minibus!* The moment I saw you, I said to my companions: 'A fellow walking here, at this time of the year, it has to be him!'"

And right then and there, she asks me to autograph her book, indicating that it was *on* the Silk Road itself that I signed it! They tell me the unbelievable news: there was an attack on the twin towers of the World Trade Center in New York. It's September 14 and the towers were struck by airplanes three days ago. But in Xinjiang, word travels at a snail's pace. The news has me so distraught that I forget to ask these tourists their names, although they know mine. I'm numb that afternoon to the wild beauty around me, devastated by what I've just been told: is the world once and for all descending into homicidal madness?

---

* TN: *Walking to Samarkand: The Great Silk Road from Persia to Central Asia* (New York: Skyhorse Publishing, 2020) and *Out of Istanbul: A Journey of Discovery along the Silk Road* (New York: Skyhorse Publishing, 2019) respectively.

It's simultaneously a strength and a weakness of a civilization like ours that, in allowing those men to learn how to fly, it effectively trained its own executioners. How could men have accumulated so much hatred? One evening, for just two seconds, I glimpse on Chinese television the images of an airplane crashing into one of the two towers. It's at the end of the newscast, after the eternal parade of overviews of Party meetings, which constitutes the bulk of news here. The official Chinese news service clearly did not, at the time, take the event all that seriously. And my imagination runs wild, not for the planes that hit their targets, but for the one that crashed in the countryside. What could possibly have taken place on board? I suppose we'll never really know. I see in my mind's eye the passengers attacking the hijackers with their bare hands in hopeless combat since the pilots have already been killed, making catastrophe inevitable. Heroism out of desperation? How many passengers rose up? Did they ever think that their plane, as has been suggested, was intended to strike the White House, and that they may very well have saved the life of the president? Refusing to be projectiles, they accepted to be victims. No one will ever do justice to the story of these heroes who revealed themselves in the heat of the action, then vanished into thin air when the plane hit the ground. In an absurd, yet sublime act, they chose death while thumbing their noses at their executioners. Not much has been said about that plane, yet those on board carried out the ultimate expression of humanity: the revolt of the lambs. They dug their killers' graves; the latter, while seeing themselves as martyrs, were, in the end, like the passengers they sought to kill, victims of their own madness.

In Yanqi, I stop to contemplate the river. I haven't seen flowing water for such a long time! But a soldier toting a machine gun forces me to keep moving. Are they worried that pro-independence militants might be planning attacks? The Chinese government didn't need 9/11 as an excuse to go after the Uyghur mujahideen; it has been doing so for many years. It was estimated last spring, that in the previous year, ten thousand people had been executed, including two to three thousand Xinjiang separatists. I'll find out later on in France that, in the aftermath of the attack on the twin towers and confident that the United States would say nothing, the only trial several hundred Uyghur militants received was a bullet to the back of the neck, all in the name of the war on terror. True to the Empire's age-old traditions, the regime applies with extreme brutality the notion of killing in order to "set an example," a philosophy summed up as: "Kill the chicken to scare the monkey."

At the hotel, when I see myself in the bathroom mirror, I'm stunned. The drizzle of tar carried by the wind did indeed land on my face: my forehead and a portion of my cheek are slathered with thick, gummy black film that won't come off with soap. The four French tourists were too polite to say anything about it.

The road continues to climb, but gently. The hills rise ahead of me in smooth, bare terraces, like ascending steps. I encounter flocks of sheep on their way back down from alpine pastures. The clouds of dust they stir up make them easy to spot. In each one, there are two or three hundred animals. They move along with their heads held low, as if resigned to giving up the green pastures where they spent the summer. The shepherds, almost all of whom are on horseback, crack long whips, while newborn foals frolic around their mothers. A few men follow on foot, each holding a rod behind his neck with two hands, their heads lowered just like their animals, lost in dreams. Perhaps they're thinking of their children again, or of the women they love. A young boy, Tan, tells me that the journey back to his village is a ten-day walk. I'm returning to those I love, too, and it won't take me any longer than Tan to reach the end of my walk this year.

My body, sun and heat soaked for the past four months, has become very intolerant of drops in temperature. At 77°F, I start shivering, and at 61°F, like this morning, I'm freezing cold! As is the woman I buy a packet of ramen noodles from, and who slept in her shack by the side of the road. She never leaves it, day or night, seven days a week. How does she make it through the winter like that? The portrayal of the Chinese as being industrious workhorses is no fairy tale. Determination is a cardinal virtue here.

I'm becoming less and less presentable. The sole of my left shoe has a gaping hole in it. I'd need a first-rate tailor to repair my pants. They were already in sad shape in Kashgar, when I had them patched by young seamstresses in a shop near the mosque. Nine hundred miles and more since have done them in. The inseam has given out from all the rubbing. And seeing that the boxer shorts I have on underneath have become, after 1,900 miles, little more than short skirts, I have to keep from bending over whenever there are people behind me! My socks, consisting three-quarters of holes, are almost gone. Two zippers on my pack have stopped working, along with the one that lets me seal up my tent. I've given up washing my shirts, I only rinse them now to remove the salt left by all the sweat. My body is also crying out: "Enough already!" I've been pushing through a case of lumbago for two days now, and my level of exhaustion forces me to stop for fifteen minutes every six miles until the aches in my left thigh and soles subside somewhat. It's only knowing that my destination is not far off that I can put all that out of my mind and cheerfully press on. Ulysses, unrecognizable with all the welds and modifications he's had since Samarkand, is in great shape now after a mechanic, in no time flat, reinforced the weaker welds.

I've finally lost my hat: my old hat, my faithful companion through both rain and sun, which I was already wearing when I took my first steps on the Way of Saint James four years ago! Fed up, no doubt, with all that I was putting it through, it finally made up its mind and went its own way. Worn to threads, scorched by my sweat, it had lost its beautiful blue denim color. It even had a hole in the front, making it look like a Stetson worn by a *Lucky Luke* character who'd suffered a bullet graze to the scalp! Other than my pocketknife, it was the one object that had been with me from the start, for over 6,200 miles. I had hooked it onto my cart as usual this morning, waiting for the sun's first burning rays. When they finally came, it was gone. I hired a taxi heading back from the village I just left, where it had dropped a passenger off at . . . a funeral. We slowly retraced the nine miles back to the hotel while I scanned the roadside. Nothing. To make up for its absence, I've wrapped my head in my kaffiyeh which, even though we haven't been traveling together for nearly as long, is already threadbare. I get too attached to things.

The cotton harvest is underway. In the fields, men, women, and children, bent over antique-bronze leaves, pick the ivory bolls, one by one. On the main road, wagons are invisible beneath unbelievable bundles billowing with white gold. Flat on their stomachs atop the highest bale, a long rod in their hands, relaxed peasants guide their stubborn, indolent oxen to the cooperative.

Wushitala is at today's mile twenty-two. I have no idea what the village looks like since the first building I come to is a hotel and I go straight in, eager to get some rest. Today's leg, on top of yesterday's twenty-five miles, has wiped me out.

"No rooms."

The woman who owns the establishment didn't flinch. But a man shows up and asks me about my journey. He's flabbergasted that I could manage over twenty-two miles in one day. He bombards me with questions that I don't understand. I take out my little "open sesame" papers, while a second, then a third man arrives. They besiege the woman and they seem to be urging her to find a room for me. She rather quickly gives in and lets me into a large, clean room with two beds. I'm delighted.

"How much?"

"It's free."

"But I can pay!"

She refuses even a single fen—a hundredth of a yuan—and everyone seems to find it perfectly normal. So, I settle in. Shortly thereafter, she brings me a pan, some cold water, and a thermos full of boiling water. Her name is Chen Chouping, and she goes out of her way to take care of me. After helping me wash up, she makes sure I have something to eat: noodles and vegetables, and once again, it's on the house. An ill-timed procession of all the hotel's guests ensues, informed by the first man who spoke to me. I'm used to pageants like this!

When the assemblage finally breaks up, three men come in and order tea for themselves. They turn to Chen and I grasp that they're talking about me. One of them comes over and, with a few words in English asks to read my little papers written in French and Mandarin that recount my travels. He then shows me a badge, saying that he's with the police and that he wants to see my passport. A little while later, all three head off.

Where will I be able to buy a hat? In the village center, Chen tells me, only a short distance down the road. So I'm about to head off, when one of the police officers returns in a jeep driven by a tall fellow in fatigues. Nearly six and a half feet tall and with a face that looks as hard as rock, he's not one to stir up people's sympathy. He's the abominable snowman sort, but even grumpier. Beating about the bush is not his thing: he comes over to me, points his chubby index finger at my belongings and then at his car, and utters the only word of English he knows: *Go.*

My Chinese is hardly any better, but I answer him, not missing a beat:

"*Meiyou.*"

He winces. He's not used to that, the old grizzly bear.

The other cop, who speaks three words of English, manages to convey through babble and mime that they want to help me and are going to take me to a more comfortable hotel.

"But I'm fine here!"

"Impossible. You must come with us."

"No. I'm not in a hotel, I'm with friends. Ask the owner: she wouldn't take my money. Do you want me to turn down her hospitality? Out of the question!"

Chen Chouping, whom I turn to, is at a loss. In this land, the police's will is God's will. So, I have to mount my own defense. But I haven't got many weapons. Why should I go along with this ridiculous transfer to a hotel where I'll be more isolated than if I were sleeping in the desert? A third police officer who speaks a few more words of English has been called in to help out.

"In the hotel for foreigners, the mattresses are more comfortable."

"Every night, I sleep on stones. I don't care about comfort! What I really enjoy is being around people who are happy to have me. And here, they're very kind indeed."

But I'm dealing with some tough nuts to crack. If I don't want my hostess to suffer as a result, I'm going to have to do as they say. So, I start buckling my pack under the triumphant gaze of the Cro-Magnon-like soldier. Chen comes running out saying that she will go and get me a hat. We have to wait for her. The soldier drives off with her in his jeep only to return a few minutes later with both Chen and a young girl who introduces herself in excellent English: she's Tu Sian, Chen's daughter. Unable to find a hat, she and her mother brought me a golf cap. Not my kind of headgear, but I'll take it if it means avoiding sunstroke! Tu Sian's very kind, and I regret having to leave right when, finally, there's someone I can speak to. So I decide to engage in a final skirmish:

"Would you mind telling these officers that I'm quite disappointed by their attitude. I'm aware that they have their orders, but they need to know that the reason I'm traveling in China is to meet the Chinese people—like you, your mother, and the hotel guests—not to get comfortable. The only comfort I seek is a warm welcome. I was greeted by your mother as a friend, not as a customer. For that matter, does anyone speak English or French at the foreigners' hotel?"

The officers reply that they have no idea.

Tu Sian translated everything I said. The cops look perplexed. The bystanders listen to the girl with mouths agape, astonished by her mastery of English. She's a girl who I'd guess is about fifteen years old—later on, she tells me that she's eighteen—with short hair and a round, expressive face. I'm struck by her elegant hands and long fingers. Her eyes sparkle, and she's graceful even in her schoolgirl uniform: a blue and white tracksuit and little canvas sandals like those nearly all Chinese wear. Above all, there's a liveliness about her, an attentiveness to others that's surprising for someone her age. The last police officer to arrive has stepped away and is engaged in a conversation on his cellphone. Now he's the one we're waiting for. I maintain my stance. My heart is heavy as I prepare to lift Ulysses up into the jeep when the officer suddenly comes back over.

"You can stay. The chief of police says it's okay."

No one is so crude as to publicly celebrate. Above all, never let the authorities lose face! I thank them all, all except for the muscleman, that is, who has already hopped back into his jeep.

Later that day, I have a long chat with Tu Sian. Six years ago, her father was killed in a traffic accident. The paramedics didn't get there in time. Tu Sian's brother was three, her sister six. So Chen raised her three children on her own and took over managing the hotel. The children help out, especially Tu Sian. The circumstances of her father's death were very hard for her to accept and she promised herself that she would become a doctor. She tells me that she has a boyfriend but that she won't get married until her studies are behind her. She's an incredibly energetic young lady beneath a very poised exterior.

That same evening, two guests who have drunk too much rice wine get into a fight. I watch as she steps in and skillfully calms them down without getting worked up. She'll surely make a fine doctor.

Chen Chouping is delighted at how things turned out and is very proud to watch on as her daughter converses in English with a big-nose. She insists on washing my shirt which she deems—and she's right—incredibly dirty. I tell her not to bother, but she makes a compelling argument, so I finally give in: "You're part of the family! Look how the two little ones have already begun calling you *yeye* (grandfather), and Tu Sian wants to call you *shushu* (uncle)!"

X
MISTER LIU

Just outside Wushitala, high on a hill, a large *obo* dominates the valley. The mound, covered in stones and planted with dead branches hung with prayer cloths, is sacred ground. Every Mongol passing this way feels obliged to set yet one more stone atop the pyramid. Three concrete yurts, their doors facing south, are empty. A road-mender, placing his palms together, tells me that shamans come every year to lead religious ceremonies. The view extends far out over the oasis as well as the plain I left behind this morning.

I find it hard to walk but manage to cover twenty-one miles despite crossing over a mountain pass at 1,700 meters (5,600 feet). It's not just any old pass. As I reach the crest, I leave the Tarim Basin behind—the largest hydrological drainage area in the world—and enter that of Turfan, which, though much more modest, is unique in that its center is significantly below sea level.

Halfway down, I discover a dozen long, parallel buildings covered in glazed tiles and in which tiny skylights have been bored. It's the former Daobangfang prison. It's said that, at one time, it could house a thousand prisoners. Other old prisons are falling apart here in the region, like painful, impure memories. I'm traversing China's Siberia here, a land perfectly suited for prison camps, for it blends the aridity of the desert with the raw hostility of the mountains. And if that's not enough, winters here are bitterly cold and summers scorching hot. An ideal prison, as it were. Lastly, any man planning an escape would have to go by way of the road I'm on. Because it runs alongside

155

the mountains, it's so narrow that guarding it is child's play. At Daobangfang, a family has moved into the former guardhouse near the road and is working a small gypsum mine. How many men were sent here to be "re-educated"?

The road climbs once again, devilishly steep. At sunset, the mountain reveals a stunning variety of rocks, and is bedecked in a palette of soft colors: bister, gray, serpentine green, black, red, and orange. I camp, having covered twenty-nine miles. My lower back pain, nevertheless, is no better.

The next day in Kumishi, the owner of a *luguan* requests thirty yuan for the night. Six times the usual price, but still reasonable. Since I don't object, he doubles the rate. And when I ask whether there's a shower, he tells me that there is, but that it will cost twenty yuan more! The "shower," which I ask to see, is . . . a toilet bowl. I flatly refuse to be taken for a fool, and head off to the next *luguan* over, where the women running it are less greedy and I'm able to eat, wash up, and sleep for a quarter of what I would have paid at the first.

I decide to devote the next morning to a little needlework. I have no choice but to assume from time to time the role of a modern Penelope! I also have to find someone to repair my shoes. A sidewalk cobbler, armed with nails and glue, puts an end to my soles' bid for independence. I do what I can to sew up my pants so people aren't offended when they see me, and I have my chin shaved (it was starting to itch something awful for a good week) by a little Chinese lady barber who wields the straight razor with a graceful hand.

I head back out in the early afternoon with fresh wind in my sails. In the evening, I camp near an especially poor hamlet. The children are covered in equal parts of mud and rags. Some of the parents are away, working in a mine to the north; I see trucks returning from it loaded with stones. A crowd watches me set up my tent. Exhausted, I'm in bed by 8:00, but one of the locals plays the guide and conducts very noisy tours until 11:00.

I have a thousand more feet to climb to get over another mountain pass. The ascent is steep and the wind, blowing hard from the east, seems to want to wrest Ulysses away from me. Leaning forward, I heave my companion up, step by step. Then there's the descent. I'll be going from an elevation of 2,000 meters to 160 meters (525 feet) *below* sea level! Rock was extracted from the mountain, block by block, to build a vertiginous road overlooking a fast mountain stream. It clings to a high cliff, suspended below the vertical wall, anchored so deeply that the sun cannot reach it. Over one hundred meters farther below thunders the torrent. On the other side of this narrow valley are high, rounded dunes of bronze, arid sand. An abandoned prison rots in a side valley, and by noon I'll have discovered two more. In each, a few people eke out a living—you have to really wonder how.

Traveling this road involves some nasty risks. The bedrock is heavily fragmented schist, and scores of rocks that have broken off lay in piles on the roadway. I understand why Silk Road caravans traveled this route in winter only. Here, before bulldozers cleared a passage, there was a viable road only when the river was frozen. After a change in elevation of 1,000 meters (3,300 feet), my legs are on fire. I camp in an abandoned house. Squealing brakes and the moan of motors pushed to their limits keep me awake all night long.

The following day, I feel as if the road has become even steeper. Is it true or did I simply not recover enough after a night of tumultuous sleep? The trucks roar as they head uphill, they heat up, whine, and force their drivers to stop every now and then. On the way down, it's their brakes that suffer. Flames burst forth from the wheel of a semi-trailer truck as it's passing me up. The stolid driver stops his vehicle, gets down from his cab holding a bucket of water, and puts out the small fire, causing the release of large billows of steam. Then he gets back underway, unruffled.

Around 10:00, three zealous cops ask for my passport and tell me to walk on the right side of the road. That's simply not something I'm going to do. The pickup truck incident is still vivid in my mind. The narrow lane forces trucks to brush up against the rock wall as they head downhill, and I no more want to try to stop one of them with my body than to have a stone hit me on the head. I bid the cops a civil goodbye, then, very conspicuously, head back across the road to the other shoulder, left of descending vehicles. I expect them to whistle and scold me. But no, they've done their duty by pointing out the law, and whether or not I wind up as mashed potatoes on the front grill of a semi is of no concern to them.

Arriving in the valley is even more spectacular than the difficult climb to the top of the mountain pass. Rock suddenly disappears. Here I'm surrounded by sand: the beach left behind when the sea withdrew. The valley opening before me is a hollow, flanked by two Tian Shan massifs. The endlessly winding road, as though liberated, now leads straight on to Tuokexun, twelve miles away, but which seems much closer given how clear the air is. Off in the distance, thirty, perhaps sixty miles away, another mountain range straddles the horizon. The day is luminous, the temperature mild. I feel a great sense of peace of mind after that challenging descent. I glance at my altimeter: a third of a mile before reaching the first houses of the city, I have reached the level of the sea. The illusion is all the more striking in that there is what appears to be a demarcation: small stones take over from the sand. I've reached the bottom of a waterless ocean.

I've never seen so many restaurants on the road leading into a city. Imagine them all . . . shoulder to shoulder for two miles along both sides of the road. There are surely more establishments than custom-ers. I choose one of them because a woman seated on a chair outside the door is rocking a child. It's a little girl, still a baby, with intense green eyes. Chinese babies are typically devilishly cute bundles of joy; from their so-very-fragile almond eyes, they seem to peek out at the world with both fear and mischief.

They prepare for me a variety of sweet potato they call *kunshu*, and a *laghman* in which rice takes the place of the noodles, and which has been renamed *camfen*, followed by juicy, wonderfully sweet watermelon.

For some strange reason, although I'm very tired, sleep is slow to come. The fact that my destination is right around the corner has me both excited and unnerved. I lie down on the bed with dozens of ideas bouncing around in my head. No matter how accustomed I am to the phenomenon, I'm still amazed how walking for long stretches of time is an extraordinary weaver of future plans. It's a three-phase process.

The first consists in lightening the load. This is the darkest stretch, lasting a good two weeks, sometimes more. You have to tear yourself away, put up with blisters and sore muscles, and combat the fears of the road. As for the mind, it frees itself—sometimes violently, always painfully—from memories, or from suffering, whether recent or old. It's an assessment, a difficult appraisal. A kind of more or less controlled mental breakdown. When packing your bag, you eventually remove any unnecessary clothing and objects. Then, over the first few days on the road, you further get rid of all the impediments, all the troubles cluttering your mind. The soul grows calm as it steps away from all the dull or dark concerns of pre-departure life.

The second phase is that of dream and discovery. Your battle-hardened body lets you forget that it's even there. You start paying attention to your environment and to the people you meet; you're ready to listen to what they have to say, and, in moments of solitude, you listen to yourself. Far from phones, demands, pragmatic preoccupations, and the daily grind, the imagination takes over. And it isn't long before the question arises: what, in life, is truly important? Answers come in flashes, in stages. Free from trivial cares, *having* gives way to *being*. And that's when walking reveals its secret: you thought you set out to find others, but now you're finding yourself.

The final phase is only half sad. Realizing that the end of the journey is near, you feel a mix of regret—the dream is ending—and joy, thinking of how you'll soon be reunited with the people you love. But this concluding phase is accompanied by unbridled creativity: new plans start running through your mind; you fill the days, months, and years to come with resolutions and intentions of all kinds. No doubt because, after such a long period of physical activity and pleased to have successfully completed a long walk, you somehow have to stop focusing on the present alone, and instead make the present relevant to the future, projecting forward the tremendous energy that has accumulated in your muscles and mind. It's probably also because doing so softens the blow of seeing your dream come to an end. The walker becomes a prospector, panning not for gold, but for nuggets of life. In the last days of a walk, I'm no longer on the road, but on the road-beyond-the-road. Reading over my notebooks, I notice that I fail to mention my surroundings much. I'm already someplace else, back home, with those I love, but in action.

After studying my maps, I decided that for my last two days of walking this year, upon leaving Tuokexun, I'd take the scenic route, straying from National Road 314, which I've faithfully followed ever since Kashgar. I located a short itinerary going east, whereas the main road heads up north. I won't find any hotels or restaurants, but I'm an experienced camper now! But above all, I no longer want to see—nor hear—any trucks. So, on my way out of the oasis, I make a right turn. Near the city's last houses, some children are playing with a live snake.

I'm in the middle of the desert, a featureless space, though not entirely devoid of vegetation: there are a few tufts of camel grass and some flowering tamarisk shrubs. But not a single car, not even a donkey cart: I'm all alone under the open sky. And I soak in this solitude, knowing that, as early as tomorrow evening, I'll just be one more face in the crowd.

It's fairly late in the day and I start looking for a suitable place to camp. It has to meet two basic conditions: there must be shelter from the wind and enough large stones nearby so that I can cinch down my rainfly and build a campfire ring. I'm not having much luck as the sun is already sinking toward the horizon when, off to the south, I notice a rather odd-looking structure: two tall columns and a kind of colossal doorway that opens out . . . onto the desert. Around the

columns in every direction, there's at least a half-mile of gently undulating sand. Intrigued, I approach the strange portico. The wind has,
little by little, shoved sand up against a high wall, silting up the wall's
round, festoon-decorated edges. Behind this portal, looking unreal
out here in the steppe to say the least, stands a one-story house with
a large terrace covered in part by an arcade gallery. Standing to the
left are buildings that would be easy to mistake for the prisons of
Daobangang. Sheltered by the wall buzz hundreds of beehives. And
among them is an out-of-place, surreal, little Chinese man in a blue
shirt and black pants, his feet in traditional black-canvas espadrilles.
He stands near a fountain spouting clear water, which, in the desert,
is always a moving sight. Upon noticing me, the little man hurries
over, his hand outstretched, a wide smile lighting up his face. He
utters a phrase: words of welcome, no doubt. I don't understand but,
moved by a welcome that had no time for diplomatic mumbo-jumbo,
I reply, in French:

"*Merci pour ton accueil. Moi aussi je suis ravi de te rencontrer!*"*

Surprised, he pauses, then bursts out in a loud, expressive laugh.

"Bernard," I tell him, pointing to my chest.

He does the same and I hear a name I've heard before: "Lio,"
which is normally spelled Liu. Mister Liu! In China, you never call
people by their first name—only the person's mother and spouse,
and possibly brothers and sisters might do that. The surname is preceded by the equivalent of "Mister."

Mr. Liu points to the house and motions me to come along with
him and to bring Ulysses with me. Before doing that, though, I can't
resist giving in to an urge to drink a few gulps of the water flowing
from the fountain. A careless move, one stemming from the fact that
I'm more relaxed now, knowing that my journey for the year 2001 is
coming to an end. And the presence of this man with a benevolent
face reassures me. So long as I'm with him, nothing bad can happen to me! As I catch up to him out on the terrace, his wife, a tall,

---

* "Thank you for your greeting. I, too, am pleased to meet you!"

slim Chinese woman, comes over to me and gives me a look full of haughty distrust. It's a look I've seen before. But what's got me so excited is Mr. Liu's incredibly friendly face. The very moment we met, I knew that this would be a memorable encounter, the very kind I've been waiting for since crossing into China. And here it is, just in the nick of time!

The house, shaped like the letter "L," has ten rooms, none of which communicate with any of the others. Some have just one door, and the window has been bricked up. My host returns with a teapot, and at that point, there's a sudden connection between us: a strong attraction, a kind of brotherly bond, friendship at first sight. For two hours, I "converse" with Mr. Liu despite not understanding a word of Chinese. And he doesn't speak a lick of English, or any other language either. Yet we exchange ideas, we understand one another. Our mutual empathy is so complete, our attentiveness to one another so great, that we come up with our own language. He speaks Chinese and I speak French; but each intonation, each mimic, each sign has meaning. Our dialogue makes use of every available tool: grimaces, expressions. We communicate, one clueless person with another! And we use the sand deposited by the wind on the terrace as a blackboard.

My friend tells me that this place, called Nong Chang, is a former prison-farm. He left his hometown of Tiendo and came here in 1981 to work as a mason, just as the walls of the penal colony were beginning to rise from the desert floor. What side was he on? That of the to-be-rehabilitated, or that of the rehabilitators? It's a question I'm afraid to ask. Two thousand goats here and many more thousands of ducks were raised in the buildings that he shows me and that are today beginning to give way. The prisoners were housed in a village that we can just see off to the southwest. The house he lives in was the prison's central office. When it closed, Liu and his wife stayed behind. He makes a living thanks to his bees and a herd of one hundred goats that returns here each evening, guarded by a herder, a simpleminded fellow from the neighboring village. Liu has two boys, one's nineteen and the other twenty-two. The older one is married and has a little girl. I had him read through my little introductory papers in Chinese, but he wants to know more and asks me a thousand questions about *Bali* (Paris).

Little by little, the sky has caught fire in the west and the sun is finally plunging into the Taklamakan. I pitch my tent beneath the eaves of the roof. It turns out to have been a smart move, too, since a dreadful sandstorm blows in in the middle of the night, which otherwise would probably have carried my rainfly away!

The next morning, my host offers me some honey and makes me promise to write and send him photos of *Bali*. When it's time for me to leave, he takes hold of my hands, squeezing them for a long time as if hoping he might keep me from leaving, then gives me a hug.

That day, I walk with a spring in my step. I mentally carry on with last night's conversation, as if this overdue, joyful friend were still by my side. Liu showed me what was once the director's office, and he mimed with incredible realism what happened when a prisoner was summoned before the head honcho and came in, with tied hands, to hear what the sentence awaiting him was. Throughout the day, I scroll through in my mind each scene of this fantastic encounter. It's true that, had I learned Chinese, I would probably have met many captivating people here. But this one evening has made up for the lack of human interaction that has plagued me from the moment I set foot in China. This little man's beaming smile is still with me as I write these lines. There are magical moments like this every now and then in life, which transcend boundaries and free us from the weight of the world, putting us on par with the gods. Thank you, Mister Liu!

I reach the Turfan Oasis from the south. It's Sunday. Families, in mule-drawn carts, are out making the rounds. A female donkey, startled at the sight of Ulysses, leaps over the ditch and gallops off across the fields, dragging an entire tribe with it; they hold on for dear life, and their screams only panic the animal more.

I take a look at my altimeter. We're 150 meters (500 feet) below sea level. Turfan, which the Chinese have nicknamed Huozhiguo (Land of Fire), can reach 122°F in the summer. The oasis is 155 miles northwest of Loulan and the dry lakebed of Lop Nor, where China tested its nuclear weapons.

The region is famous for its seedless and very sweet grapes. At the entrance to the city stand countless low buildings with well-ventilated walls: they were erected leaving a large gap between each brick. The buildings are used once every year for drying the clusters, which are hung from wires. The heat helps remove water from the grape berries while preserving their juice. I watch on as peasants out in their yards strike the clusters to free the raisins, which can then be stored indefinitely.

On September 23, 2001, I set my pack down in the lobby of the Oasis Hotel. I have just completed a journey of nearly 1,900 miles (3,000 kilometers). I celebrate the event that evening by prancing about with a troupe of Uyghur dancers performing in the hotel's courtyard. It isn't until the following day that I finally throw open the floodgates of fatigue. I walked the Chinese portion of the journey at the insane pace of 620 miles per month. Until now, I had never covered more than 500 miles in under thirty days. But having succeeded once again this year, life is beautiful, and I'll have plenty of time from now until I embark on the final stage of my journey to regain my strength and the twenty-six and a half pounds I've lost since setting out from Samarkand.

On a first visit in 1997, I found the heart of this city extremely charming, resembling a beautifully decorated movie set. Years earlier, grapes had been planted, and the vines climbed up their trellises, forming arbors over the roadways, providing both shade and fruit. It was a striking sight, streets beneath heavy clusters of grapes. Unfortunately, the very success of these streets led to a series of decisions by city council that have taken away much of their charm. Plastic columns have replaced the old wooden posts, and there are marble tiles where blacktop used to be. Decorated with an overabundance of small, multicolored bulbs, the place has taken on a gaudy, ridiculous look. Schoolchildren mop down the walkways twice a week, and I noticed that they do so reluctantly. Finally, to keep people from stealing the clusters once the grapes have ripened, the streets are literally teeming with overseers and they slap fines on anyone picking even just a single grape.

There's no river running through Turfan to supply it with water; instead, there's a rather tight network of underground canals, the *karez*. I saw these canals back in Iran (where they're called "qanats"), and the techniques used here originated in Persia. The Turfan Oasis owes its existence to these little streams that fetch water in the foothills and carry it, cool and pure, to the city. The region boasts three thousand miles of underground canals. The Uyghurs, who are very proud of them, are quick to point out that, although they're not as visible nor spectacular as the Great Wall, it took two thousand years and just as much work to build them. Two thousand shafts provide maintenance access to this network, on which the very existence of the oasis depends. The *karez-kan*—those who drill the underground tunnels—enjoy tremendous prestige and unanimous respect.

Turfan, which the Chinese have renamed Tulufan, is also an important site with respect to the region's history. Before Islamization in the eighth century, Buddhism was widespread, as evidenced by the sites and grottos that can still be visited, and which have, by and large, escaped devastation of all kinds. When the Uyghurs left Mongolia and settled in this region, a kingdom sprung up, with Gaochang as its capital.

The day after my arrival, I tour the ruins of the ancient city of Jiaohe. Perched atop cliffs at the confluence of two rivers, it boasts origins so ancient that no one knows who its first inhabitants were. In the second century, the Han dynasty established a garrison here to ensure the security of the Silk Road. Unfortunately, a thousand years later, the city was visited by Genghis Khan, who left behind him hardly more than can be seen today: ruins and earthen walls rising desperately to the sky. That said, the place is not lacking in nobility: it's one of those corners of the planet where the void is so filled with the past that the present falls away.

Some distance north of Turfan, on the Gobi Desert side, is the "Black City" of Khara-Khoto. Marco Polo reportedly visited it one year before it was destroyed, and he named it Etzina. The master of the city, Khara Bator, had vowed to overthrow the emperor of China. He declared war on him, lost several battles, and took refuge here in this city, reputed to be impregnable. The Chinese diverted the river that supplied it with water. Knowing that the end was near, Khara Chiang Chun placed his treasure in eighty chariots and buried them at the bottom of shafts that had been dug—in vain—to find water. He immolated his two wives, his daughter, and his son, attempted a sortie, and was killed leading his horsemen. Despite numerous excavations by both the Chinese and the Russians, his treasure has never been found.

These two days off in Turfan have passed quickly. I have a thousand things to do. I've notified Paris over the Internet that I'm on my way home. I also pack up Ulysses's two wheels, which I leave in the care of the Oasis Hotel, advising them that I'll be back to retrieve them next spring. But I need to take the cart itself back to France: I have too many upgrades to make to my prototype and traveling companion, hoping to boost his performance, and many of those couldn't be done here.

Ürümqi, Xinjiang's regional capital, is a large city where Han Chinese and Uyghurs coexist, but don't mix. There, I meet up with Wang Wan Ping, who, as you'll recall, is the travel manager who helped arrange my border crossing. I have no idea why, but I had pictured him as old and plump; instead, I find a svelte, energetic young man. He hands me the airline ticket for my journey out of China to Almaty, the capital of Kazakhstan. From there, I'll head back to Paris. Biding my time, I stroll around Ürümqi, recalling what Peter Fleming once said about the city: "The death-rate at

banquets is appalling," he writes, in his very British sense of humor.*
Indeed, during a banquet in 1916, General Yan Tsen Hsin ordered
the heads of people he suspected wanted to overthrow him cut off,
while an orchestra played on. He then calmly finished his meal. In
1928, another banquet: but this time, it's he and his friends who are
unable to digest all the bullets served up. In the nineteenth century,
the heads of convicted persons were clamped in a *kapas*—a kind of
pillory—set up in the middle of a street, to the total indifference of
passers-by. The torture victim's feet were set on a plank that, over the
course of a week, was progressively lowered until the fellow's neck
broke. Man, decidedly, in both pleasure and horror, is staggeringly
sophisticated.

In my mind, I'm already back in Paris. Common sense would
have me sleep in for a few mornings. But my biological clock, which
has become used to waking me up at dawn every day for the past
four months, isn't quite ready to change routines. So, I head out into
the streets before sunup. There's a serene ambiance in the large park
called Renmin (meaning "people"). I spend several delightful hours
there, watching as the first workers come to perform group gymnastics before going to the office. I notice that there are only Han
Chinese there. Once the workday is underway, a swarm of retirees
arrives in a display of uncommon energy that must save Chinese
social security some serious money. Every corner of Renmin Park is
worth seeing. Beneath the trees, the innumerable birds are inaudible
given that there's music playing everywhere. First off, there's a little
island where, to the rhythm of Strauss waltzes or the paso doble,
some rather mature couples are twirling away. Groups armed with
toy swords perform slow, calculated movements in perfect unison.
There are those who engage in gymnastics, and others who gambol

---

* Peter Fleming. *News from Tartary: A Journey from Peking to Kashmir* (New York:
Charles Scribner's Sons, 1936). Reprinted by arrangement with the Estate of Peter
Fleming by the Marlboro Press/Northwestern University Press (Evanston, Illinois,
1999), 249.

about to the music of *"Chérie je t'aime, chérie je t'adore. . . ."** In one alleyway, an old woman, accompanied by three traditional musicians, sings Chinese operatic arias, her voice as high-pitched as that of a little girl. A hundred women or so, scattered about beneath the trees, a scarf in each hand, rehearse rhythmic dance movements. Few have the routine down, but they're all learning. For each discipline, there seems to be one or two people who serve as leaders. The others carefully listen or follow along. A few truly elderly individuals who can't keep up with these frenzied rhythms relentlessly perform stubborn little gymnastics movements while walking about the alleyways or standing beside a large tree.

At an intersection, I lunch on donuts that I dip in a kind of hot milk under the tender eye of other customers who teach me how to proceed. Here, as elsewhere, I've grown accustomed to wiping my mouth and hands with . . . toilet paper. There's none to be found in bathrooms, but in large cities, a restaurant table wouldn't be quite right without its own roll.

Seated in the shade of the park, as I'm about to take leave of this country for several months, I ponder how energetic the Chinese are. I'm hardly surprised that technology-wise, the country is quickly catching up with the West. Work is a cardinal virtue here. Staying active is raised to the rank of a state religion. But how can one not be surprised by how quickly the Chinese have adjusted to a market economy after sixty years of hardline communism? There's no denying that buying and selling never completely disappeared during that time, despite the Party's stranglehold on the economy. It struggled along nevertheless, conserving its energies in the back alleys of the bazaars, where competition never lost its rights. No sooner did the doors crack open than it blossomed once again. Things went almost

---

* TN: The song *Ya Moustafa, chérie je t'aime, chérie je t'adore* ("Here is Mustafa, I love you, darling, I adore you, darling") was made famous in Europe in 1960 performed by Bob Azzam, an Egyptian singer of Lebanese origin.

immediately from pure economic socialism to aggressive, savage capitalism, and stragglers were shown no mercy.

On September 28, I board a Chinese airline's Russian-made aircraft bound for Almaty, and from there I'll fly to Paris by way of Istanbul. Since I didn't know in advance when I'd be returning home, a ticket was purchased for me and I'll have to pick it up at the Turkish Airlines counter in the Kazakh airport.

Exiting the plane, I'm in for a surprise. There's no special passageway for in-transit passengers. Arrivals and departures are in separate buildings. So all passengers have to go through immigration. When it's my turn, a vocal and aggressive female police officer, thumbing through my passport, expresses surprise that I don't have a visa.

"I'm in transit, so I don't need one. I'm on the flight for Paris tonight."

"If you don't have a visa, you can't enter Kazakh territory."

"But I just told you that I'm in transit . . ."

She turns a deaf ear, pushing me away while pointing to an office. There, a Kazakh consul explains that, in order to get from where I am now to the departures terminal, I have to cut across Kazakh territory, so I need a visa for his country. The price: twenty dollars. Quite the little scam and I'd love to put up a fight, but decide against it while asking to retrieve my bags: they tell me that I'll need the visa just to get to the baggage claim area! Their dollar trap is a perfect setup. A group of Danes is in the same boat as I am, and despite their guide's ranting and raving, he has no choice if he wants to free them from the snare. The scheme suddenly turns Kafkaesque:

"Your passport and ticket for Paris, please!"

"I just told you that I don't have my ticket for Paris, it's at the Turkish Airlines office, where I have to pick it up."

"Then I can't issue you a visa!"

With a zany, half-baked bureaucratic system like this, how, without a fierce sense of humor, would the citizens of this country ever survive? I initially take it as a big joke, but I quickly change my tone of voice and throw quite the tantrum when the consul declares that there's absolutely nothing he can do for me. It appears I'm condemned to remain in this little room until the end of time since there's no way to break the vicious circle, barring—who knows?—a revolution . . . or the Apocalypse. I can't get a visa without a ticket, but to go fetch the ticket, I need a visa. The consul, whose honor is impugned by my Homeric, ironic laugh, tries phoning the airline, but since the plane isn't scheduled to take off until 4:00 in the morning, the airport office isn't open yet and the one in town, given how late it is, has already closed. I ask permission to simply go get my bags, but I'm turned down point-blank by the uniformed harpy who smokes cigarette after cigarette while laughing it up with her coworker.

For an hour, I'm chomping at the bit. Then the consul, behind his window, motions for me to come over.

"Have you resolved your problem? The office is closing."

I pounce on him.

"How do you expect me to get out of this prison since you've locked all the doors?!"

He appears genuinely sorry. But I have no doubt that, come dinner time, he'll leave me here high and dry. And since there's only one flight per week . . .

"Please understand. I'm only enforcing the rules."

He scratches his head for a moment, then, in a flash of inspiration, he asks to see my passport again. He thumbs through it, then smiles.

"You came by way of Kyrgyzstan! That's perfect! I can't give you a visa if you are coming from China, because then, I have to also have the plane ticket of your final destination. But if you're coming from Kyrgyzstan, there's a land border, and in that case, there's no problem, since your Kyrgyz visa is still valid! We'll just pretend that you came by road."

I'm speechless.

"But I'm in an airport that's 124 miles from the border. I couldn't possibly have come all this way without a visa."

"A mere technicality! Your Kyrgyz visa is valid. Everything's in order."

The employee who had returned my twenty dollars to me takes the bills back and checks them over once again, for one can never be too careful! Finally, the female cop, wearing a smug little smile, plants a stamp on my passport. My bags are fortunately still in the arrivals area, orphaned but intact.

In the deserted airport, waiting for the airline office to open, I meet an American en route to Tajikistan. He has been here for three weeks and was unable to resolve a similar situation. After spending a third night in the airport, he was granted permission to check into a hotel in Almaty, even without a visa. But he still can't leave. Fortunately for him, a pretty young Kazakh woman who runs a store in the airport has taken a shine to him and is helping him enjoy his stay.

When the airplane finally takes off for Istanbul, my eyes glued to the vast steppe passing beneath the cabin windows in the morning sun, I think about how it will take us ten hours at the speed of five hundred miles per hour to reach the city I set out from three years ago now. And to think that I have covered this distance step by step suddenly strikes me as unbelievable. As though the man who sweated it out down there, thirty thousand feet below, wasn't the same one now comfortably seated in the plush cabin where a flight attendant leans over to ask in a hushed voice: "Would you like something to drink, sir?"

For the first time since beginning this Long Walk, I'm starting to think that I just might make it to the end. But let's not get ahead of ourselves: I still have 1,900 miles to travel, I have to cross the Gobi Desert, and China is hardly noted for its hospitality. I have just over six months to prepare for this final stage, the goal of which is to reach Zhonglou, that legendary Bell Tower rising at the heart of Xi'an.

PART II—THE WINDS OF THE GOBI
FOURTH VOYAGE

(Spring-Summer 2002)

I

SANDSTORM

Upon reaching the National Road, my heart sinks into my boots. The fine cement distance marker, painted white and planted atop a rounded mound, displays in black a terrifying figure: 3,981 kilometers (2,474 miles). Route 312 is the longest in all of China. And the world. It runs from Shanghai to the Kazakh border, a distance of over 3,100 miles. Xi'an, my destination, is 600 miles from the coast. Until early this morning today, April 18, 2002, I was hoping that one of my documents was wrong. Unable to find a reliable map, I stuffed three questionable ones into my backpack. The first shows 2,400 kilometers (1,491 miles), the second, 2,650 (1,647 miles). Desperately contemplating the baleful marker, I have confirmation that, unfortunately, it's the third map that must be right: there are indeed 2,900 kilometers (1,802 miles) between here and Xi'an, China's imperial capital until the ninth century, and the final kilometer of the Great Silk Road. My spirits, at half-mast since I left Paris, sink to an all-time low. Can pitiful, twenty-six-inch strides really carry a person so very far? And that's on good days!

I must admit that for two weeks now, I've been down in the dumps. I left France this year in poor health: in winter, a nasty bout of the flu laid me low. A relapse, complicated by bronchitis, struck just three weeks before I was supposed to board my flight. My cough sounds like I'm suffering from the whooping cough, and I'm spitting like they do here in China. Pain, especially in my left foot and knees, make me doubt whether I'll be able to see the journey through to the end. For the first time since I started walking the Silk Road, I'm feeling every one of my sixty-four years.

On top of these physical woes, I'm somewhat emotionally drained. The country I left behind is mired in a presidential campaign marked by such mass hysteria that it has me doubting democracy. Since I don't speak Chinese, but will be traveling 1,900 miles in a country where, as I saw last year, hospitality is by no means a cardinal virtue as in Central Asia, I know that the only person I'll be able to count on is myself. In short, our troubled human race has me greatly distressed, so I tell myself—small comfort, for the Gobi truly frightens me!—that heading out into the desert might not be such a bad thing: sometimes a strong dose of solitude is just what the doctor ordered to fight depression. The first year, a certain recklessness with respect to what I might find got me started on this mythical, magical, albeit dangerous road. The following two years, delighted by the people I'd met, I found walking admittedly painful, but my spirits held high. But tearing myself away from those I love was more painful this year than ever. To add to my distress, as soon as I arrived in China, I learned that my beloved Aunt Raymonde had passed away, a little old lady I loved dearly and who departed this life just as I was boarding my plane in Paris. In short, physically and psychologically, since first setting out from Istanbul three years ago, I doubt now more than ever that I'll succeed in dragging my body past that three thousandth black-and-white kilometer marker, and into unattainable Xi'an.

When I arrived in Beijing the day before yesterday, the streets were cloaked in what I first took to be fog: the city had, in fact, just weathered a sandstorm, and, their faces covered with scarves, all the Chinese women I saw might have given the veiled women of Turkey or Iran a good run for their money.

From there, I boarded a connector flight for Ürümqi, Xinjiang's capital city. Some mysterious cargo containing yellow paint exploded in the baggage hold, brightly decorating all the suitcases. With my backpack striped in yellow and black, I'll have a tough time not standing out from the crowd! From Ürümqi, I had to board a bus for Turfan, the city where I ended my walk in September 2001. I've given myself a full day here to do a little grocery shopping; I want to pick up some vitamins (raisins and apricots), a few apples, and a supply of freeze-dried noodles. They'll be the staple of my diet for the three or four months I expect this final stage to last. I also picked up the wheels belonging to Ulysses, my demountable wagon. I'd left them in the care of the manager of the Oasis Hotel last September. The tires have gone flat, but for one yuan (about $0.09), the corner mechanic has them pumped back up in no time. The cart itself, which I had safely transported back to France with me so that it could be reinforced by my friend Marcel Lemaître, is now ready to weather any storm.

Xinjiang is three times as big as France but has only a third as many inhabitants. It boasts two of the planet's most uninhabitable deserts: the Taklamakan, whose northern edge I skirted last year, and the Gobi, which straddles Mongolia and China and which I'll have to brave this year. Today, April 18, as the sun is peeking out above the horizon, I've just covered—after going in circles for an hour—the four miles that separate Turfan from the National Road—and now this devastating distance marker. This is where the real journey begins. The weather's good—the air's a bit cool, but it's perfect for walking. I've chosen to get an early start this year to make the most of the mild spring temperatures and reach Xi'an sooner than I did for my previous destinations; although I won't be able to avoid the hottest weather altogether, at least I'll suffer from it for as short a time as possible.

Walking makes me feel good. The first few miles lift the cloud of apprehension that had been weighing heavily on me for the last two weeks. The road gently rises. From this oasis, located 154 meters (500 feet) *below* sea level, I know I'll have to ascend nearly 2,000 meters (6,600 feet), since the Gobi Desert is, in fact, a plateau. Before I get there, though, I revel in a spectacle that has always delighted me: the pruning and tethering of grapevines by local farmers, who work with the same care and diligence as do all vine growers the world over. Local grape varieties are sweet; they're dried after harvest, and it's certainly grapes that have made this oasis's reputation. Harnessed to my belt, Ulysses follows along in my footsteps without a fuss. He's carrying my backpack, a mariner's duffel bag (streaked in yellow since my arrival in Ürümqi) in which I store my camping and cooking gear, and without which I would never be able to endure the deserts. I've also lashed on two large water bags (the third is on my back), such that I can carry a total of twelve liters of water. I disinfect these with chlorine, not wanting to relive the tortuous experience I had in Doğubeyazıt, Turkey, a couple years ago.[*]

At noon, having gone twelve miles, I make a first stop in a Uyghur restaurant. The owner, Ma Ching Chang ("Ma" is Sinicized "Muhammad"), is especially warm and generous. He carries on the tradition of hospitality I came to know so well in Turkey, Iran, and the three ex-Soviet republics of Central Asia I visited.

For my first day, I had decided not to walk more than twelve miles, but true to the crippling stubbornness that propels me on and on, come hell or high water, I flout my walking schedule. I turn down Ma's invitation to stay in a room he usually rents out to truck drivers, under the pretext that I need to put my camping gear to the test.

So farther down the road, I take out my extremely lightweight tent. I fall right back into my old nomadic practice of picking up kindling along the way, then cook my noodles over a fire lit in a three-stone firepit, happy as Robinson Crusoe! But the wind begins to blow in gusts, and I'm forced to acknowledge that my shelter is completely unrealistic. The salesman accurately stressed that this model, designed with large mosquito netting on three sides, prevents the well-known effect of condensation formation. But when the sandstorm suddenly blows in, this particular advantage proves to be a serious drawback. I slip into my sleeping bag and wrap my head

---

[*] *Out of Istanbul: A Journey of Discovery along the Silk Road, op. cit.*

in the eight-foot-long *cheche* I intended to use as my pillow, neck covering, and bath towel. For several hours, I listen to the gales howling in the guy wires, nervous that the stakes will pull out of the ground.

I must have finally drifted off to sleep. I wake up literally smothered: fine dust has penetrated the mesh, burying me beneath a powdery layer! I have sand in my eyes, mouth, nose, and ears. What a great success this first night camping in Xinjiang has been!

I'm back on the road, dog-tired. My feet hurt, especially my left foot, which suffers from a bunion caused by the fashionable Italian shoes I wore in my youth. I pass nineteen miles to the north of Gaochang, a city I won't be visiting. Although it was an important stopping point on the Silk Road prior to the seventh century under the Tang Dynasty—and the capital of the Uyghurs, when they first settled in the region over a millennium ago—it was destroyed by the Mongols in the thirteenth. Today, there's nothing left but an empty ruin. The same is true of the Bezeklik Caves, located on cliffsides four miles off my route. The grottoes had filled with sand. When? The answer is lost in the mists of time. And the sand, that true friend of the arts, perfectly preserved the treasures they contained: rock paintings, sculptures, and statues happily escaped both theft and deterioration. It was around the year 1900 that European Orientalists' craze for the region began. These "foreign devils," as the Chinese called them, discovered the site, then looted it for themselves. Albert von Le Coq, it's a well-known fact, shipped everything back to Berlin. But let's not be chauvinistic: a French Sinologist, Paul Pelliot, for his part, stole seven thousand manuscripts from the Dunhuang Caves. The Germans gave Albert von Le Coq a tremendous reception when he returned home bearing his trophies. They even built a museum to house the treasures . . . which allied bombs pulverized in 1945. As they say, "Gains badly won, profit none." Local populations, however, were not to be outdone: convinced that the paintings would make excellent fertilizer and fearing, furthermore, that the painted eyes and mouths might be representations of the devil, they took it upon themselves to obliterate once and for all anything that had remained. Whatever providentially managed to survive the plundering was finally destroyed by Muslims, who rarely admire works of art inspired by rival religions.

If luck is with me, during the final segment of my journey, I'll be able to visit some better-preserved Buddhist caves. So I turn down invitations from impromptu guides waiting for tourists along the road. And I ignore calls from a man behind the wheel of a minibus who cannot fathom why I would want to walk. "But it's free! Free!" he yells, without getting me to give in, though I'm strongly tempted: I'm off on the wrong foot: I've lost the sacred flame within, and I'm haunted by the Gobi, which I'm beginning to see as the handiwork of the Evil One!

After the sandstorm, the dust that remains suspended in the atmosphere makes it hard to see. I've only had a vague glimpse of the "Flaming Mountains"—hills of red earth that, if I'm to believe my guidebook, literally burst into flames when the sun reaches its zenith. The road climbs higher and higher, without end. Yesterday, I was at 154 meters below sea level; at noon today, I am at zero, having traveled only nine miles.

An inn in the village of Sheng Jui is a welcome sight. After eating, I can't even get up from the table. As thin and bony as a bamboo tree, the tall Chinese man who just fed me a platter of spiced noodles suggests that I rest up in a bedroom adjoining the restaurant. He even brings me a pan of water, afraid no doubt that I'll dirty the place up. But I instantly collapse onto the bed and take a three-hour nap. Upon waking, I remove the ochre foundation that last night's storm applied to my face and hands. I can't seem to get moving again; I'm too spent and lack the motivation. Too bad. I have an early dinner then lie back down in a larger room that the innkeeper rents out to me for a sum he probably considers astronomical, for he prefaces his announcement of the rate with a speech of which I don't understand a thing, but which was delivered in a tone meaning unquestionably that "times are hard, gullible tourists are rare, and taxes in this country are fierce!"

The wind continues to bluster in gusts, and to make matters worse, it's blowing from the east, which is to say, directly in my face. Brave Ulysses, who offers a rather large surface area for the wind to catch, is ripping my arm off, and, to make any headway, I have to lean forward like Volga boatmen must have done. A fog, made up of fine, suspended grains of sand, obscures the landscape. I'm suffocating—my lungs, weakened by bronchitis, make the sound of a dismantled pump—and I'm freezing in the icy wind in spite of a waterproof jacket, my multipurpose *cheche*, and a pair of wool gloves, which I was wise to bring along. My watch that evening indicates an elevation of 260 meters (853 feet); there's no village or inn, the wind is still blowing, and it would be delusional to even attempt to set up the tent. Under a heaven-sent bridge (I'll later find out that there are many along Route 312), I construct a wall of stones for my shelter. Then I dive into my sleeping bag after wrapping myself in my survival blanket, and, my head completely buried beneath my *cheche*, I somehow manage to fall asleep.

The next day's route is, in all respects, identical to that of the day before. It seems that the wind will never stop. At Shanshan, I note that I've covered sixty-one miles in four days. A snail's pace. I'm going to have to speed up if I want to make Xi'an before Christmas! I only have a two-month visa, having abandoned the idea of requesting special permission from Chinese authorities: I still have the bitter taste in my mouth of their refusal to let me walk at Torugart. For the time being, I'd rather put my trust in my lucky star. But my lucky star is dim, the distance I've gone rather short, and Xi'an is incredibly far! In these first days on the road, I'm like those sailors who see the coastline fading into the distance where they have left their beloved behind and fear that they'll never make it to the other side of the sea. Still, at least they can have pleasant conversations with their traveling companions. Whereas I left Turfan on a solo journey through a barren land and, even when I do meet men, I can't converse with them.

They're like fish to me. I see their mouths move but I haven't the slightest idea what they're saying. Will I make it to the finish line? Right now, I have no idea. My lungs are full of phlegm from bronchitis. My autonomy is my weakness. At the least sign of depression, all I have to do is wave my arms and climb up into a truck in order to head back to home port. I alone, and my pitiful strength, will decide how long this journey lasts. I knew this as I boarded the plane back in Paris. So the gamble is whether I'll be stronger than the desert, with its emptiness, cheerlessness, and winds. And now here I am, face to face with it.

Here's to the two of us, Gobi!

II

THE POOR

At the hotel in Shanshan where I've only just settled in, two men—a Uyghur and a Chinese Han in civilian dress, waving a "police" badge under my nose—barge into my room, alerted by some mysterious phone call. My passport and visa—but above all, it seems, the laminated paper that sums up in ideograms the walk I've undertaken, starting in Istanbul—soon have them smiling. Then they indicate, giving me the thumbs up—which in Chinese, as in so many languages, is a sign of admiration—that a guest of such stature is entitled to stay at the "Hotel for Foreigners," which, no doubt, is far more comfortable. It's of course more expensive, but I've earned special treatment: they won't charge me a higher rate. Their kindness goes so far as to want to take me in their jeep on a tour . . . of the desert. You'd be correct to guess that the last thing I want to do right now is jump the gun on my sojourn into the Gobi! What I really need to do is to get my letters for Paris in the mail. That's no problem, they'll take me there and even help me cut to the front of the line; after all, I'm a distinguished guest! I reckon they'll open my letters, but what difference does it make? If it's because they take me for some godawful dreadful traitor to the Chinese homeland, then my words of affection for those I love will leave them sorely disappointed.

I learn that a Frenchman, a viticulture researcher, had been working here for four years on improving the vinification process so that the wine could be exported to Europe. He told people that he was going to spend Christmas holidays in France with his Chinese fiancée. Four months have now gone by . . . and the carefree run-aways have apparently decided to get drunk in French vineyards . . . on freedom. Perhaps that explains why people are suspicious of me.

In Central Asia, I got used to having incredibly hospitable strangers come up to me and invite me to partake in their *shashlik, plov,* or balls of *kurut* cheese. There's nothing like that here. But I'm in no danger of starving. Every evening in Xinjiang, a swarm of little Chinese men invades the small squares in every town, where they set up tables, chairs, and portable kitchens. It's a beehive of activity, everything comes together in a flash, and, before you even know you're hungry, they've cooked up the very dish your stomach was yearning for. This evening, it's a *pai gu shao guo*, a stir-fry that tastefully blends black mushrooms, mutton, fish, and noodles, all served in a large terracotta bowl, and I have no trouble wolfing it all down.

At the hotel for foreigners, which the two cops swore had "every comfort," I fall asleep at 10:00; the hot water that had been promised for 8:00 still hadn't arrived. Early the next morning, I take an invigorating cold shower and get underway on an empty stomach: breakfast won't be served, apparently, until 8:30. Official time in Xinjiang, as everywhere else in China, is that of Beijing, which is two true time zones away. No one pays any attention to it, except government offices which open and close in sync with the capital. It's easy to imagine misunderstandings: is that local, or Beijing time, that we have our meeting, or breakfast is served?

A kind Uyghur, astounded to see Ulysses and a harnessed European on the road at dawn, offers me a bowl of noodles that I'm by no means unhappy to gulp down. These sedentary people of Xinjiang's oases, whose language is related to Turkish, were referred to as "Uyghurs" by the Soviets first, then by the Chinese communists. Yet these people have very little in common with the infidel Uyghurs who migrated from Mongolia shortly before the tenth century. These people are Muslim, and they make up no less than half of Xinjiang's population, or about one percent of the People's Republic of China as a whole.

On my second day walking, I had come across a young woman whose dress and attitude I found both troubling and moving. About twenty years old, she was a sight to behold. She carried a bundle under one arm, which must have contained all of her possessions. Most striking was that she was coated—literally encased in dirt—to such an extent that one might have thought she was wearing some ridiculous Halloween costume. When she noticed me coming her way, she crossed to the other side of the road and continued on. Was she afraid of foreigners, or ashamed of her condition? I couldn't help but wonder . . . are there, in China, those who are poor even among the poor, outcasts who have reverted to a natural state and to whom no one in society extends a helping hand? I banished the thought. China, a communist country, was necessarily focused on those most in need, on the *Lumpenproletariat*, and would never allow such a situation to exist.

That same day, I met another vagrant. I had seen poor people before, but this one was exceedingly so. Covered in filth, he had a canvas bag with him, hanging from a stick carried over his shoulder, in which he had stuffed a few pans and empty food tins. His face was grimy, covered in patches of incrusted dust. He stopped without saying a word and, when I gave him a few banknotes, he returned a smile, his mouth full of yellow stubs. Then off he went.

Now seven or eight miles farther on, I drop down under a bridge to eat a few pieces of dried fruit away from the wind. Behind an old oven that had been built there by highway laborers, a woman is sleeping beneath a thick pile of rags. She's only slightly less dirty than my vagabond. His lady friend? I can only speculate. Perhaps he has gone off in search of food and drink, since the bridge is nine miles from the nearest habitation. She points to her stomach. She's hungry. I offer her some packages of ramen and hand her a few banknotes which she must regard as a king's ransom judging by the silent laugh she offers me in thanks, like the other fellow.

The driver of a large yellow crane truck comes to a screeching halt and runs over to me. He heard from "Ma" that I was headed to Xi'an and, by an incredible stroke of luck, that's where he's going, too! He's so certain that I'm going to jump for joy, that he has already grabbed Ulysses by one hand. My *yok* ("no" in Uyghur) devastates him. When he insists that the ride is free, I hand him another *yok*, along with a thousand smiles. He goes back to his vehicle without a word and, fifteen minutes later, drives past me without so much as a glance. It's decidedly tough to go against the grain these days! Walking is acceptable only if it's classified and reduced to the concept of "hiking"; otherwise, you're an eccentric. And heaven knows, there's not much room in the world for eccentricity these days. But it still stirs arouses curiosity: a perfect example is the television crew returning from Lanzhou (pronounced *lan-jo*)—they hurry over to film me while a journalist blandly interviews me about my trip.

In the China that I'm traveling through, there are two kinds of sleeping accommodations for travelers. The *binguan* is what I'll call a "luxury" hotel—although they're not necessarily comfortable. They're relatively rare and reserved for Westerners. Then there's the *luguan*, which is a kind of motel for truck drivers and locals. The yard out front serves as a garage, around which are hard-walled cabins containing the bare minimum: the bed's a wooden crate, the mattress a mat, the pillow a bag of beans, the comforter a wool blanket, and there's typically a shared hand pump for washing up.

The *luguan* where I spend the night in Qitekai offers me the ultimate luxury: a desk . . . although there's no chair to go with it. The young woman who comes to rectify this oversight offers me "love for sale" as well. I never faced this kind of proposition at any of my previous stopovers, but in the end, I'm not all that surprised. I've noticed that the Chinese—in addition to monetizing everything—are rather obsessed with virility. Their questions, translated for me, frequently address the subject: How could I remain abstinent for four months? It's a question that could only be asked by someone who doesn't know a thing about walking twenty-five miles per day: the body pours every ounce of energy into the muscles and desire vanishes into thin air! There are no sexual cravings for walkers, who are merely passersby: they observe, admire, and are back underway before the crack of dawn. I've always refused to get involved with prostitutes. And at sixty-four, I'm not about to start.

The scenery past Turfan has been pretty much the same as it was. Upon leaving the oasis, a barren, gray expanse of stones and sand extends to the south, with a few high rocks here and there that have held up to the wind, and on which cling a few twisted tamarisk trees. I'm still hugging the Tian Shan range to the north—the Celestial Mountains—one of the least-explored high-mountain regions in the world, but all I can see of it here is the piedmont: gray dirt hillsides full of ravines, cloaked in an eternal bluish mist. It's clear that Qitekai will be my last stop in the inhabited world, and that I'm about to confront what I've been dreading since leaving Paris: the notorious Gobi Desert.

For my seventh day on the road, after a brisk twenty-two-mile walk into the wind, I note that my body's quickly adjusting to the routine I'm putting it through. Seeing how windy it is, I forgo setting up my tent and I'm starting to think that I'm going to have to get used to sleeping out in the open. But after all, no one pressured me into this! So no more whining! I light a fire between two gusts, then force myself to enjoy a noodle dish that, all things considered, is not so unpalatable after all.

Come morning, I realize that, caught up in a thousand thoughts and clearly not entirely back in the groove of walking and its needs, I neglected to get groceries in Qitekai and refill my third water bag! With only four liters of water and food for a day and a half, there's no way I'll be able to make it to the next village which, according to my map, is ninety miles away. Should I turn around? Return to Qitekai? Too lazy, I decide to try my luck, which typically turns out to be better than I expect.

The miles go by, my water reserves drop, and nothing! I walk past a restaurant, but it was boarded up many years ago. Once I reached

Kashgar, I started noticing scores of little red and white cement posts connecting buildings equipped with automatic telephone equipment. They're repeaters, powered both by solar panels installed on each building's roof and small turbines whirling in the Gobi's winds. Each time I spot one of these buildings, I start thinking it's an inn. Unfortunately, they're all empty.

Can a person embark on an adventure as crazy as this without the conviction that Lady Luck will show her face every so often? Of course not! And at that very moment, several workmen suddenly appear, to whom I present my "open sesame" papers, which, written in Chinese, provide an overview of my odyssey. They whoop it up, they surround me, and they fill up my water bags for me! A couple hundred yards down the road, Wo Chi, a jolly little round woman who cooks up food for the workmen, serves me a revitalizing helping of spicy rice. This tiny Chinese woman, who's swimming in a multicolored jacket, has cleverly enclosed the underside of a bridge with plastic tarps, inside which she has set up a temporary kitchen. She stuffs my pack with several packages of noodles and I now feel sufficiently rich to brave the desert.

I have to turn down the offer of yet another truck driver who wants, come hell or high water, to give me a ride. One more fellow I'll have disappointed! But what's to expect from a European who's crossing the Gobi without a vehicle? Perhaps he'd be interested in talking about soccer? I expect him to mention Zinedine Zidane, but he brings up . . . Platini!* News is decidedly slow to reach the far-flung Gobi.

Deserts, as everyone knows, are by no means deserted. But here, there are no natives or animals: no nomads, snakes, scorpions, or spiders. Nothing but refinery flare stacks lighting up the night like stars brought down from the sky, and trucks carrying drill pipe back west,

---

* TN: Michel Platini, considered one of the greatest soccer players of all time, played for French teams in the 1980s, and coached the French national team in the 1990s. Zinedine Zidane's professional soccer career, on the other hand, began in the 1990s.

evidence that oil exploration is booming. There's nothing romantic or poetic about the desert here. The one threat I could possibly face is from men. So, roughing it tonight, I lie down with my knife clenched in one hand. The only birds in the sky above me are plastic bags carried on the wind, which, sadly, the Chinese consume in great quantities, like we do in the West.

III

THE CELESTIAL
MOUNTAINS

I've slowly increased the distance I cover each day until I'm averaging nineteen to twenty-two miles. In the village of Yiyanshang, there are two houses. The largest belongs to the Chang family. The man of the house, burly and affable, manages a tire repair shop along with his son. The women tend a small beverage and cigarette stand. They give me a warm welcome. We share the meal together. Tau, Chang's wife, and his stepdaughter Shing Koa, cook up a dish of eggs, chili peppers, and tomatoes, and my stomach, saturated with never-ending noodles, finds it a welcome change. The grandson, his backside peeking out from underpants that have been intentionally split in the back so that he can do his business whenever and wherever he pleases, is kissed, caressed, and coddled by the entire family. Worried about thieves, Chang sleeps in the beverage and cigarette booth. They rent me a room in which in which I'm unable to find the switch when I'm ready to turn off the light. The lamp, it turns out, is wired directly to the generator. When they turn the generator off, the lamp does, too. But tonight, too many trucks have flat tires, so the light wakes me up and the noise of the powerful screw gun they use keeps me from falling back asleep.

In the morning, now that they trust me, Chang's son shows me the family treasure. Some time ago, while digging into the red soil behind the house, they unearthed a veritable quarry of fossilized wood. A forest of tall trees grew here thousands of years ago. The family plans on generating income from it: every Chinese is an entrepreneur at heart. His wife, Shing Koa, is very proud to pull from a drawer a tiny, intricately embroidered shoe, shorter than my pen. It's one of those shoes women wore, when it was fashionable to bind their feet. It's not much over four inches long!

After walking for four hours, a mirage suddenly appears out of nowhere: straight ahead, on the distant horizon, I take it for a clump of trees. It's been several days since I've seen any. But no, it's not a forest, but something far better: I've come across a magnificent fire tower, and, my heavens, it's in rather good condition! A square, earthen structure, it must stand at least fifty feet tall. It's the first vestige of the Silk Road that I've seen, having walked over 1,200 miles in China. To keep the peace, the Empire maintained small garrisons all along this highway, one traveled by merchants, diplomats, and pilgrims. Each fort was surmounted by a tower. If an enemy army were to appear, bonfires and loud cannon booms carried the news from one tower to the next, by day or by night, until it reached the capital, much faster than the swiftest horsemen could have managed.

The relic that I explore was spared from the elements because it was covered up and used for agricultural purposes. There's a well of clear water at its base. And down the hill a bit, behind the building that must have served as soldiers' barracks, a water hole surrounded by willows. The fort's ramparts have partly crumbled. The moat is entirely dry, but it's still recognizable.

I refill my water bags from the freshwater spring before leaving for Tiziquan. Two and a half miles in advance of the village, an innkeeper, a slight Chinese woman with a childlike smile, assures me that there's no *luguan* in the village. But *she* has rooms for rent. A half hour later, I find myself wondering whether stopping here was such a good idea. Two ill-tempered characters arrive who, one after the other, drag a petite, bleach-blond employee into a bedroom, only to come back out . . . pulling up their pants! Have I once again landed in a brothel? Son, the owner, keeps smiling, as if it were all perfectly normal, yet she hardly has the look of a Madame! The next morning, she prepares a dish of fried eggs for me, with brined onions and tofu.

I traveled thirty-one miles in one day and, for the first time, felt no worse for it; admittedly, the road was straight and flat, and the wind had miraculously veered to the west, such that it was pushing Ulysses and me along. It certainly seems that, both in body and spirit, I've at last found my stride.

Since I no longer have to stare at the pavement in order to fight an east wind, as I have for the past several days, I now take my time and enjoy the scenery. To my north are the towering Celestial Mountains, and to my south, the desert. It's unsettlingly monotonous, for it varies only in color: there are patches of golden sand, vast seas of black stones, white flows where salt has risen to the surface, and infinite stretches of ochre soil.

How can I keep my mind busy in this cosmic void, out here in nowheresville, where there's nothing to grab my interest? The other years, I busied myself learning the languages of the countries I was in. For Chinese, for some reason, I've already thrown in the towel. My mind wanders, and I take refuge . . . in the moon and daydreams. Mulling over the life of women in Central Asia and comparing it to that of European women at the time of George Sand, I start imagining a storyline. It could even be a novel, and, were I to bring it to life, I would title it: *The Story of Rosa Who Held the World in Her Hand.** As the days go by, I'm going to try to breathe life into the story's characters, and they'll be my companions in the Gobi.

To reward me for my performance (thirty-one miles!), that evening, near a bridge where I bivouac, the desert offers me a fabulous spectacle. With the snow-painted Celestial Mountains for a backdrop, the mountains nearby turn crimson while the desert arrays itself in bluish light. An eagle circles lazily, and a little rat with a tufted tail and pointed nose cautiously emerges from its hole to contemplate

---

* TN: Ollivier did indeed finish this novel, entitled, in French: *Histoire de Rosa, qui tint le monde dans sa main* (Paris: Phébus 2013).

this strange biped that has invaded its territory. Is there life in the Gobi after all? I lie down to sleep along with the sun and dream of Hami, where I'm going to indulge in pure joy: a full day's rest and a good scrubbing down!

I'm awakened by an awful din. A violent wind has kicked up, and it's driving sand low to the ground, pelleting my face and skull, the only parts of me protruding from my sleeping bag. The gale blows through my down bag, puffing it up like a sail and chilling me to the bone. I hastily construct a stone rampart, wrap myself in my survival blanket, and bundle my head in my *cheche*. I then succeed, helped along by fatigue, to fall back asleep. By dawn, I'm once again buried beneath a layer of sand.

The first drops begin to fall around 7:00. By 8:00, I'm soaked in a driving, ice-cold rain. My boots are veritable buckets, and I have to empty them out at regular intervals. Pushed along by the wind (from the west, fortunately), no matter how fast I walk, I can't seem to get warm. Around noon, I go for shelter under a bridge—blessed be these new, albeit extremely ugly structures: they're godsends to the poor walker! The colder I get, the more it convinces me that my only solution is to reach Hami by the end of the day. Thirty-four miles: is it even possible, after yesterday's thirty-one, and thirteen days of walking without a break since Turfan? My hands have turned to ice.

A mounted-crane truck is kind enough to offer me a ride. More out of habit than conviction, I refuse. I'm beginning to hate myself for being so obstinate. What difference would it make if I were to go nineteen miles by truck? Not one. But my fear is that at some point later on there would be nothing to stop me from doing it again. Truck when it rains, truck when it's hot, truck when my feet hurt, truck when food supplies begin to dwindle . . . I know instinctually that, feeling less motivated than previous years, given that my encounters don't energize me the way they did in Central Asia, the risk that I'll give up is quite high. If I give in to weakness once, I might as well kiss my resolve goodbye. I really want to complete the walk I began in Istanbul and honor the agreement I made with myself.

And so I walk. I walk quickly, running at times, propelled by the gusts, my boots sloshing with every step. Here's hoping my feet's soft soles also hold up! At 5:00 p.m., I turn off the National Road, but it takes me another hour to reach downtown, where I find an excellent hotel, the Hami Binguan. Freezing from head to toe, I drown myself in a scalding shower, then dive under two comforters, one on top of the other, where I sink into a deep sleep for two hours. There'll be time to assess the damage inside my pack later on: my notes and waterlogged papers. As for my clothes, they'll have all night to dry out.

The city of Hami is famous for more than just its delicious melons. In the days of the Silk Road, it was reputed for offering travelers first-rate hospitality. Here is what Marco Polo said of this city, which was formerly called Kumul, and which he refers to in his notes as Camul:

> Camul is a province which in former days was a kingdom. It contains numerous towns and villages, but the chief city bears the name of CAMUL. The province lies between the two deserts; for on the one side is the Great Desert of Lop, and on the other side is a small desert of three days' journey in extent. The people are all Idolaters and have a particular language. They live by the fruits of the earth, which they have in plenty, and dispose of to travelers. They are a people who take things very easily, for they mind nothing but playing and singing, and dancing and enjoying themselves. And it is the truth that if a foreigner comes to the house of one of these people to lodge, the host is delighted, and desires his wife to put herself entirely at the guest's disposal, whilst he himself gets out of the way, and comes back no more until the stranger shall have taken his departure. The guest may stay and enjoy the wife's society as long as he lists, whilst the husband has no shame in the matter, but

indeed considers it an honor. And all the men of this province are made wittols of by their wives in this way."*

Alas for travelers, times have changed in Hami-Camul!

As for its inhabitants, they're proud and independent Uyghurs. When their ancestors rose up against Beijing in 1910, the city was razed by the Emperor's troops.

On May 1, in a communist country, one could well expect large public festivities, parades, music, speeches, and more. There's none of that. The human ant farm is still busy working just as hard. A junior high school has organized a rather pitiful event: in the school courtyard, uniformed students circle behind a marching band while buglers play dreadfully out of tune. To drown out the cacophony, their teachers crank up a sound system, and drive me away.

Razwan, a young Uyghur university student who must have detected my disappointment, invites me to her cousin's wedding, taking place at the hotel. There are over two hundred guests. As in Central Asia, families go broke marrying off their children. The ancestors of the groom's clan, sporting white goatees and the embroidered, traditional square hats of Xinjiang's Muslims, are seated at the front in a row of chairs. The bride is introduced to them, her face hidden behind an embroidered white veil. The food arrives, and we graze in the Chinese way, helping ourselves to savory or sweet dishes in no particular order. When it's time for gifts, since the ceremony doesn't offer anything different from weddings I've attended before, I slip out.

Liza, the hotel's only receptionist who speaks English—and who's delighted to be able to put her language skills into practice today, given that Hami is not on most Western tourists' itineraries—takes

---

* Marco Polo, "Of the Province of Camul," in *The Travels of Marco Polo*, trans. by Henry Yule. Edited and annotated by Henri Cordier (London: John Murray, 1920). Wikisource. https://en.wikisource.org/wiki/The_Travels_of_Marco_Polo/Book_1/Chapter_41.

me to an Internet cafe so I can consult any messages I might have received. An email from Mathieu, my oldest son, whom I asked to vote by proxy on my behalf, has let me know how the French presidential election turned out. How fragile the Republic is!* And it's all the more frightening viewed from a country where anyone who dares to challenge the Party is imprisoned, and where, out of ten thousand executions each year, a great many are members of the political opposition. After 9/11 and the attack on the World Trade Center in New York, the Chinese authorities, delighted at such a boon, have vociferously supported the American war on terror, while using it for their own purposes to liquidate more than a few Uyghur separatists. I've heard talk of three thousand executions. . . . But who knows what the real figure is in a country as vast and tight-lipped as China!

On May 2, with Ulysses loaded up, I'm about to leave my room when Liza shows up with her arms full of cucumbers and fruit. She's worried that I'm going to waste away in the desert. She then hurries off, claiming to be late for work, but it's pretty obvious that she doesn't want me to take her offering as a come on. Of course it's not: in both East and West, motherly impulses easily kick in when a woman sees a man all by himself who's clearly in need. I'm so moved by her gift that I behave like a lout: I neglect to reimburse her for her purchases.

---

* TN: Ollivier is referring to the first round of the 2002 French presidential election, which took place on April 21, 2002. It resulted in a run-off election on May 5, 2002, between Jacques Chirac of the center-right RPR (Rally for the Republic) and Jean-Marie Le Pen of the far-right FN (National Front). Many were surprised to see a far-right candidate finish ahead of Socialist candidate Lionel Jospin, and garner enough votes to move on to the run-off. Le Pen went on to lose to Chirac by a wide, 64.4-percentage-point margin.

IV

THE CORPSE

The next city, Xingxingxia, near the Xinjiang-Gansu border, is six days away. There's no wind, the sky is clear. The desert stretches off to the north until it butts up against the foothills of the nearby Celestial Mountains, whose summits glisten beneath a spring sun— icy fangs tearing at the blue sky. To the south, the desert is drowning in infinity. I'm spryly walking along when some young motorcyclists come into view, providing some entertainment. Where are they headed? To Dunhuang for Youth Day on May 4, and they'll make the most of it by visiting the famous Buddhist caves in Mogao. In the region's oases, new grapevines are being planted and the older ones are being pruned. Grapes are a valuable resource here, but what Hami is most famous for throughout China is the high quality of its melons. According to legend, in the eighteenth century, the king of Hami sent melons from Lukexin—a small village just southwest of Shanshan and south of the Flaming Mountains—to the Emperor. He absolutely loved them, and so inquired: "Where do they come from?" Caught off guard, they replied: "From Hami." That little fib has endured for three centuries!

I should have stopped in Luotuojuanzi, after the more reasonable distance of twenty-two miles. The name means "camel corral." But— was it because there were no camels, only far too many trucks?—I just kept right on going, energized by all the rest I got on May 1, adding five miles to my planned stage. When I finally stop, it's in a hamlet that bears an unusual name, one which remains a mystery to me despite my repeated questions: "second company of the fourth production unit." The innkeeper, delighted to have a foreigner, calls for his son, Xuan Chun Lai, an English major. Unfortunately, all Xuan can say is "hello." His father is disappointed but doesn't hold it against me that I made his son lose face: he shows me to a room that I can almost call comfortable, and I'm even provided with a pitcher of hot water while his wife makes me *jing jiang rou si*: very thin slices of caramelized pork served on a bed of fresh onions. During the meal, I noticed that Xuan reads and writes English just fine, his only handicap is how shy he is. Their warm hospitality is topped off by a very reasonable rate, since, for the room, dinner, and a generous breakfast, they ask only for three dollars. And I'm supposed to consider getting a sponsor?

Since leaving Kashgar, I've been walking for nearly 1,250 miles in the shadow of the Tian Shan. I've tracked along these Celestial Mountains, which close the arc formed by the Himalayas to the south, and the Pamirs to the west. The Tian Shan—which is the name they're known by in Central Asia, and among geographers— boast several summits that soar to nearly 7,000 meters (23,000 feet), and their largest glacier could, it's said, fill the entire Aral Sea, drained by the diversion of the two rivers that formerly fed it.

Squint as I might, I cannot find Yandun. Still, the village appears on all three maps I brought with me. My GPS tells me that I'm getting near. Then that I've arrived. Then that I've gone past it! Too tired to push on any farther, I bivouac under a bridge, without ever having seen Yandun. I have to blame my ignorance. The city did indeed once exist, but it has completely disappeared, like many other cities in Xinjiang. Someone ought to let geographers know, too . . . that would spare poor travelers who stubbornly persist in trusting maps a few disappointments!

Once again, a storm rolls in in the dead of night. Sand pummeling my bald head wakes me up. It has gotten into my eyes, nose, ears, and mouth. I stack my two bags and a few stones to protect my head, but it doesn't help. The wind is diabolical; to make matters worse, search as I may in the dark, I can't find my survival blanket, gone missing in the depths of my pack, which would effectively trap my body heat. I'm freezing cold in a sleeping bag "guaranteed to 5ºF." I put my clothes back on, but it's no use, I spend the rest of the night shivering. The next morning, after trying unsuccessfully for half an hour, I finally manage to light a fire and warm up a bowl of soup, which I gulp down piping hot.

Out on the road, the wind in my face is unbelievably violent. After a two-mile Herculean struggle, I sit down on a distance marker, short of breath, pooped. When I set out once again, I have to lean into the wind, towing Ulysses along with both hands. Every now and then, one foot remains frozen in mid-air, like in a still-frame photo of a runner, the moment the starting gun fires. The wind stops me dead in my tracks. To get going again, I have to set both feet on the ground, lean into the wind even more, find the angle of least resistance, then throw all my weight into it.

To catch my breath, I stop first every mile, then every half-mile. My face is numb, paralyzed by the freezing wind. My nose stings. My fingers burn inside my gloves; the wind drives drips of nasal mucus onto my cheeks, where they stick but I can't wipe them since my hands are busy tugging on my friend Ulysses. Then I notice that the mucus is red! Small blood vessels in my nose have burst, and the bleeding has stained my jacket red. I wrap the *cheche* around my face, leaving only a tiny slit for my eyes.

The Gobi Desert regions are "terrifying in their loneliness," declared Mildred Cable and Francesca French, two missionaries who visited the area in the 1920s and 1930s.* Today, I couldn't agree more. A popular saying describes the Gobi this way: "No birds in the sky, not a sprig on the ground; years pass without a drop of rain and

---

* Mildred Cable and Francesca French, *The Gobi Desert* (London: Hodder and Stoughton, Ltd., 1942), 97.

the wind blows so hard it sets the stones rolling.""* A flawless description, and one, I suspect, not intended to lift my spirits. How long will
this storm last? There's no telling, but my water and food reserves
won't let me wait it out forever. And how can I make a fire if I have
no wood? The watch-barometer I wear on my wrist keeps dropping
toward "storm." I have to keep moving, but where to? Xuan warned
me: "all the way through to Xingxingxia, there isn't a single house."

I've been walking for four and a half hours but have covered just
seven and a half miles. By this time yesterday, I'd gone seventeen. A
very steep, mile-long climb finally drains my last drop of strength.
For heaven's sake, why was I born with such a stubborn streak?!
Why am I so hell-bent on traveling—and never straying from—this
insane Silk Road, which, right here and now, no longer brings me
joy? Sure, I wanted to keep my promises: to hang in there, come what
may. But what good is running on and on without even looking up
to see where I am, hunched over like a donkey, my eyes glued to the
stones, climbing like a mule to the top of this hill that leading me
. . . to yet another hill, which will leave me wiped out under some
god-awful bridge or, at best, in a dingy *luguan*? No, I honestly have
no clue what keeps me going. All that stands between me and giving
up is a single step . . . but it's a step I do not take, for, miraculously,
I reach the top of a hill where . . . a tire repairman has set up shop.
The man opens his door for me, and his wife promptly serves me a
tureen of noodles and vegetables with a few cheap cuts of lamb floating on top. I fill up on water and get back underway knowing full
well that I will probably face more disappointments: my maps show
three villages, but since Yandun doesn't exist, the two others may
be ghost towns, too. Furthermore, when I bring the matter up with
my hosts, they tell me they've never heard of them. After covering a
total of twenty-five miles, completely spent and numb with cold, I
reach Kushui. There isn't a single building, but I see that the place
is identified by a sign bearing two ideograms, meaning, in Chinese,

---

* TN: Some attribute the saying to Xuanzang, 603–64 CE.

"bitter water." Before that, I went through Tienshan Dunzi, another ghost town. These former encampments or villages were abandoned when their wells ran dry. I tip my hat to the geographers but, for the moment, I would most gladly strangle them! I have no other choice: why don't I try pitching my tent in defiance of the storm? It will provide better shelter than a bridge. So, I remove the bag it's in, and pluck out the rainfly. But it unfurls, and a gust of wind rips it from my hands! In one fell movement, I throw my heavy backpack onto the rest of my camping gear and make a mad dash to catch the tarp, now dancing in the wind and taking flight like a will-o'-the-wisp. Picture it: I must look pretty sharp, running like a rabbit after a runaway rainfly! Four times I'm about to grab it, and four times it gets away, catching an even stronger gust and climbing high into the sky like a kite. I'm short of breath, I'm out of energy, I can run no more. And at that very moment my guardian angel reappears, and one of the lines catches beneath a rock. I jump with both feet onto the canvas, then carefully fold it up. Hugging it in my arms, I carry it back to my "encampment." I remember something I read long ago. On the nuclear base in the province's north, the wind once blew so fiercely it knocked over a fifty-ton fuel truck! One young woman, whose travel diary had been ripped from her hands by the wind, took off after it. Her body was never found.

In the morning, the desert wind is still stiff. After ten attempts and an entire box of matches, by using my jacket as a shield, I finally manage to light a piece of paper on fire and slip it beneath some dried grass. Success! I soon have a roaring fire, whipped about by the wind.

At 10:00 a.m., having walked for two and a half hours, I break, as I do every day, for the all-important apple ritual. It's my morning entertainment. I stop near a distance marker—they're the only high ground around—and, from my pack's left ear, I extract an apple, stowed there earlier that morning or the day before. I carefully peel it, slipping the blade under its colorful skin, trying hard not to lose even the tiniest bit of white flesh. One of the benefits of the apple ritual, besides being a wistful reminder of my native Normandy, is that it forces me to stop, whereas walking always makes me want to keep on going, ever further, often faster, almost against my own will.

Today, I also make the most of the stop to check Ulysses's tires. They've had me worried for several days now. Back in Hami, Mr. Li reassured me: "These tires may have three thousand kilometers on them, but they'll easily carry you all the way to Anxi!" My bet is that he had never seen this brand before but didn't want to admit it, for I still have 124 miles to go before I reach Anxi, and the right-side tire already has a gash in it. The inner tube seized the opportunity and is poking through it. Another mile and it will burst. I make a quick decision. I pack Ulysses up and flag down a truck that drops us off nine miles down the road in the small town of Xingxingxia. I rent a room and make inquiries: no, one fellow warns me, I won't find a new tire here; he then cobbles together a patch and places it over the spot where the tire is punctured. "Perhaps in Anxi," he suggests. But a fellow assisting in the operation is unequivocal: "No, there are none there." As you can imagine, I'm absolutely delighted by all this uncertainty, given that Anxi is 124 miles away! The tire is threadbare. I can't chance breaking down out in the wilderness.

I leave my belongings in my room, take apart Ulysses's two wheels and wave down a truck on its way back to Hami. The trucker hands me off to a cabbie who drives me to a department store where, for the sum of six euros and sixty cents (about $6), I purchase two brandnew tires. The woman running the cycling section has hands of iron and takes off the old tires without levers. In the meantime, I go back to the hotel where Liza had so kindly spoiled me with an armful of cucumbers and fruit, and I leave an envelope containing what I owe her. The taxi takes me back to the hotel in Xingxingxia, where I drop off the newly-fitted wheels. I then hop back in the taxi for another nine miles to the exact spot where I first hitched a ride in the truck. As I step out of his vehicle in the middle of the desert, his eyes say it all: so that's it, he has been dealing with a madman! As for me, I still haven't forgiven the Chinese military for having "stolen" sixty miles of the Silk Road from me! And it's not on account of a tire that I'm going to be shorted out of nine more!

I begin the journey back to the hotel in Xingxingxia, my hands in my pockets. The wind has let up, and it's pleasant walking without Ulysses the desert, which the sun has now painted blood red as it plunges toward the horizon.

On May 6, I get up before dawn, refreshed and fit as a fiddle. It doesn't take me long to load up Ulysses, who's now sporting brand-new boots. I grab a hearty snack for later on and chuckle when the owner hands me the bill for my dinner, room, and breakfast: an amount that I estimate to be four times the normal rate. She knows how to play the game, but so do I. I don't mind being taken advantage of a little bit, but there are limits. I give her only half, but, with a wide smile, she accepts, as it still leaves her with a pretty hefty profit, and no one has lost face.

Today, I'll be leaving Xinjiang Province and entering Gansu. As much as the former is vast and empty—with fewer than three inhabitants for every ten square miles—Gansu Province, a thin strand stretching northwest to southeast for nine hundred miles, has a total population of twenty-five million, or, on average, one thousand four hundred and twenty inhabitants for every ten square miles. The Silk Road, which splits into two routes through Xinjiang—one to the north of the Taklamakan, the other to the south—is, in Gansu Province, a single path once again. Travelers of yore heading to Xi'an had no other option in this poor and mountainous province but to wander from one oasis to the next by way of Lanzhou, the territorial capital. That's still the case today.

The landscape changes radically beyond Xingxingxia. The endless desert has disappeared, but I know that, unfortunately, I'll be seeing it again later on. I'm walking on a road that climbs gracefully rounded hillsides, then heads back down into little valleys or cirques that rein in my field of vision, allowing me to experience nature on a human scale. An occasional wide valley offers an unobstructed view to the north or south. The road is no longer that infinite straight line vanishing at the horizon, which makes the emptiness we all carry within feel particularly present. The road ahead is alive, winding, unpredictable; sometimes even attacking the terrain, wherever bulldozers have decapitated a hilltop.

The wind has died down. The weather is mild, ideal for walking. I finally feel on the right side of life. My muscles, seasoned in the battles I fought against the wind, are now ready to handle whatever I require of them. They work smoothly. The miles have grown shorter; they come to me now; they no longer flee out ahead of me beyond reach, as they do on certain evenings when I'm overcome with exhaustion. I'm generating tons of endorphins, and they soon have me dreaming. I walk quickly, side by side with one of the characters in *Rosa*. I've decided to walk with a different one each day until they all come alive and begin to have voices of their own. I'm distracted from my thoughts only by an eagle asleep on the wing, and a little lizard that suddenly darts out from under my feet and heads for shelter beneath rocks in the ditch. I meet a nonchalant horseman who's leading a second little bay horse by the bridle. I even spot a few tufts of camel grass. Life here is clinging on.

Around 1:00 p.m., I'm surprised to find that, without the wind, I've walked like the wind! Twenty-five miles! I take out of my pack a few pieces of dried fruit and some of that famous Uyghur *naan* bread. It's made daily by bakers in vertical, terracotta ovens called *tandir*. These flatbreads are especially delicious fresh from the oven. They dry out in only a few hours, and by the second day, they're covered in unfamiliar green mold. The first few times, I simply scratched it off, convincing myself that, like "noble rot" on certain Bordeaux grapes, it wasn't toxic. I must confess that a glass of wine, with or without noble rot, would at times help wash such stale bread down!

I settle in for a nap but—keyed up about how good I felt all morning—I can't fall asleep. My familiar walking fever takes over once more, accompanied by an obsessive desire to push on and on: the road is so pleasant, I've moved along so quickly, and I still have plenty of time ahead of me, so why stop now? If I keep up this pace, I might even break my one-day record of thirty-eight and a half miles, set on the Anatolian Plateau! Current conditions are practically the same: the air is cool, the altitude between 1,600 and 1,800 meters (5,200 and 5,900 feet), and the route I'm on isn't particularly difficult.

I fold up my mattress, pull my boots back on, and get going again. Leaving Xingxingxia, the distance marker read 3,396 kilometers. If I want to match my record, I'll have to keep going all the way to marker 3,334, and if I want to beat it, I'll have to push on to 3,333. I rather fancy that figure! I enjoy playing with numbers, keeping an eye out for unusual ones, such as three figures that repeat (3,666), or stutter (3,636). But the marker in question with its four identical digits is unique. In any case, it's the only one like it that I'll come across throughout my entire journey. Yes, there's a marker 2,222, but I'll be taking a different road beyond Lanzhou and won't set foot back onto National Road 312 until I reach Xi'an, well past stone marker 1,111, which I'll also miss. You must be thinking that I'd be better off taking my time. That, after all, might be the best way not to waste it! You old number cruncher! Bedeviled bean-counter! Ridiculous infinity-reductionist! What's the point of all these calculations, anyway? The excuse I'll give for my failings and this pitiful obsession is that I'm bored, that I need to fill a void, and so on, and so forth. When it comes to self-justification, I'm no scrooge! What a culpable indulgence! Yes, I'm nothing but a hopeless calculator. I should have studied to be a surveyor, that way I could measure the world. Instead, surveyor of my own life, I wind up imposing limits on my world.

This critical look at myself ought to weigh me down . . . but instead, it lightens my load. Here's once again proof to myself that we don't walk with our feet but with our heads. Walking originates in the brain. That's what tells the body to move forward—today at a rapid pace, yesterday and the day before in a struggle with a wind so strong it could have stopped me once and for all. The body only responds to what the will tells it to do.

As the sun is swallowed up behind the hills, I reach the post marking the day's sixty-second kilometer; then, ten minutes later, marker 3,333. I snap a picture of myself straddling it, laughing, claiming victory, oblivious to fatigue, next to Ulysses who, on his new feet, followed along without a hitch. I've pushed back the limits of my endurance. The bridge I opt to sleep under is located just short of the day's sixty-eighth kilometer. My muscles will make me pay for this record distance tomorrow. But the next stage is trivial compared to what I've just accomplished: only thirty-two klicks, a mere bagatelle!

I sleep well. It seems that the Gobi's winds can't reach this hilly landscape, and instead remain locked up further north. In the morning, I'm moved more than ever by the fabulous spectacle of dawn. The fires lit by the sun behind the hills set several clouds ablaze before the golden disk finally leaps into the sky. I'm going to try to make Hongliyuan by noon.

Having traveled six miles or so, I suddenly stop, at a loss for words, thunderstruck. Sticking up from the ditch below is a clenched human hand. I draw nearer and discover what I first take to be a mannequin, then realize that it's a corpse. A man is lying on one side, curled up in fetal position. Given his location, he can't be seen by passing trucks. The man had put on several layers of jackets and pants, and is wearing a fur-lined leather cap. What's most striking is his skin. His face and hands, the only visible body parts, are desiccated, full of cracks, bronze. The skin of a lizard. His remains have apparently been there for a long time but, given how dry the air here is, instead of decomposing, they've mummified. Lying alongside him are several plastic bags in which the man must have kept his belongings. An egg carton, probably carried on the mischievous wind, is stuck between his legs. It's a surreal sight, a gruesome take on a painting by Magritte or Duchamp.

I flag down the first car to go by. The distrustful driver comes to a stop a rather far distance from me. The sight of the corpse doesn't seem to bother him much; I'd dare say he finds it perfectly ho-hum. I forced him to drop his average speed and he's by no means pleased;

he makes it clear that he has no time to use the cellphone taunting me on his dashboard. So I decide to keep on going and get help in Hongliyuan: I can't just leave the body of an unidentified man to the vultures like that.

I grab Ulysses and realize that I've lost the harness that lets me tow my companion hands-free. It was a backpack belt that I had cobbled together for the purpose. Made of canvas and stuffed with foam, it fell off without my hearing it. The little bolt holding it to the tow bar must have worn loose. There's obviously no way I'll find one like it here. So I turn around and, scanning the road far ahead of me, I retrace the six miles I traveled this morning. Nothing. I make the return trip, vainly keeping an eye on the ditches, and find myself once again beside the corpse, which I must be drawn to. He was clearly a vagrant, like the many I've met since first setting foot in China. Central Asia, though formerly communist but still very religious, doesn't seem to give rise to this kind of destitution. There, at least, almsgiving is a common practice. It's absolutely incredible to think that I can draw this conclusion from first-hand observation.

A three-wheel motorized taxi stops two hundred yards away. One of its tires is flat, the driver and passenger are trying to figure out what to do. I tell them about the mummified man in the ditch and they burst out laughing. They know all about it; it was discovered, they tell me, last summer. I'm aghast. You mean that the corpse has been lying there for over a year, and no one has ever bothered to bury it? I get back underway, obsessed with the image of the clenched fist and the glib laughter of these two men. The vagrant must have died long before his body was found. His fur hat and layers of clothes would seem to suggest that he died in winter, so it would have to have been a year and a half ago. I was once in Beijing in January and the temperature dropped to 5°F. I saw old men playing chess on the sidewalks and they were dressed in the same way: they had donned everything they owned, making them look like Michelin men.

How can a corpse, though it has nothing to do with you, make you laugh? I think back on the dead wolf I saw by the road in the mountains of Kyrgyzstan, left where it couldn't be missed, to set an example. A wolf, I get that, but a man? Heaven help the wolves of Kyrgyzstan! Heaven help the poor in China!

A wave of fatigue suddenly sweeps over me. The search for my lost harness will have forced me to travel not twenty, but thirty-two miles. On top of yesterday's forty-two, that's seventy-five miles in two days. That's a lot, even for someone in top shape. I walk woefully, unable to get my mind off the one question haunting me: what if I, too, were to die by the wayside, or under a bridge? Is the indifference I encountered peculiar to Gansu men, or does it reflect the way all Chinese view death? To what extent does it reflect Taoist, Confucian, or Buddhist culture? I've seen, on many occasions, how their cruelty to animals affects no one. And the long history of China offers abundant proof that the death of one man, or of a group of men, has very little impact on public opinion. Five thousand miners die each year in this country, but no one has done anything to improve the safety of those working below ground. Images resurface in my mind. Like that of a poster I've seen several times, intended to combat delinquency: a police officer holds a man by the scruff of his neck. The thief is on his knees, his head lowered in submission. The handcuffs are so tight around his wrists that they're bleeding. Hoping to silence these sad images, I recite to myself a poem by François Cheng:

> *Before they bloom*
> *The flowers of the day*
> *Must see the night through*
> *To the bitter end . . .*

Around 6:00 p.m., at the Hongliyuan toll booth, the uniformed men guarding it inform me that there's a hotel, five kilometers away. Five kilometers? There's no way I can walk that much farther, so I tell

---

* François Cheng, *D'où jaillit le chant* (Paris: Phébus, 2000).

them that I'm going to camp right here, just off the road. They consult one another. Their commander takes Ulysses by the tow bar and motions me to follow. They offer to put me up in their barracks—for a price. I tell them about the corpse at Kilometer 3,318. Their phlegmatic reaction reveals just how little the matter interests them, so I give up. I grab a quick bite to eat in a nearby tavern, lie down for two hours, then get back up, my stomach growling once again. I wolf down a second plate of sautéed noodles at 10:00 p.m., then jump into bed, where I toss and turn all night, disturbed by visions of the mummy. Early the next morning, no sooner have I gulped down my usual noodle soup than they tell me that I'm due in the mess hall for breakfast. It wouldn't be right to offend my hosts. In just twelve hours, I'll have eaten four times!

V

POLICE!

It's warm out and, for the first time since the Iranian border, I can walk with my legs uncovered. In Iran, that wasn't not an option. In the deserts of Turkmenistan and Uzbekistan, and in the Taklamakan in summer, I would have risked serious sunburn. In Kyrgyzstan, it was cold, and I had to cover up. In China, going about in shorts shocks no one, although I'm still the only one doing so this early in the season. I'm back in a peneplain-and-desert region, although it's a little less rugged than it was on my way into Xingxingxia: there are, here and there, tufts of camel grass.

The latest vagrant I run into, though not yet thirty, is terrifyingly gaunt. I hand him a fistful of bills and point him to a restaurant I just walked past. These unfortunate fellows all wear the same uniform: a plastic bag full of their meagerly belongings in one hand, and, on their backs, their entire wardrobe. I see an undershirt, shirt number one, shirt number two, a sweater, a light jacket that was once white, a second jacket that was once pink, a third one that's gray, and a parka resting on his shoulders. Hunger makes one cold-sensitive. His hollow cheeks have been eaten away at by a beard, and it's mangy, too. But what's most disturbing are his eyes: he has the stare of a vanquished man, of a dying, pleading animal. Off he goes, clutching the bills in his hand, taking slow steps, as if each stride were his last. As I watch as he walks away, and the memory of the dead man in the ditch comes back to haunt me.

As I near Anxi, the ground becomes perfectly flat. It's so horizontal that the horizon itself is invisible. That bluish spot over there, is it six, thirty, or sixty miles away? And that fog gleaming in the sun, is it a mirage, a sea, or a cloud that, demoralized by all this flatness, has at last lain down to die? My slow steps work on the distance like photographic developing fluid, revealing details bit by bit. Six miles, and the white fog is emblazoned with a dark line at its center. Two hours farther along, the black line reveals its true nature: it's an oasis that looks to be sliding into the desert. Six miles more, and the trees stand out more clearly, like Chinese shadow puppets. An extra boost and I'm suddenly there. A few stores, the inevitable tire repair shops, and a long string of restaurants in front of which young streetwalkers call out. Just to annoy them, I choose the only one lacking feminine bait. A busty Chinese lady is busy munching on the products she sells: *da dou*—thinly-hulled grilled beans and she invites me to try some, too: they're deliciously starchy.

Anxi used to be called Guazhou* and was a major center at the crossroads of two very popular places back in the Silk Road's heyday: the Yulin Caves, and especially those of Dunhuang. The Buddhist communities that had settled there were very rich. They collected donations from merchants traveling the Silk Road, who paid them when they first went by, so that good fortune would smile upon them, then paid them again on the return trip, thankful to the gods for having spared them. I will not return to visit the dozens of historic sites there, they're simply too far away; I went there five years ago, on my first trip to China.

Anxi was perhaps once a major crossroads for travelers. Nevertheless, all I find here today is a room with neither water—hot or cold— nor electricity. Chen Xiping, who has an impressive command of Oxfordian English, tells me that it's because of a power outage and that it will last all day, but that everything should be up and running again by 8:00. Chen is a Chinese engineer who's tagging along with

---

* TN: In 2006, four years after Ollivier's walk here, Anxi was renamed Guazhou.

Gayle Hall, an ex-nurse's aide from the United States who gave it all up out of love for China . . . and for the three-thousand-mile-long Great Wall: she intends to walk its entire length from here to the sea! Zhu Yunsu, who has a head as round as a marble, teamed up with the pair. He had a job in Beijing, but the allure of adventure got the best of him. An adventure that's off to a bad start: an official in Anxi, unearthing a document from 1991, claims that it's "illegal" to walk the wall. So at least as far as Jiayuguan, they're going to walk along the road instead.

I hang out in the city for a little while trying to find a barber to give me a shave. The young woman who takes care of me doesn't use soap; instead, she softens my beard by applying hot towels. That's how barbers do it for the Chinese, who don't have much in the way of facial hair. After scalding me several times, now she's trying to remove my epidermis! It's as if she were plucking my chin hairs; and so, with a smile, I decide to flee!

Given that the power outage has put the kibosh on my plans to check my email, I revert to one of my long-time habits: visiting the post office, a ritual I've practiced religiously since my teens. I love these places, through which so many destinies pass. Today, I have a large stack of postcards to mail, as well as something more precious still: the notes I've kept since the last major city I was in. Chinese stamps aren't pre-glued or gummed, and postal rates vary from one office to the next. The stamp salesclerk, a deadly serious Chinese woman as surly as a gendarme, has clerk's sleeves on, much like the postmistresses of my childhood. She has fully understood the importance of her role and, with the slowness and care of someone in a senior position, she places a small assortment of stamps on each of my envelopes, but not without first folding each one in two to make sure that the address is correctly written on the envelope's right side. The line behind me grows longer. Unflappable, the postal worker calculates the postage on her abacus, in flagrant disregard of the computer in front of her. A letter for Europe costs as much as two bowls of noodles in a restaurant. But there's a final step to the operation: the stamps have to be glued, an activity accomplished at a counter in the middle of the room. The clever, jury-rigged system that spits out adhesive doesn't quite do it for me: I only manage to glue my fingers! Before I'll be fully Chinese, I still have an awful lot to learn.

My body, which didn't much appreciate my personal best of forty-two miles, lets me know that it's had enough, and lets others know as well: my lip is now swollen from two large cold sores, giving me the mouth of a grouper. I'm lying in bed when, at 11:00 p.m., the phone rings. Someone offering a "massage"?—Hotel employees sell the room numbers of single men to prostitutes, especially if they're westerners. But no: it's Abdul, a Uyghur tour guide who speaks French well enough to have adopted the name of Guillaume. He accompanies French tourists on behalf of the Orients Travel Agency, a group that has come to my rescue more than once since my journey began. Guillaume was speaking with the owner of the hotel and learned that I was here. What a surprise! Over a beer, three of us—myself, Guillaume, and Emmanuel, a visiting lecturer from France—chat for two hours. I can't stop talking. I haven't spoken French for a month, and I enjoy it so much I can't stop talking. Emmanuel was in Kashgar last year, and he's delighted to be following in my footsteps. When we meet up again later on in France, he tells me how tired I looked during our get-together here, and, above all, how dirty I was!

I keep meeting new people. Leaving Anxi, I run into two cyclists from Hong Kong on their way to Pakistan. The man is from Italy and the woman from Sweden—a Swede with almond eyes and jet-black hair, more likely of Filipino or Japanese origins than Scandinavian. They work in Hong Kong and speak Chinese fluently, which helps streamline their interactions with locals.

"I started out making trips by car," Mario tells me. "But I couldn't stand the noise of the engine, so I switched to biking. I believe you're right that the slow pace of walking is the only way to capture travel's magical moments!"

I think to myself how true that is when one's spirits are flying high. But when the soul is dark and in the doldrums, it closes you off from the world, and you no longer even notice your surroundings.

This year, I feel like a zombie stumbling along, impervious to the scenery and any self-reflection that might delve into the metaphysical. There's no place this year for questions like "why am I here?" and "what is my destiny?" If I were to ponder, even just a little, the motives keeping me going, I'd promptly turn around and head home! This is where I am, where I am is no paradise, and that's all there is to it.

The Hui people are Chinese Muslims. I have a hard time telling them apart from the Uyghurs, who are also Muslim, but of Central Asian origins. The Hui man I meet is here to try his luck in the big city. While motorists endlessly offer me a ride, for this frail beanpole no one stops; I guess he's not exotic enough for them. There are millions of young countryfolk like him who, tired of starving on a tiny patch of land, are drawn to the cities of the east. There, they're exploited to no end, for they're motivated, hardworking, not too particular about salary, and have no qualms about showing up at the worksite day or night. The government rounds up a few thousand of them every now and then and ships them back to their villages. And the migration begins anew.

Boredom wells up from the stony desert I'm walking in now. To keep my mind occupied, I reconnect with Rosa, the heroine of the novel I'm trying to write, word by word. In Xiaowan Daoban, formerly a prison, a museum was built with fake castellated walls intended to look like the old penitentiary, now in ruins. According to a billboard, the star exhibit is a drum set with drumheads made from human skin. I opt out. Not only have I never been a fan of guidebooks and generally usually prefer chance encounters and surprise discoveries, from the moment I set out on this walk, I've felt a sense of kinship with vagrants. I've come to see Ulysses as the ultimate in luxury—although without him, how would I avoid dehydration in the Gobi? I'd like to be freer still, to cast off the few things I'm lugging around. To eliminate everything and reclaim freedom; to shed the unnecessary, and liberate the self. And when all that's done, will the mind follow?

In the greasy spoon where I stop, a wimpy-looking beanpole with all the trappings of an undercover cop comes to have a sniff around. He tries to "pigeonhole" me, which, for obvious reasons, is an utter impossibility: our homelands are worlds apart, and I'm an eccentric, even in my own country! His eyes rummage about, interrogating me, dwelling on me. He doesn't belong to the immigration police, which forces its flock to make their rounds in pairs and be kind to tourists, while speaking a smattering of English. Expecting to terrorize me, he writes on a piece of paper: "I am a policeman." I take his pen and I add just below: "I am a tourist." He reads my note and appears surprised. He clearly has no idea what it means. And so, in a state of doubt—perhaps a *tourist* is someone important?—he changes tactics, becoming jovial, bestowing upon me countless favors, bringing me back a toothpick, and pouring tea into my bowl. He then takes his pen back out and writes "14" on the piece of paper. Fourteen yuan for a bowl of noodles and tea? The couple running the place put on a self-congratulatory look: obviously, since a cop handed me the bill, I'll pay without batting an eye. I rarely contest a tab; the exchange rate is so skewed in my favor. And that must make me look like a chump in the eyes of many Chinese, for whom money is not a matter to be taken lightly. Most often, I'm charged twice the price, even though the practice—illegal, but widespread—sometimes annoys me. This time, I don't even haggle. I count out four yuan coins, set them on the table, get up, grab Ulysses and head out like a prince, never once turning around.

I dive straight into the desert. It's broiling. Heat waves make everything in the distance appear to dance. A lake seems to sparkle, then vanish: a mirage. I'm beyond exhausted. My mouth hurts: fever blisters caused by fatigue and the sun—two of which are festering—have disfigured my lips. I have to conserve energy. I will not exceed—hand on my heart—the twenty-two miles planned for today. But the Shoulder Devil is restless and, as I'm about to raise my tent, a cyclist tells me where there's a *fandian* (restaurant) only a short distance away. I make a beeline for it. It turns out to be two and a half miles down the road and, as if that weren't enough, it's closed. Then, yet again, as I'm about to set up my bivouac, a trucker, his vehicle spewing oil onto the asphalt, assures me that there's another *fandian* three kilometers away. The dialogue in words and gestures goes more or less like this:

"You're sure? Three kilometers, no more?"

"Three kilometers!"

"And it's open?"

"Yes, I had a fish there this noon."

"And they have rooms where guests can sleep?"

"*You*" (They have).

That would be more comfortable than camping. I toss the wood I've gathered for my fire and set off once again, my fatigue forgotten. I count the kilometers: one, two, three, four . . . but no *fandian*! To make matters worse, the road clambers up a steep hill and Ulysses starts to get heavy. Two kilometers farther, still nothing. I give up and pitch my tent, going to bed without dinner. In the morning, just three kilometers more, there's the inn, on the shores of a lake, with a naïve-art billboard featuring a fish jumping out of the water and into a skillet. At this hour of the day, it's closed. I'm angry that I keep falling into the same trap, even though I know that most Chinese are unfamiliar with distances, and that they'll say anything with such assurance that it lures you in every time.

I'm closing in on Yumen, the Jade Gate. A substance arrived by way of this road that, in Chinese eyes, was as precious as gold. Jade, so the legend goes, is frozen dragon semen that had been deposited at the center of the earth. In Chinese literature and in the country's collective imagination, dragons hold a special place. Great ceremonies are devoted to them. In spite of their terrifying appearance and privileged relationship with those in power, people absolutely love them. There are dragons of all shapes and sizes: they come in the form of men, serpents, or birds; they sometimes bear horns, and can be covered in scales or fur; they may have claws; their mouths may contain long, pointed teeth. They're most often green or blue. Irrigating one's land is very easy. You simply lure a dragon by attaching a beautiful woman to a rock. He comes running. At the final moment, you hide the woman. Furious, he begins spitting thunder and rain. The year of the dragon is a very auspicious one. And what does it bring? Wealth, of course!

The Jade Gate also marked the border between the territory the Hans considered their own, and that belonging to the "barbarians" farther west, though they, too, were governed by the Empire. The Chinese didn't hold these neighbors in high esteem, and it was only in the mid-twentieth century that the ideogram designating foreigners was changed. Until then, it was identical to the one signifying "dog."

Yumenzhen Oasis is huge. It takes me two days to cross it. Nothing but wheat and cornfields as far as the eye can see, and thousands of dark spots: bent-over or crouched peasants cutting weeds with a tiny metal blade. Here, treating the soil with chemicals is unheard of.

I've been looking forward to this day for a long time. Today, May 15, I'll be crossing over the one thousandth kilometer since I got underway in Turfan. But the day's going to prove emotionally tumultuous. As I'm walking along a little-used road, Ulysses's right hub freezes up. This year, I didn't take the time to oil—or rather, grease—my cart, and in particular, the ball bearings; once they'd dried out, they quickly wore down. Fortunately, my guardian angel sends in a motorist who, fortunately yet again, has an oil can, which he generously splashes over the wheel's axle, getting it turning once again. But it goes without saying that it's only a temporary fix.

Around 1:00 in the afternoon, while napping like a hobo under one of the countless bridges located at regular intervals the entire length of this road, a young Chinese fellow dressed like a London businessman comes charging down in my direction and, the moment he sees me, stops dead in his tracks. I greet him with a laugh, given the surprised look on his face.

He doesn't respond to my greeting but motions to someone else to come down the embankment. The other fellow scrambles down the incline, too, and also fails to answer my "*ni hao.*" It's a regular running gag routine, since the second man waves in the direction of the road, too. The third fellow comes down to us so slowly that I take him to be someone important. Surprise: it's a police*woman*. About forty years old, she's sporting high heels, and has an off-putting expression on her face. She looks me over with a mix of surprise and condemnation. I get up, and, to put an end to all the suspense, I present my little "open sesame" papers. They typically give rise to smiles, leniency, pity, or admiration: *Fancy that! All the way from Istanbul. And on foot!* But here milady-perched-on-high barely glances at them and, in a tone of voice she expects will go unchallenged, accompanied by a flick of the wrist, her forefinger out, she orders me to pack up my gear and follow her. But I'm in a dissenting mood:

"*Meiyou!*"

The lady's not used to resistance. She thinks that I've misunderstood and repeats both what she said and the gesture.

"*Meiyou.*"

Bemused, she turns to her two companions. Equally flabbergasted, they motion her over with their fingers, then the three of them step away in consultation. The woman comes back and looks me over with growing puzzlement. These cops, real or not, are having a decidedly hard time putting a label on me. I have the look of a nice guy, a harmless fellow, but these days, as everyone knows, a wristwatch can hide a miniature bomb, and an old man's boots might be full of explosives. Still saying nothing, she motions to the older man and they head off, leaving the younger chap to keep an eye on me. The boss and her assistant, whose car I hear start up, are headed off, either for instructions or reinforcements. I lazily lie back down, acting nonchalant, though my brain is hard at work: my papers are in order with respect to the police, and my visa is valid for another full month. But fearing that I might get lost in the desert, I brought my GPS along with me, that ingenious device about the size of a cellphone that picks up satellite signals and lets you know where you are and where you need to go anywhere in the world. I'm fully aware that, for military reasons, the device is strictly forbidden in this country. Of course, satellites have been equipped with more sophisticated technology for some time now. Still, the fine for carrying a GPS is one thousand euros ($950), the annual salary of a laborer. But more importantly, I risk forfeiting my chances of being able to renew my visa, or worse yet, being deported. In short, to be unable to make it all the way to Xi'an.

If the two others went off to get reinforcements, then they're going to take me away forcibly and search me. The device is in one of my backpack's side pockets. There's no way even an absent-minded novice would miss it. I pretend to be dozing, but careful!—I take it that I'm already imprisoned and have a close eye on my jailer. If he was making his way double quick down the hill a short while ago, it's clearly because he had a sudden urge. So he still hasn't relieved himself. Surely, he'll do so soon . . . that remains to be seen. If he heads off for two minutes, I'll remove my GPS from my pack and hide it on the other side of the bridge. But the whippersnapper stays put. Ten minutes go by. I have to try something. I get up, pack up my things and set them on Ulysses. The chap wants to stop me and manages a few words in English.

"What are you doing?"

"I'm done with my nap. I'm heading off."

"But you can't! You have to wait."

"Wait for what?"—I hold out my two joined fists, as though I were handcuffed: "Are you arresting me?"

"No."

"Then if I'm not arrested, I'm free. And off I go. If you want to talk to me, you'll find me on the Yumen Road."

Resistance like that is unheard of. The man's a bit lost. I haul Ulysses back up onto the bridge. But I'm all nerves: everything boils down to right now. What's he going to do? Stay put and wait for the higher ups, or follow me? He hesitates, vainly dialing numbers on his cellphone. I have no time to lose. Without turning around, I set off

lickety-split. Five hundred feet on, I pretend to be arranging my bags
on Ulysses and take a glance back. He's still standing on the bridge,
his phone stuck to his ear. I have to act fast. About 650 feet from him,
the road goes over a hump. He'll therefore only be able to see my head.
Making sure he can't see what I'm doing, I take the GPS from my bag
and quickly slip it into my pocket. Then I conspicuously take some
toilet paper out of the pack's other side pocket and go off about three
hundred feet from the road. I squat down where he can only see my
head—normal protocol when you don't want anyone to have a view
of your bum. I take out my knife, dig a hole, and drop the forbidden
device in and cover it back up. Then, no doubt brought on by the fear
gripping me, I find I actually do have a little business to take care of,
catlike, on the dirt I just dug up! I head back over to the road, conspicuously buckling my belt, as I attempt to play up the ploy. I'm still very
afraid. Did he see what I did? If he gives it some thought, he'll find my
sudden urge suspicious, though it turned out to be very real.

The cop's waiting for me on the road. Milady-perched-on-high
instructed him to follow me. He smiles, happy to have me back in his
clutches, and that reassures me. We start walking, the police officer,
Ulysses, and I, at full speed. I want to put as much distance between
me and my GPS as quickly as possible. It's extremely hot out. The
young man starts sweating in his city clothes, but he doesn't let me
get ahead of him. I'm flying. To gain his trust, I rattle on:

"How old are you?"

"Thirty-four."

"That's my eldest son's age!"

He plays along, asking me how many children I have and telling
me that he loves to walk. A steep climb quiets him down. I don't
know if it's because I solved my problem, but I suddenly find him
rather likeable.

At this point, a black Volkswagen with tinted windows pulls up
alongside of us. Out steps our lady, a fellow who's second-in-com-
mand, and a scrawny young man who appears embarrassed. I ask
him in English:

"Are you the interpreter?"

He nods. The officer in charge takes over once again. But then with disconcerting friendliness she asks: "Your passport" in Chinese, followed by "please." The first time around, she didn't even ask for my papers. Not very professional, Milady!

In a very urbane, almost high-class manner, I smile at her:

"But of course."

At this point, I feel very relaxed. If the young cop were even slightly suspicious about my little shenanigan a short while ago, he'd tell his boss about it straightaway. While she's thumbing through my passport, I show the young cop a photo of my children, since we had spoken about them. Above all, I want to keep him from thinking. The policewoman finishes looking over my papers and hands them back to me without even verifying the dates on my visa.

"Thank you. Sorry."

Good heavens, she even apologizes!

Giddy from an adventure that has ended well, I allow—somewhat through my teeth—that it's no big deal, that she's simply doing her job. I know that the young interpreter will translate that for her, but for the moment, he says nothing. They climb back into their car and drive off.

With their vehicle out of sight I sit down on the pavement, my legs like jelly. Then I burst out laughing—one of those deep belly laughs, the mad laughter of someone who just escaped a close brush with disaster.

When I finally regain my composure, I ask myself: Should I go back and get my GPS? It's not impossible that milady could be waiting for me just a little farther on. But is the device really indispensable? By comparing the ideograms on road signs with those on my map, I'm able to translate city names. If I tempt it once again, will luck smile upon me a second time? My goal isn't to make it back to Paris GPS in hand, but to make it all the way to Xi'an. So there we have it, my mind is made up! And off I go, with lighter heart and lighter feet.

VI

THE FUNERAL

It's never hard to find a place to eat in China. As I've said before, it's easy for anyone to set up an eatery and sell food here, and cook stoves are portable. I've grown thin very early on this year. I have to do something about it. I have a bowl of soup at 7:00, at 10:00 I have chicken fricassee with noodles offered by a merry band of truck drivers, and at noon a generous portion of sweet and sour pork, sopped up with two bowls of rice. I'm eating five meals a day, like an infant!

The driver who catches me doing a little jig on the road with Ulysses as my partner must think I've lost my mind. He couldn't possibly know, of course, that I'm celebrating my one-thousandth kilometer since Turfan! This ritual of spontaneously whooping it up as I complete stages in my journey got started on my first long walk. Such festive self-gratification bolsters my spirits. Ridiculous? For sure! But since I'm not the reclusive type—as my solitary walk might suggest—I have to recreate situations that make me feel as though I'm celebrating with others.

Here's a pretty little mosque. I've seen hundreds of them since Istanbul, but this one stands out: it's an unusual mix, part-Buddhist temple and part-mosque. With respect to the latter, it has the bulbous dome and crescent atop the roof; but it has the former's shape, and its roofs of glazed tiles curl up toward the sky. The prayer service is over. The Hui faithful who just gave thanks to Allah are friendly; they invite me to join them for tea, which we sip while munching on delicious little sweet cakes. There's a heated fight over the last one remaining;

222

it's rightfully mine, but I'm a well-bred boy and offer it to the imam, but he wouldn't think of it! This game of trying to see who's more polite goes on for some time, but in the end, I lose, amid laughter. At the mosque's entrance, incense sticks are burning in two large bronze vases. The carpets are Chinese or Persian, as are the inscriptions on the wall, some written in the language of Muhammad, others in ideograms. The adjacent room, the one beneath the bulbous dome, is almost entirely taken up by a finely crafted sandalwood reliquary. Tapestries hang from the ceiling, reminding me of the Buddhist temples I visited in Xiahe, five years ago. The imam, a man with a long white beard, suggests that I stay with him, that he would gladly put me up. I'm tempted, but how could I, with my visa expiration date hanging over my head? I'm especially tempted because, although the Islam that I encountered Central Asian cities sometimes set me ill at ease, the way it's practiced out here in the countryside is good-natured, family oriented, and kind.

I cover six more miles before a sandstorm blows in. In no time at all, the gravel turns to bullets. A providential bridge shelters me through the night and, contrary to what I was expecting, I'd even say I almost slept well. By morning, the wind has changed direction and nudges me along. It's around 3:00 p.m. when I finally get my first glimpse of the Jiayuguan Fortress, known as Cheng Lu. I had been living among Barbarians; here I have stepped into the Middle Kingdom, home of the Hans. Built in the fourteenth century during the pinnacle of the Silk Road, the fortress, which was given the name of the "impregnable pass under heaven," is impressive. It rises up in the middle of the pass formed by the Qilian Mountains to the south, whose snow-capped summits are visible in good weather, and the Heishan, the Black Mountain, to the north. Dominated by three towers, each with a three-tiered pagoda roof, the fortress was the last bastion protecting the Empire against invasions from the west. The Great Wall—which formerly ran farther west, past Anxi (Guazhou)—at the time, ended here. Half fallen into ruins, little by little, Cheng Lu was rebuilt, starting in the 1960s. And since the Great Wall had disappeared—no worries—they simply erected a new one in 1987. There had to be something to show tourists, who flocked to the city in large numbers. Students were enlisted to rebuild its heavy, mud-brick walls. They were paid, it's said, one *fen* (one one-hundredth of a yuan) for each brick. They had to stack six hundred and fifty of them to earn the equivalent of one dollar. The reconstructed Great Wall, which is very photogenic, ascends a mountainside, then comes to an abrupt end past a tower. Another section is being built that will connect the mountain to the fortress. The latest in antiquities.

When I get to Jiayuguan, feeling very tired, I spot a taxi whose driver—a woman—looks to be waiting for customers. I let her know that she's now got one. She smiles at me in a show of dimples and explains that she's not free. Then her passenger shows up: a fat fellow on the verge of a heart attack. But he's not selfish and, without any fuss, sets about helping me disassemble Ulysses so that he'll fit in the trunk. Five minutes later, I've shown them my little papers and we've pulled up in front of the comfortable tourist hotel where I've decided to stay. I desperately need to get back in shape and have chosen the one the guidebook claims is the best. The cab driver and the man—a friend of hers—go with me to the reception desk. My new friends balk at the rate, 350 yuan (about $45), and they manage to get it reduced by half. They then ask for breakfast to be included, which the women at the reception desk agree to, while giving a thumbs up in a show of admiration. There's no paying my driver. I want to take her picture, so I can send her the photograph and, more selfishly, so that I won't forget her dimples and smiling eyes, but she refuses that, too, and runs off with a laugh, delighted we'd met.

My room's mirror reflects back to me the image of an emaciated hobo with dark circles under his eyes, hollow cheeks dirtied by a week-old beard, and a mouth disfigured in scabs left behind by cold sores. It's time I get some rest! So, despite my tight schedule, to hell with reason, I decide right then and there to stay put in Jiayuguan for not just one, but two days.

The city's tourists don't look too happy. It's quite chilly out, and the sandstorm I suffered through yesterday stirred up dust, a kind of white haze, such that, from atop the brand-new Great Wall, the snowy summits of the Qilian Shan aren't visible, as promised in their guidebooks.

The Xingcheng Weijinmú Museum, which boasts a reproduction of one of the countless tombs scattered throughout the region and which dates from the Wei and Western Jin Dynasties, keeps me busy for a while. Each sepulcher is composed of two or three funerary rooms constructed to a depth of thirty feet. The technique used is rather clever: the workmen, after digging a single well, bore vaulted rooms and then reinforce their sides and ceiling with oven-fired bricks. There's no need for cement or binder. The walls are covered in painted earthenware tiles that depict daily life during the first four centuries of the common era: plowing, blackberry harvesting, banquets, hunting and war scenes, music, and more. In short, nothing that isn't already known. Museums, as I've said before, excel at boring me! I'd rather poke around the working-class districts where, as in Turkish cities, a host of tasty little treats can be enjoyed all day long. The *migao* merchant has spotted me. Each time he sees me, he calls out and hands me sumptuous portions of a kind of rice cake stuffed with prunes and drizzled with syrup that I'm absolutely crazy about.

I converse for a long time with a solemn and talkative Chinese woman, an engineer who came here for work. When I express my astonishment that China is one gigantic construction site, she points out that what I've seen is nothing compared to the four large-scale projects that have been underway for several years and which the government has made one of its top priorities. The first two involve transporting energy from the sparsely inhabited west to the over-populated east, which needs it desperately, and is suffocating due to the use of low-grade coal. Electricity will come primarily from a monumental dam being constructed along the Yangtze River. Natural gas and oil will be brought from Xinjiang, where there are vast reserves. But the project faces some considerable transportation challenges, both by rail and especially by pipeline. The third priority is the railroad line planned to extend all the way to Lhasa, in Tibet, scaling the mountains of the "roof of the world." The last major project that the regime has decided to undertake involves bringing water from the south, where it's abundant, to the country's north, where it's in short supply. At least two of these prodigious projects have obvious political objectives: ensuring China's greater grip on Tibet and Xinjiang, and speeding up colonization already in progress. The construction of the railroad between Xi'an and Ürümqi in the 1950s made it possible to send Han Chinese by the millions into the Uyghur homeland. Before the line was built, Uyghurs made up ninety percent of the population. Today, they account for barely fifty. One clearly deliberate consequence: the Hans have monopolized jobs in the manufacturing, construction, and service sectors, as well as in industry and administration, while leaving agriculture to the natives. Tibet will undergo the same process.

Leaving Jiayuguan, I notice once again that Chinese people *listen* to what I say in English, but don't seem to *understand*. It takes me no fewer than ten minutes to explain to an English-speaking receptionist that I need her to write down instructions that I can give to my taxi driver. Unable to figure out directions in large cities, especially now that my GPS lies asleep somewhere beneath the Gobi's sands, I need a taxi to put me back on the right road. I want to be dropped off just outside the city in the direction of Lanzhou, on Route 312. To make sure there's no mistake, the woman orally repeats to the female taxi driver what she jotted down on the note. Both of them tell me not to worry: they've understood. We load up Ulysses and ten minutes later, the taxi pulls up . . . in front of the bus station. Whenever I say that I'm going to Xi'an on foot, only those who see me sweating it out on the road actually think I'm serious. The others, despite assurances to the contrary, don't buy it. For them, it's truly UN-I-MA-GIN-A-BLE!

Nine miles separate Jiayuguan from Jiuquan, a city of no touristic interest, but which is home to the region's administrative services. It's was here in Jiuquan, in 1607, that brother Bento de Góis died. He was a Jesuit who, five years earlier, had set out from India in search of a land route to Cathay. At the time, Westerners knew very little about the vast continent of Asia. The Silk Road had been impassable for nearly a century. De Góis, taking the name of Banda Abdullah (The Servant of God), pretended to be an Armenian merchant and joined up with immense caravans that took months, sometimes an entire year, just to convene. In those days, Cathay and China were believed to be two distinct countries. But de Góis met Muslim merchants returning from Beijing who mentioned another Jesuit, Matteo Ricci, whom they had seen. He then realized that China and Cathay were one and the same. His finding would bring an end to expeditions attempting to discover this "terra incognita."

The route detours around the city, and so much the better. But from a distance, I'm stunned by how much real estate development is going on. As far as the eye can see, there's a veritable forest of cranes. The apparatuses' beams, each one decorated with three red flags, turn this way and that in a sky that's growing overcast. Here, it's not enough to simply bulldoze and rebuild a neighborhood, they're erecting an entire city! Large painted walls celebrate, in Soviet-style realism, the brave Chinese men and women who constructed these dreadful skyscrapers. Several days later, someone tells me why so much building is underway. A nuclear-testing facility has been built in Qinqshui, north of Jiuquan, out in the middle of the desert, and the city serves, in a sense, as the center's staging ground.

The wind picks up and a freezing rain begins to beat down on the oasis. I walk in a torrential downpour for a distance of six miles before finally throwing in the towel and pushing open the door of Niu's inn. The young man there is truly one of the kindest, friendliest, and most urbane fellows I've met this year. His two elderly parents rely entirely on him to manage the business. He does the housework, the cooking, and he cleans the rooms, although he seems to have forgotten mine, which, as usual, is dirty. He cooks an excellent meal for me, lights a fire to warm me up, and even strings a wire so that I can hang my soaking-wet things out to dry. He's an impressive homemaker. At 2:00 in the morning, he's still serving meals to truck drivers on break. At 6:00, I wake him up to ask if he'll make breakfast for me. I take out my maps in preparation for the day's stretch.

"That dot, that village on the map, thirty kilometers away, does it have a place where I can eat and sleep?"

"*You*" (It has).

"And there?"

"*You*."

Somewhat suspicious, I point to a blank area on the map, where there isn't a single village.

"And here?"

"*You*."

Niu doesn't know how to say "*meiyou*." If he thought it would make me happy, he'd swear there was a five-star hotel atop Mount Everest!

It rained and blew all night long. The downpour is still just as cold. I'm shivering despite my jacket, gloves, and quick pace. In no time at all, my waterproof poncho is just as wet inside as it is out. I protected my packs with an oilcloth tarp, but the wind gusts have gotten the better of them. For the first time since the Kyrgyz border, there are more peaked roofs alongside the traditional flat, earthen roofs, perhaps indicating that it often rains here.

At noon, the rain has let up and I watch as several young people come charging down the street on bicycles: ten, fifty, then a hundred . . . it's a veritable Tour de France peloton! Two hundred, three hundred or more. The explanation is that there's a junior high school here, and it draws children from several villages. They all ride their bikes to school. Issuing from the road is an uninterrupted stream of calmly pedaling young people dressed in lively colors. Riding three or four abreast, they take up the entire bicycle path, though it's as wide as the road intended for trucks. The trucks charge on ahead, continuously honking their horns, without any effect whatsoever on the young people. I wait for the flow to dry up. I must have seen five hundred kids go by. The more alert ones bid me a sonorous "hello" in English, the one foreign language taught at school.

The rain is back, as if it had wanted to spare the youngsters. My hands are blue from the cold, my joints stiff. In a welcome inn, I'm served a piping-hot cup of tea and *moo shu ru*, pork with eggs and mushrooms. I'm reluctant to head back out into the rain, but really have no choice. I still have nearly 1,250 miles to go before I'll get my first glimpse of Zhonglou, the Bell Tower of Xi'an. And in one month, my visa expires. Will I succeed in getting it extended for another month? I have bitter memories of the refusal I received in Torugart, where, try as I might, I wasn't able to persuade the soldiers to let me walk those sixty miles! So nothing is certain. And even if I do manage to get one, I'll still have to walk at the pace of 620 miles a month, which is something I'd never done until last year in the Taklamakan. If they refuse to give me a new visa, I'll still have the option of going to . . . Hong Kong, where they're issued without hesitation, and then make a quick return to finish my journey. Compounding this problem is another quandary: I have to request the extension one week before it expires. In the next two large cities, Zhangye and Wuwei, it will be too soon, and in Lanzhou, it could very well be too late. Since I can't slow down, I'm going to have to pick up the pace if I want to make it in time. There are days I detest bureaucrats.

Those are some of the dark thoughts bouncing around in my head when Ulysses's tow bar breaks. That's the problem with prototypes: they're perfect for identifying and eliminating all the weak points! I do a makeshift repair . . . only to notice that the right tire is nearly flat. Fortunately, I'm not too far from Xiaheqing. Two miles ahead of the village, luck is once again on my side.

Shi Shao Feng's family (the name means "little stone summit") welcomes me with extraordinary kindness. The man himself is a mechanic by trade. His mother rushes off to brew liters of tea; the grandfather and his daughter-in-law set about repairing the inner tube, one of them applying the glue, the other pumping air; and their son welds Ulysses's broken arm. I'm delighted, but they're even more delighted than I. They all speak at the same time; I can't understand a thing, and they laugh at the lack of understanding on all sides. A neighbor drops by and adds to my aura: he saw me in the rain yesterday, on my way out of Jiuquan. The family, happy to learn that they haven't helped out some namby-pamby, offers me a room and a seat at their table. But on account of my visa, I have to turn them down. If I dared, I'd give them all big hugs! I'm nervous that the hardest part will be paying them. And indeed, they're not having it. I try to stuff a banknote in the son's pocket, but he steals away laughing. His wife does the same thing, and his father makes it clear that it would be impolite for me to insist. I pull out a wad of yuan notes to prove that I'm a well-heeled Westerner, but still, no dice. All I'll be able to do is send them the photograph I took of them while they were busy at work.

Rainy day number three. The wind has died down. The weather report, which I caught on television (a TV set blares in every restaurant) confirms that all of China is underwater except north of the Gobi. The desert is blooming. Plants are poking out from between the pebbles. The tufts of camel grass that were nothing but dry, thorny stems a short while ago, are now covered in little green leaves. Delicate yellow flowers (I don't know their name and until now didn't even know they existed) are springing up here and there, and the tamarisks are already mauve. The kiss of the rain has roused these sleeping beauties from their long slumber in the sun.

The woman running the *luguan* in Qingshui sends her daughter to fetch the kid of the owner of the restaurant across the street since he supposedly speaks English.

"What's your name?" he asks me. He doesn't quite grasp my reply, so I point to my name on my passport. He transcribes it under the admiring eyes of those who came to watch the boy wonder: the little guy speaks English and even writes it! The next morning at 6:00, another kid, a girl this time, who has been waiting for me for an hour not wanting to miss me, hands me a note written by her boyfriend: "Can you sign my book?" I'm the second person to have signed her autograph book; the first signed in Chinese.

The ceiling of clouds has lifted. In the south, the Qilian Shan are covered in snow. We're at 1,600 meters (5,250 feet) and the freezing rain that has been soaking me over the past three days is falling as snowflakes three hundred meters farther up. This is ideal for local farmers. The rain means they don't have to irrigate, and the snow melt will fill the canals. But for me, it's a terrible deal: water and mud stagnate beneath bridges, and the soaked soil, sticky as clay, makes camping difficult. So each night, I'll have to try to find a *luguan*.

Qingshui is of special significance for the Chinese military. It's the departure point of a "secret" railroad I cross, one not on maps. Two hundred miles away, it provides service to the super-secret center called "Qingshui Base." The word "secret" makes me laugh, since the railroad has certainly been photographed by every American military satellite since ground was first broken. Qingshui Base is where military rockets are assembled and launched, and where Chinese nuclear warheads are built. But in the large market town, no one says a word about this. The nuclear site at Qingshui is located far to the north of the little city of Jiuquan, and, according to some sources, covers as an area as big as the island of Taiwan, some 14,000 square miles. Building the base required over one hundred thousand workers. Gansu is home to most of China's nuclear sites. Nuclear testing takes place south of Hami, in the Lop Nor region, on a base in Malan. From time to time in the past, there was concern that radioactive fallout might rain down on the Hexi Corridor, which bustles with tourists heading to Dunhuang and elsewhere in the region.

On the road to Xuan Tang, as the sun is finally breaking through the clouds, I'm drawn to voices and laughter and intrigued by dozens of bicycles lying just off the road. A canal is being dug. But in the Chinese way. There are no bulldozers or cement mixers here. The trench, already quite deep and approximately fifteen feet wide, is a beehive of activity. Men and women, young and old, are digging. Those in the rear fling their shovelfuls onto a platform, where they're picked up by other shovels and tossed onto the side of the canal where a few valiant workers, all standing in a row, dispose of them. Everyone's talking and laughing. Some are taking a break in the sun. Those who are having lunch have planted their shovels side by side, creating what looks like a bouquet of shiny handles. It's their only tool, one ridiculously small given how big the canal they're digging is; but what they lack in size they make up for in number. Over a distance of two or perhaps three miles, thousands are tirelessly working together. I have before me what's all-too-often called—though not always judiciously—"Eternal China." This is an industrious, numerous people. The same people that built the Great Wall. Back then, laborers were conscripted and forced to work. Do these workers enjoy greater freedom? I'm in the Gaotai kolkhoz and, if not obligatory, this corvée is likely at least strongly recommended by local authorities.

I've come to the conclusion that people are more interested in Ulysses than in me. I should have applied for a Chinese patent! But now a young woman in a restaurant in Beidalu contradicts what I just wrote by implying that she doesn't find me unlikable, then discreetly invites me to follow her. She's not a prostitute. For a second, I'm tempted . . . and if I abstain, to be perfectly honest, it's more for lack of protection. That should come as no surprise: true adventurers, as everyone knows, only take calculable risks.

    As I near Zhangye, the landscape abruptly changes. There's not a square foot that isn't being farmed. The villages are increasingly spread out, meaning that I can now find water just about everywhere. Have I left the Gobi? I'm walking merrily along that morning, when I set foot in the little village of Sohata. A noise attracts my attention. Music? But the sounds that reach my ear are discordant, a little like an orchestra tuning up before the conductor steps out onto the stage. Hanging from a tall pole in front of the house from which the noise is coming is a giant paper lantern shaped like a four-story pagoda. Each level of this imitation, multiple-roof tower is approximately three feet high. Its colors are bold: carmine red and buttercup, with patches of blue here and there. Against the wall is a display consisting of two large wheels of multicolored paper. They're funeral wreaths, intended, it seems, to be burned atop the tomb of the deceased. A crowd mills about. An old man with a white beard motions me to come into a small courtyard where six musicians, seated at table, are making one hell of a racket. Three young people are playing *suona* flutes, which have bell-shaped ends like trumpets. A fourth is clanging a pair of cymbals, another is using a wooden mallet to strike an impressive bronze bell on a tripod, and the last is playing the xylophone. Each is throwing his or her heart and soul into it without any regard for what the others are doing. They're there to chase away the silence of death, to drive off evil spirits ever-ready to steal away the soul of the departed. Harmony would be inappropriate, for it would draw evil spirits in!

On the doorstep, laid with a thick carpet, two men are kneeling; clothed and capped in white, their hands on the ground and heads lowered, they're perfectly still. Candles are burning beside a small altar, banners flutter all over the place, coloring the sky. Amid the racket, the colorful streamers and lovely votive candles, an old woman is sobbing her heart out. Mixing death with life—which our Judeo-Christian civilizations refuse to do—is, to me, heartening. And for starters, as the color of mourning, white is so much more attractive.

Then the attendees turn away from the corpse and take an interest in me, the foreigner. Here, for once, it's the women who put their hands on Ulysses, checking the tire pressure, seeing how it rolls, and squeezing the large water pouch with their fingers, clearly wondering what the soft bag has in it.

I've been back on the road for two or three hundred yards when an out-of-breath monk catches up to me. He hands me a piece of paper covered in ideograms, which, upon my return to France, Sofy translates for me. It's a word from the widower and it says: "Honorable Friend, you can take things (photos?) if you want. Please give us some." He then indicates his name and address in the small town whose name, it turns out, means "village of the little river." He will have his photos.

Zhangye, a city of four hundred thousand, is significant to me for a perfectly pragmatic reason: it's the halfway point in my journey. Looking back over these past forty-three days, I have no choice but to rate them mostly positive in spite of the Gobi's cursed winds and my mindset, which, ever since Paris, has had me barricading myself in, rather than opening myself up to the world. There's no denying that Route 312 is not all that much fun. What, of that legendary Silk Road, still remains? The books I read had me thinking it still existed. Reality has reduced it to nothing, and I have to confess that I've covered these last nine hundred miles on the edge of an abyss, like a child just having discovered—but still refusing to believe—that Santa Claus is nothing but a myth.

At the hotel, my appearance and my pull-cart grab people's attention. I'm offered a room in this three-star hotel for ninety yuan, which must be the unadvertised Chinese rate. The only rate I see is the one for foreigners: 380 yuan.

Zhangye was not always Chinese. The emperor Wudi, who reigned in the second and first centuries BCE, built military forts in Gansu, in Dunhuang, and here, and he shipped in colonists in for the forced Sinicization of the population. Nearly two million soldiers and peasants, accompanied by their families, took control of the region. In the seventh century, the Tang dynasty generals, who owned seven hundred thousand horses here, used this place as a staging ground for their campaigns against the Mongols and Tibetans.

Three centuries later, it was these latter groups who occupied the region, until Temüjin—aka Genghis Khan—finally drove them out.

Bad news in my email inbox. The Seuil Association, founded with a few friends and a great many supporters, seeks to rehabilitate at-risk young people through the therapeutics of . . . walking.* In pairs and accompanied by an adult, they backpack for 2,500 kilometers (1,500 miles) in a foreign country. This novel approach, practiced for many years in Belgium's Flemish-speaking region, is reputed to yield very good results: post-hike, sixty percent of juvenile delinquents resume a normal life and the courts never hear from them again. Seuil's first expedition set off for Italy a month before my journey began, led by my friend Marcel. Accompanying him were two young men: Christophe, a hard-core repeat offender, and Nicolas, who also had some run-ins with the law. The group planned to arrive back in Paris at the same time as me. Well, a message informs me that, after a series of confrontations, Christophe apparently threw in the towel and ran off, convincing Nicolas to flee with him. It's devastating news. I was counting on the success of this first experience in order to convince judges and public authorities that it's a recipe that works. I respond to my friends and ask them to keep me informed, knowing full well that I won't be able to read their reply until the next city I'm in with an Internet cafe. The news pulls the rug out from under me, and for several nights I'm unable to sleep. Seuil is an adventure I truly believe in! And, before handing it off to someone else, I want to be sure it's successfully up and running. Only then will I be able to "rest."

---

* See the appendix.

VII

THE GREAT WALL

Seven hours after setting out from Zhangye, I finally see it. In fact, I couldn't possibly miss it, for the Great Wall stands directly in my path! They bored a hole in it to allow the ribbon of asphalt through. "Great" is a bit of a misnomer. It ought to be called the *Long* Wall, given that it stretches for over three thousand miles, or perhaps the *Immense* Wall, or better yet, the *Immortal* Wall. Unlike what tourists see near Beijing, or the brand-new wall I saw at Jiayuguan, here, it shows its age. No stone- or tile-rejuvenating creams have been applied. It's a wall of raw brick and dry mud, approximately sixteen feet wide at the base and thirteen at the top. On the "barbarian" side, the railing elevates it to about twenty-five feet. Time has taken its toll. But after two thousand years, it still stands. Holes have been drilled in it here and there, wherever men wanted to put their roads through. In the valleys, spring floods have carried it away, but *Changcheng*— the Great Wall—still endures, in defiance of wind, rain, barbarians, and bulldozers. I walk in its shadow, fascinated by this long yellow ribbon, which sprouts a square tower every third of a mile. The towers have suffered more than the wall, for rain has destroyed their roofs, and mud has invaded the rooms and the stairways that, on the "defenders" side, once provided access to the rampart walkway. All that remains of them are compact slabs of earth. I vainly search for an incline or staircase I could use to climb to the top. But the soil they're made of is too friable and the wall is too steep for anyone to scale them.

The road runs along the yellow wall as if it, too, were admiring the structure. How many men, soldiers, merchants, pilgrims, and diplomats have walked in its shadow over the last two thousand years? How many thousands of cavalrymen have ridden past, searching for an opening? How many armies have defended it? One hundred thousand soldiers guarded these walls. The small garrisons served less to defend them than to sound the alarm should troops of Mongol nomads arrive at breakneck speed on their short, jittery, Przewalski's horses. As soon as an adversary was in view, news traveled from one tower to the next, all the way to Xi'an. Communication at the speed of sound and light. Light—in the form of the fires that carried the message, weather permitting. Sound—that of the cannon that confirmed the dispatch, rain or shine. The code consisted of one to five signals. One bonfire and one cannon shot: the arrival of a cavalry of fewer than one hundred men. Two cannon shots and two bonfires: a company of five hundred men. Three times two signals: one thousand men. Five cannon shots and five fiery lights meant that an army of over five thousand men was advancing on the Middle Kingdom.

In consideration of the distances, garrisons had to be self-sufficient. The soldiers, therefore, took up farming and ranching. The Empire reaped double benefits: it sent convicts—gallows birds released from prisons on the promise that they would protect the border—to the country's farthest reaches, thereby getting rid of thugs, and simultaneously putting them to good use in locations where it was most vulnerable.

When it comes to the Great Wall, we find ourselves navigating between myth and reality. I once read, for example, in a well-respected guidebook that "the bonfires were fueled by wolf droppings." There's no question that in Kyrgyzstan, cow dung is the nomads' main source of fuel for their fires. But to suggest that wolf droppings were all that was used to keep the Great Wall's warning signals burning is clearly exaggeration designed to embellish the story.

In terms of its length, the venerable old wall is quite impressive, but its height is less so. As compared to the walls of medieval European castles, one would think that resolute troops could easily scale it. All it would take is a simple ladder. But that would be neglecting the fact that attackers were on horseback and that, without their steeds, they were nothing. From this standpoint, the wall was more of a speed bump than an insurmountable obstacle, allowing those under attack to organize their defense. Genghis Khan, who cleared the Great Wall without a fight, defined it differently. "A wall," he said, "relies less on height than on the valor of its defenders." And he bought off the general in command!

This wall, incredibly sound despite its apparent fragility, sets me dreaming. In the evening, I decide to camp nearby. And, in my tent, invaded by Silk Road ghosts, I dream of the slow camel caravans that, protected by the wall, undulated over this vast plain with their precious bundles, guided by resolute merchants under the watchful eyes of soldiers—distracted momentarily from their vigil, but always alert—fearing riders from the steppe.

If it needed to be defended, it's because it was immensely rich; "The Great Shiny One" made the Mongols' almond eyes gleam with envy. The Chinese called them the Xiongnu (the "Stinky People"). With respect to how the Han people regarded their neighbors, it's a revealing epithet! They claimed that the Xiongnu were born of a union between a white doe and a blue wolf. During the siege of Beijing in 1215, sixty thousand young virgins committed suicide rather than serve as birth mothers for the Xiongnu's children.

The Mongols, for their part, showed no mercy and it was unusual for them to leave any survivors once they had conquered a city.

Thanks to Silk Road trade, the Middle Kingdom had an abundance of gold. Pliny the Elder estimated that Rome disbursed over fifty million sestertii each year to buy silk and other products from China, especially pepper—which was used as a tonic, a drug, an aphrodisiac and . . . a moth repellent.

I've been on the road for a half hour when a thought brings me to a halt. Where did I put my notebook and map? I could probably manage without my map. But not my notebook! It has all the addresses of the friends I've met and to whom I need to send photos and news after I return home! My negligence infuriates me: how could I have been so careless? Too bad for the lost time and fatigue, I turn around and head back . . . all the way to my campsite where my notebook is waiting for me, next to the fire I made last evening. As for the map, it sprouted wings and wedged itself at the foot of the wall. I overlooked the one rule I repeat to myself every day: "Think to close all your pockets, for goodness's sake!" And I immediately bury my notebook deep within my pack and start a fresh one. So as to limit the loss were I to be forgetful yet again.

Two days later, in the wee hours of the morning, it's a real joy to head out onto a poplar-tree-lined road with the sun coming up; the feeling is tempered, though, by an inauspicious grinding in Ulysses's right hub. The rising sun casts long shadows crosswise, creating what looks like a stairway to infinity. That's when I notice, coming on foot in the opposite direction, a startling little man. When he sees me, he bursts out laughing, and, walking toward him, I do the same. He's a Tibetan monk on his way to Labrang Monastery in Xiahe, from where he will continue on to Lhasa. We could be brothers: his head is shaved, he wears a graying, three-day-old beard, and his face and hands have been baked on and off by the sun and rain. My "little Buddhist brother," Shu Bao Sheng, is fifty-six years old and has a resounding laugh that makes him almost close his eyes, reducing them to two slits beneath very black eyebrows, like circumflex accents. He's wearing a blue silk outfit, a large vest, and roomy pants cinched below the knee by white stockings. His shoes, or slippers rather, are brown canvas with thin plastic soles. His backpack is a perfect example of Chinese ingenuity: two articulated panels formed by a bamboo structure lined with a mesh net. The two panels, closed by a string, contain a burlap bag in which he keeps all his belongings—the bare minimum, judging by the bag's size. His face is protected by a large straw hat; in his right hand, he holds an iron-bound staff, and in his left, a string of yellow-amber prayer beads.

He greets me with a courteous bow, his palms joined as in prayer. He sets down his pack, unties a small horsehair rug, and, spreading it out on the side of the road, we sit down face to face, oblivious to the traffic. From my pouch, I take apples and grapes; he offers bread and dried apricots. We're instantaneously on the same wavelength. He reads my little papers, albeit with some difficulty, since Chinese isn't his mother tongue. But, as was the case when I met Liu last year, the mutual affinity we have for one another has no need for words. We understand one another through signals and laughter. He takes from his pack a precious relic: the book of a sage, whose photograph appears on the flyleaf. It shows a relatively young monk seated in lotus position, who, through a photomontage, looks to be floating on air in front of a small Buddhist temple. This is the guru my monk is going to see in Labrang. He happily shows me a photograph in which he himself is standing beside the sage. Shu could be the young monk's father, but that doesn't keep him from expressing great reverence for him.

He has come from Xi'an, and has traveled over 746 miles. I'm astonished at how modest his pack is; he makes fun of all my gear perched atop Ulysses. East confronts West! I still have a long way to go before achieving true simplicity. His pack, which I pick up, must weigh less than a dozen pounds. This man has cast off every unnecessary thing. But he maintains, nevertheless, exemplary cleanliness, whereas I look dirt poor. On that account as well, I have a lot to learn. The Westerner owns things, and therefore dirties them. Now there's something for me to meditate on.

When we feel that we're full up on smiles, affectionate gestures, and displays of sympathy, he buckles his little bundle and, with one sweeping motion, lifts it onto his back. He stows his glasses, book, and photos in a fanny pack he wears around his belly, salutes me with the same bow as when he arrived—palms together once again—and, smiling just as brightly, decisively turns away. He walks off with a quick step, his staff setting the tempo, and he never once turns around to look back. This man lives every moment of his life intensely, with keen awareness, having learned to do without non-essentials, those bonds that dupe us. I must learn from his example!

Fengshenbao is a village perched high atop a mountain at 2,350 meters (7,700 feet). The Great Wall doubles back here to encircle a tall mountain atop which was constructed, back in the day, an observation tower and signal lights. From so high up, there must be a view to the ends of the earth! As there's neither a hotel nor a *luguan* in the village, the restaurant owners suggest that I sleep in the same room where I have my meal, on a sofa. News of my arrival having spread through the village, Xu Zang Ming, an English teacher at a nearby junior high school, drops by to pay me a visit. Like most teachers who have studied English in China, his book-learning is very good, but he has practically never spoken the language. The man has an honest, friendly face. He suggests that we go to see his students.

"At 8:30 in the evening? Are they still in class?"

"In after-school studies."

Chinese children work very hard. Their day begins at 6:30 a.m. with a fitness and gymnastics workout. Classes run from 7:00 a.m. to 6:00 p.m., followed by two and a half hours of study hall and independent work.

The students are very taken by my presence. Xu asks them to speak with me, but they just sit there, mute as fish. One girl, less intimidated than the others, brings me her English book and asks me to sign it. Then there's a stampede. Forty kids stand in line, a book, workbook, notebook, or piece of paper in hand. Xu tells me that in ten years of teaching, he has hosted two foreigners: his university English professor, and me. He invites me for tea at his house, a single-room apartment on the school grounds where he lives with his young wife. They're so wrapped up in their work that they've placed their little daughter with Xu's mom. Deeply honored by my visit, the director of the junior high school comes over to greet me, and suggests that I spend the night in the school building. They're going to let me use a room. I'll be better off here than on the innkeeper's couch.

Xu makes one thousand yuan a month (about $125). The school-teachers, eighteen men and four women, are all housed on school grounds. Most of the kids bike back to their village each evening. Compulsory elementary school lasts five years in China, so-called "middle" school three, and "upper middle" school another three. Those who want to keep going have to take the University entrance exam. The school year is split into two semesters: from September 1 to January 15, then from February 28 to July 15, with six weeks of vacation in between. Each child pays three hundred yuan per semester. It goes without saying that poor farmers don't send their children to school beyond the five compulsory years. By the time most girls are thirteen, they're working on the farm, and there are only a few in the class I've stopped to see. Before I leave, the children ask for a photograph, and a schoolmistress offers to snap the picture. I'm literally smothered by all the kids who want to pose right next to the foreigner. Could you even imagine such a scene in a small French city . . . in Auvergne, for example?

The next day, Ulysses is off for a visit to the village mechanic. A true master. In no time at all, the wheel is dismounted and examined. A child who appears out of nowhere brings over some ball bearings picked up who knows where, and the wheel is promptly remounted.

For today, a mountain pass at 2,500 meters (8,200 feet), then arrival in Xiaoquanzi. Changcheng—that's the Great Wall's name—splits the village in two. In the courtyard of a house, one square tower still stands. The person living there has rebuilt the collapsed upper wall and covered it with a sod roof. And for privacy, he surrounded it with a small wall. Thus protected, it will last several more centuries, if, that is, a bulldozer doesn't decide one day that it's in the way. Behind the village, an old earthen fort is nearing total collapse. It was once home to a garrison of reinforcements ready to intervene at any point along Changcheng, should someone sound the alarm. A dungeon, square like the tower, was used as the soldiers' place of final retreat in the case of an attack. Today, it serves as the village's public restroom, and should only be visited wearing boots.

The inn where I lodge is a *luguan* in name only. The couple puts me up in their own bedroom, one sufficiently vast—and honorable—for them to also park their most prized possession in it: their motorcycle. The big bike stands right in the middle of the room, decked out like a bride. Wool sleeves have been knitted for its handgrips and a splendid paper rose artistically accents its large tachometer. The rims have been polished with love. The remaining space is for human use: a clay platform—the *kang*—on which mats have been set. This is where the entire family sleeps in the winter. The *kang* is, in reality, a stove, and it's fueled through holes bored in the house's rear wall. The fire heats both the bed and the room. I go around to the building's "backside" to see how it functions. It's an open-air stable. Cow dung patties, once they've been carefully collected, are tossed against the wall where they stick and dry in the sun. Once they've hardened, they're thrown onto a pile to be used as next winter's fuel.

At an elevation of 2,200 meters (7,200 feet), the scenery is magnificent, the horizon rises to infinity in a series of levels, and I stop to describe them. The first is Changcheng's long yellow ribbon, followed by a soft green band of cropland, that leads up to the darker line of poplar trees. Farther behind is the black stripe of mountains, then, between these dark peaks and the blue of the sky, the line of eternal snows.

Shortly before Yongsheng, the Great Wall veers northeast, and I, southeast. It's the last we'll see of one another. My thoughts go out to Gayle Hall, who will pass this way in a few more days—if, that is, she was ultimately allowed to continue her walk along the Wall.*

In my stopover city, all I find is a filthy *luguan*. Manure from the stable sits piled up in the yard and the room next to my bedroom is, in fact, a pigsty, and in it, an oinking pig that reeks almost as badly as I do. I just hope I won't keep him from sleeping!

---

* TN: She was.

VIII

DEPRESSION

I've left the desert once and for all now. I traverse two or three villages each day. There's farmland everywhere: wheat, corn, and cotton. I no longer have to worry about finding a table or a bed. Just to be safe, though—maps can be full of surprises!—in my pack, I keep two full water bladders, and a two-day supply of food.

June 1 is Children's Day. In Fengle, the parade they held yesterday was such a success that they've decided to do it all over again today. There are about two hundred kids aged eight to fourteen, and they're all decked out in costumes. First come the flag-bearers, waving brightly-colored banners atop long bamboo poles. The boys look like sailors in the uniforms and berets of the Chinese Navy. Next come the trumpets—also just boys—in fancy white officers' costumes, trimmed with gold. The third group, that of tambourines and cymbals, is made up of boys and girls sporting the traditional orange costumes of Tibet. The girls, in long white robes with large red polka dots, are bringing up the rear, dancing and waving large pink-and-green hand fans. Clearly, vivid colors are a must.

I look on with admiration, amazement, and amusement, while across from me, people look at *me* with amazement and amusement. It's a game of who can out-astonish who!

I draw a great deal of attention. At the market, everyone—men and women—stops what they're doing to watch me go by. Of course, I'm inured to it. But the boy who offers to take me to the *luguan*, upon seeing how many people are staring at us, is bothered. He's suddenly not so keen on accompanying me there and, without a word, takes off running. But I, on the other hand, have no choice, so I continue my way up main street, unruffled, gawked at by a thousand pairs of amazed eyes. To tell the truth, I feel a bit uncomfortable, despite how accustomed I've become here to being gazed at so intently and with such curiosity. Our culture doesn't prepare us to be stared at like this, to be examined without restraint. Here, curiosity is natural and people don't hide it. But what could I do about it anyway? I don't speak their language and even if I did, I could never explain to every person I meet who I am and what I'm up to. A billion and a half Chinese makes for quite a few!

Another onslaught when I arrive at the *luguan*. My bedroom is invaded by twenty or so Hui who grope Ulysses and loudly comment on my arrival. Loneliness—feeling isolated because of language, I mean—has taken a heavy toll on me this year. But this rabble rush bothers me even more. Will I soon find myself longing for the winds of the Gobi?

The designers of the *luguan's* bathroom planned for a crowd, and there are six seats; that is to say, six holes in a concrete slab. Two are already occupied by young men smoking cigarettes and conversing as if they were in a sitting room. I choose the fourth hole, as I'm not here looking for conviviality. But no sooner have I squatted down than a band of teens comes in and makes themselves at home, sitting down across from me, to my right, and to my left. What does a Westerner look like when he's taking a dump? Do male big-noses have just one big-appendage, or two?

I'm horrified to learn that a rock concert is scheduled to take place in the hotel courtyard this evening. For heaven's sake! I console myself: if I'm unable to sleep, I'll draw up clean copy of my notes.

For heaven's sake once again! So that these miserable noise-pollution perpetrators have all the electricity they need for their sound system, at nightfall—around 8:30—power is shut off to the entire neighborhood. So I decide—though I have to say I'm not too happy about it—to attend the concert! The audience is rather thin: do the tickets cost too much? Is the music too modern for the Fengle Chinese? The show is just like those I've seen many times on Chinese TV: a singer performs against a backdrop of male and female dancers. The more famous the star, the more elaborate the choreography. Here, there are six singers and four musicians. The music is awful, but at least in terms of decibels, the audience gets their money's worth. Four musicians manage to keep the entire city awake, despite it being plunged into darkness on their account. And when they finally take a well-deserved break, it's only to make way for a glamour girl recruited, no doubt, more for her magnificent jet-black hair than for her shrill, overly-syrupy voice—one that has me uncontrollably grinding my teeth. In fact, a lamb tied up in a corner of the courtyard finally decides it can no longer bear the ordeal, and makes sure everyone knows by letting out a long, mournful bleat—one in remarkable harmony with the young soprano's quavering voice. I'd even go so far as to say that the lamb bleats more musically than the pinup. I'm no animal rights extremist, but when, in the morning, I see them killing the poor beast, I find myself thinking that they ought to have sacrificed it the night before and spared it from having to endure the concert!

Fengle is home to many Muslims. But the farther east I travel, the deeper I find myself in lands where Buddhism is the principal religion.

I've decided to try my luck at extending my visa in Wuwei, since waiting until Lanzhou might be too risky if I'm slowed down even a little. In the meantime, I find a hotel and head out for my first visit of the city. The spot I discover is extraordinary. A massive gate opens out onto a large courtyard in which ten hangars have been erected. Each one is big enough to house a commercial jetliner. But instead, they're filled with rows of tables that together can seat hundreds of guests. The Chinese enjoy eating in large crowds. Each hangar offers a culinary specialty. There's one for grilled meats and kabobs, another for noodles, and yet another for poultry, where one can taste chicken feet—a real treat which the Chinese relish—and crispy Peking duck.

Two or three other hangars are designated for selling clothing, mostly women's apparel; another is used for parking bicycles; the next-to-last houses chess players; and there are billiards addicts in the last. Everything takes place beneath kaleidoscopic, flashing neons, and in a clamorous cacophony provided by a diverse music mix playing full blast, jazzed up by the screeching of scooter motors, the cries of itinerant vendors, and delivery men on tricycles who, instead of ringing bells, tap their handbrakes against the frame. In short, I have before me the principal Chinese delights: buying and selling, noise, crowds, games, and good food.

I head off in search of an Internet cafe to check my email. I've been waiting for news of Christophe all week. It's a major disappointment: nothing. I return to my hotel demoralized and am up all night, discouraged and depressed; I alternate between feelings of anger and defeat. I begged my friends to send me news of the young men on their first hike in Italy. It was a simple question: "Is Christophe still walking, or did you send him home?" The fact that after two weeks I've received nothing but silence is maddening. Has my career as a journalist conditioned me to feel this way? Once a question has been asked, say whatever you want, but say something, dammit! I imagine all the possible scenarios. Are my friends not replying in order to spare me some particularly devastating news? Do they think that, with my walk in China, I already have enough to worry about as it is? Or that, after all, since I'm traveling, I shouldn't be involved? In the morning, I dash back to the Internet cafe and send an unforgiving email, railing against their "conspiracy of silence." But once again, in light of the difference in time zones and the fact that I have to leave, I won't hear back for another week. I'm so flustered by it all that it doesn't even cross my mind to phone them.

In the days that follow, I start brooding, blaming myself as the main reason for this setback—after all, something must have gone wrong! It serves me right. I set off on my final Silk Road journey with somewhat of a guilty conscience. I left my friends fully in charge of Seuil's first expedition, the most important one! It's all my fault: I could have stayed in Paris or delayed my walk until the following year. That will teach me to stick my finger into too many pies. And if that first journey turns out to be a fiasco, then why did I waste so much energy on it, since it's all for nothing? I'll willingly endure the solitude of the desert and loneliness due to my inability to communicate with the Chinese; I'll gladly contend with the fatigue of walking, and the various dangers that lurk in these lands. But all these hardships are only worth it if they lead to something more. Otherwise, what's the point? Perhaps I'd be better off going back home and pruning my rosebushes, which must be struggling by now in their lonely battle with powdery mildew. For the first time since Istanbul, the temptation to give it all up is unbearable and I can't get it out of my mind. This serious setback is going to get the best of my iron will.* But, for the time being, since I can't make any decisions until I have the answer to my question, there's another urgent and rather important matter I have to attend to in Wuwei: to try to get my visa extended for two months.

I've been warned that my chances are next to zero, since the Chinese grant visa extensions in dribs and drabs. At the third address, I finally locate the office of the MPS, the Chinese Ministry of Public Security. I ask for the visa office. They tell me to wait. A half hour goes by. Time, in Central Asia and China, passes more slowly than back home. It's been an hour. I force myself to keep my cool. A young woman, back from the market carrying a variety of plastic bags, comes over to me. It takes me a moment to realize that *she's* the visa office. Speaking halting English, she asks for my passport. She sets down her bags, takes a seat on the guard's cot who had me wait in his lodge, and at long last takes a look at the document. I explain to her,

---

* Christophe, after walking 900 miles across Italy, did indeed give up. But the teen, a repeat offender, was placed in the charge of two intelligent people back home: a judge and an educator who rightly considered that his efforts deserved their reward. Our outstretched hand was not in vain! In 2005, three years after his walk, the youth-turned-adult had not even once gone back to his old ways. He was out of the woods and was learning a trade.

speaking English as slowly as possible, that my visa will soon expire and that I'd like to extend it for two more months so that I can reach Xi'an. After an eternity, she looks up: "Your visa is no longer valid."

I leap to my feet. My visa is valid for two months and I have been in China for only a month and a half. But I avoid raising my voice. Sofy had given me good advice: "Don't get worked up, smile. In China, you must never get angry. To do so is to lose face. Smile."

"No longer valid? Really?"

"Your visa is valid two months starting March 8. Since May 8, you've been in the country illegally."

I smile, as promised. Is she doing this intentionally or what?

"No. March 8 is the date the visa was issued. I entered China on April 16, so it's valid until June 16."

She dives back into the document. She's honestly confused and doesn't understand how the visa is formatted. I was ready for everything *except* a bureaucrat in charge of visas who doesn't know how to read them! I've occasionally confused the *period* of validity with the *limit* of validity in the past. But it's not what I do for a living! Three, four, five times she repeats the sentence that's about to make me "lose face," no doubt about it: "Your visa is no longer valid." But if it isn't linked to the date of arrival in a country, a visa is meaningless. I smile, I smile! Each time that I try to calmly explain the issue, she balks. What business is it of mine, anyway, a lowly tourist and a foreigner to boot, who has had it drummed into him that cops are always right? I explain over and over again, ending each time by: "Do you understand?" She consistently replies: "Understand." But the line across her brow is clear proof that she doesn't "understand" a word of it.

Finally, I'm asked to follow her up to her fifth-floor office. There, I find two of her colleagues, and it's in them that I place all my hopes. But one offers me a cup of tea, then returns to his work; the other ignores me. The young woman—she can't be more than twenty-five years old—will have to figure it out all on her own. When she tells me for the hundredth time that my visa is valid only until June 8 (the last day by which it can be used to *enter* the country), I take offense . . . and a piece of paper. I sketch a timeline on it, and explain:

"Look: my visa was issued on March 8 and I have to enter China within three months, no later than June 8. That's the *period of validity*. If I enter *before* the first date or *after* the second, I'm in violation. Do you understand?"

"Understand."

This time, she smiles. The first inning is a win. Smile, Bernard, smile!

"Okay. Take a look at the stamp issued by the border police. I arrived on April 16. That falls between March 8 and June 8. Understand?"

"Yes."

"Perfect. Now, look at this number: my visa is valid for sixty days, or two months. We have to count down this period starting with the day I entered the country, that is to say, April 16. If we add two months to that date, we arrive at June 16. So I can remain in China until June 16. Understand?"

"Understand."

"Now, the problem I'm facing is that I still need a month and a half more in order to reach Xi'an on foot. So, I'm requesting a two-month extension."

She thinks about it for a long time, fixing the dates in her mind, and making sure that I haven't been talking gibberish. Finally, she picks up her telephone. I smile and smile. I sip my tea. My heart must be pounding at 110 beats per minute! After what seems like an eternity, she hangs up and tells me that she had her boss on the phone, and that he concurs, and so she's going to give me an extension.

"All right! For two months?"

"No, for just one. I'm not allowed to give two months."

It's as if she had poured cold water all over my enthusiasm, but I smile and smile. If it isn't one problem, it's another. The young woman informs me that she'll need an hour to fill out all the paperwork, then naively admits:

"This is the first time I'm extending a visa."

You don't say! One hour and many teas later, she hands me back my passport with a visa on it marked, as clear as day: "Issued June 3. Valid until July 16, 2002." I return to my hotel, hardly any cheerier than when I left my room this morning. Yes, I have my visa. But I'm once again going to have to hurry along if I want to reach my destination before it expires: I still have something like eight hundred miles to cover in forty-one days.

In a kind of grotto hollowed out beneath a temple, I visit the "flying horse," a small copper figurine made in the image of a galloping horse, its back leg planted on a swallow. It was discovered in a rather strange way. During the cold war, China, fearing an American attack, had called upon the Chinese people to dig underground shelters. That's how some peasant farmers wound up exhuming the age-old tomb of a general, in which had been placed the sculpture in question along with several other bronze horses and carts. One of the farmers figured they ought to inform a university professor, and the sculptures were transferred to a museum. China decided that the "flying horse" would be the country's tourism emblem. The sculpture's elegance and the way it captures movement are extraordinary.

After another night plagued by the question preying on my mind—What has become of Christophe?—I head back out on the road having received no reply. I've often said that, when traveling such great distances, you don't walk with your feet, but with your head and your willpower. My feet are in pretty good shape, other than that the bunion on the left one has flared up, and the right one has the beginnings of a plantar wart. But if I tell them to move, they move. Only now, my head's no longer in the game. I'm dragging. Every mile feels like a marathon: I push on mindlessly; this has turned into a joyless hike. In the days that follow, the only word I jot down in my journal is *RAS* (French for "FED UP"). I've grown completely numb, I'm an automaton walking only because I've been programmed to. I'm dry, devoid of dreams and imagination. I'm blind to the world.

Villages are many and I could easily find some *luguan* to stay in, but I'm so angry, and my morale so low that I prefer to steer clear of humankind. I set up my tent on a whim. But the moment I stop, country farmers come running from out of the blue. Aside from in the desert, there's no escaping mobs in a country teeming with people! Women farmers offer me turnips. Turnips! All I want are answers from Paris!

The countryside on the way to Gulang is beautiful. After extremely flat terrain leading up to Wuwei, now I'm in the mountains. That means, of course, that I'll have to cross over a series of mountains and drag Ulysses, who doesn't help much. But these green curves, these passes at over 2,000 meters (6,600 feet), these alpine meadows where peaceful herds of goats, sheep, horses, and, less frequently, cows graze on low, flowering grasses—it all perks me up a bit. Here and there, so high that you have to crane your neck to admire them, temples with glazed-tile roofs, and pagodas, either cleave to slopes or sit perched atop ledges reachable only by vertiginous pathways opened up by the footsteps of pious believers. On the mountain, beyond the torrent, clinging to a near-vertical wall, are men who, from my location, look minuscule, armed with digging bars; they're dislodging chunks of rock, which hurtle down a slope for two or three hundred yards, bouncing as they go, then finally shattering on the banks of the stream. They work with one hand, holding on with the other. Were a man to plummet to the bottom, he would shatter by the banks of the stream, too! In the village street later on, I run into a few former quarry workers hobbling along on crutches.

The village *luguan* is quite filthy, but I decide to stay there anyway as it's threatening to rain. It begins to fall during the night. In the morning, nasty weather has settled in. There's no point in waiting for it to clear, it looks like an all-day rain, and I have no time to lose. The rain is intense and ice-cold; the sky is black and heavy; we're at 2,300 meters (7,550 feet). Wrapped in my large cape, I terrify a young boy on his way to school. Spotting me from afar, he crosses over to the other side of the road. I let go of Ulysses in order to empty a boot sloshing with water. I don't know what he's thinking, but he turns back and takes to his heels. A group of three young girls is heading down the hillside and the coward places himself in their protection. They greet me cheerfully. It's raining harder than ever. For three hours, I walk in a deluge.

Arriving in Anyuan, a village clinging to a hillside, I find streets that have become torrents of red mud, swept down from the mountains. I'm soaked, frozen, numb from the cold. I go into a restaurant and immediately create a large puddle, but no one minds. While they're cooking up a large serving of noodles for me, I change from head to toe in an adjoining room and wring out what I was wearing, creating new puddles on the dirt floor, then hang my clothes on a line that the manager has strung across the room. After gulping down a scalding cup of tea and the huge meal, I'm soon ready to head back out.

The rain hasn't lessened one bit. There's no way I'm going to let the only dry clothes I have get soaked. I donned them only a moment ago, and I'm going to need them tonight. So I undress and put back on the icy clothes that had almost no time to dry. Only two steps into the street-torrent, my boots are buckets once again. But you get used to it. Two hours later, I cross over the mountain pass at 2,950 meters (9,680 feet). The curtain of rain robs me of what must be a fine view on clear days. I curse all the earth and begin the descent. I'm five miles from Dachaigou when a bus stops, after a woman asked for a bathroom break. As I'm passing nearby, the driver asks using sign language:

"Where are you heading?"

"To Dachaigou."

"Hop on."

Well, against all expectations and contrary to everything I stand for, I climb aboard! In the valley, a truck that had gone down into the river to take on a load of stones got caught in the rising water. All that's visible of it now is the cab's rooftop. A little farther, a truck that had driven off onto the soggy shoulder has overturned, spilling its logs into a field of wheat. At Dachaigou, I take shelter in a restaurant and do another striptease routine like the one I did this morning. A plate of caramelized pork with a bowl of rice, washed down with a Chinese beer, cheers me up. I kept up a brisk pace this morning and am tempted to push on all the way to Tianzhu given that the heavy downpour seems to be letting up a bit. That will put me a day ahead of my walking schedule. If I want to arrive before July 16, I'll have to leapfrog many more.

No sooner am I back out on the road than the rain picks up again. At 6:00, I reach the city. It's a Tibetan settlement and is, in theory, off limits to foreigners unless they get a special permit available on site. I don't bother. I'm too cold. At the hotel, I run the lengths of string I have in my pack around my room and manage to hang all my things out to dry. Some are soaked through, such as my sleeping bag. The oilcloth I placed over my pack did nothing to keep the wind-driven rain from getting in. I go for a Pantagruelian meal in the restaurant opposite the hotel, then return to my room, and dive into bed. As I fall asleep, the sky continues to empty itself out over both city and mountains.

In the morning, though the sun's still not shining, the rain has let up. Villages and streets have been transformed into quagmires and, to get from one house to another, the residents jump from stone to stone, or skirt around immense puddles of thick, red mud. The trucks, which power through, never slowing down, splash waves of ochre mud onto the facades. In the river, where the water level is dropping by the hour, families are out looking for treasure that the current might have carried from upstream and deposited onto the banks. But all they find are old, dead trees.

IX

THE YELLOW RIVER

At his inn in Wushangye—a name which, as Sofy later explained, means, "place where one changes horses"—Yuleh sticks me in a corner as far from his other customers as possible. A classy place like his has a hard time accepting a filthy guy like me. But eventually, eaten up with remorse, he comes over to my table.

"Where are you from?"

"Turfan."

"And where are you going?"

"To Xi'an."

"There's a bus every evening, the stop is right out front."

"I'm not taking the bus; I'm traveling on foot."

Yuleh suddenly looks a little green around the gills. I show him my little papers, which he reads aloud. And to top it all off, I'm a retired schoolteacher? In other words, a learned man? He dashes off to the kitchen and brings me back a cup of tea. He has a second dish brought out to me that I didn't order, crosses the street, and returns with two melons. He shares one with me and stuffs the other in my pack. Since I praise his tea, which is deliciously sweet, he loads me down with two bricks of sugar candy that I have the hardest time refusing. I compromise by accepting one crystal as big as a carrot. I enjoy going through the motions of breaking off a piece and dropping it into the cup of tea where it slowly dissolves, still sweetening it even after several cups. Yuleh goes around the restaurant turning me into a sensation. I've become a *persona* très *grata*, and I heard him repeating the word "*laoshi*" at each table, driving it home: Yes, yes, "*laoshi!*" to his customers' disbelief. He even sends for another *laoshi*, a taciturn old roly-poly who must have been a professor before I was even born. But I still don't speak Chinese and the learned old man hasn't the slightest command of French or English, which makes for a trying face-to-face. Yuleh is deeply saddened by this. One of his bubbles has just been burst: two educated people can actually fail to understand one another!

Along the road that day, I lose my two maps of the region between Wuwei and Lanzhou. My little Swiss knife, Ulysses's harness: it's starting to add up to quite a few losses, due to my own absentmindedness! But it's made up for, fortunately, by my foresight: in Paris, I traced my route onto a large map, then cut it up and glued the pieces into a notebook. All I have to do here, then, is to turn pages as the journey progresses. I've had maps stolen before: they fascinate those who've never seen one. They let people who live low to the ground see their region as if from an airplane. I have thirteen road maps with me this year, and ten topographic maps. The latter indicate changes in altitude.

That very evening, someone steals the bungee cord I use to secure my pack on my cart. I made the mistake of leaving it on the ground while unloading my bags at the hotel. The owner, outraged that one of his fellow countrymen would swipe something just outside his establishment, offers me one of his motorcycle bungees. Although these seemingly inconsequential devices are very important to me, I've gained a certain detachment. I have only to resurrect the image of my monk and his light smile to realize that it's not that hard to do without what we once considered indispensable.

Hekou should be called "the dirtiest city." A string of factories spews black smoke into the narrow valley in which the city is nestled. It then quietly mixes with fumes from trucks moving single file along the main drag. They zigzag from one shoulder to the other to avoid deep potholes, stirring up gray dust, thick yet impalpable, which evenly coats the little brick houses lining the road. Refuse has piled up on the sidewalks. Wherever the mound has become too big or the odor too unbearable, it's set on fire and the acrid smoke of smoldering plastic adds to the city's stench. The ruts, who knows why, are full of putrid, stinking water.

So by the time I arrive at the great bridge straddling the river, I'm suffering from smoke inhalation, and the sight of brand-new buildings across the water gives me hope that the neighborhood there may be less stinky. It is; but it proves to be a true pedestrian's nightmare. Running between this city and Lanzhou, the provincial capital, a highway has been built, with three lanes in both directions. A market once took place here, and the construction, not surprisingly, forced the farmers out. But no sooner was the highway completed than they reclaimed the site: the lanes in the Lanzhou direction have been reoccupied by hundreds of farmers. They've come on foot, bicycle, and tricycle; by car, and in carts, pulled either by themselves or by donkeys. And so trucks, cars, and tractors are forced onto the other lanes . . . which, perversely, are back to handling two-way traffic! Imagine the free-for-all. And imagine me trying to worm my way through all the commotion; Ulysses is, after all, a full-fledged vehicle! A fact which, of course, all drivers of four-wheeled vehicles dispute. There's no escaping the chaos. Vehicles rush in wherever space opens up; I even somehow miraculously manage to jerk Ulysses out from under the wheels of a crane truck. They're all honking their horns, people are screaming in order to hear one another, and the restaurants that line the road have turned up their loudspeakers hoping to lure in truck drivers who would clearly be better off switching off their engines and grabbing a bite to eat. But they'd rather just keep honking one another to death. A little farther along, I discover the cause of all this muddle: the last few days' rains and a few broken irrigation channels have resulted in a landslide two hundred yards away, transforming the brand-new highway into a swimming pool. The lanes are impassable in either direction—it's a real hazard.

It's no trouble navigating to Lanzhou: the city can be spotted from faraway thanks to the pall of smog hanging over it. Of the ten most polluted cities in the world, nine are Chinese. This one, squeezed between two high cliffs that prevent it from sprawling anywhere other than along the river, stretches on and on for over twelve miles. Its three hundred thousand inhabitants of fifty years ago have become three million today. A swatch of cotton over my nose, I walk in circles for two hours before finding the hotel I'm looking for; then, scrubbed clean and groomed like a postman's horse, I dash off before nightfall in order to survey the famous Yellow River, the Huang He. The Chinese themselves claim that it's the muddiest river in the world, and indeed, the liquefied loess, flowing lazily between the river's high banks, makes it look like a long ribbon of muddy silt.

And this yellow soil is, in fact, inextricably linked to Chinese civilization. According to the founding myth of the Han people, Nügua was the mother of the first human beings. Like her brother and her husband Fuxi, she had a human head, but her body was that of a serpent. The first thing she did was to create noblemen, kneading them out of the Yellow River's silt; she then went on to create foot soldiers, which she fashioned out of mud. It's said that she also went on to invent writing and marriage. So much for the legend. As for the reality, the Yellow River Basin was indeed where the first Chinese civilizations were born.

I'm in dire need of rest so I decide to spend two days in Lanzhou. I want to make time to visit the famous grottoes at Bingling Si and to see the city's museum the *Gansu Sheng Bowuguan*—the Gansu Provincial Museum—which includes a permanent exhibition entitled "Cultural Remains of the Silk Road." Since I've encountered practically no traces of the Silk Road along China's highways, I'll go looking for her where she can still be found: in the repositories of History! But to my great dismay, the museum is closed for construction. As for my expedition to Bingling Si, it would require a two-hour journey by car followed by an hour-and-a-half-long boat ride, all at a prohibitively high cost, if I'm the only one making the trip. Which happens to be the case. So too bad yet again for these mythical grottoes carved by sculptors who were veritable trapeze artists, for they worked while hanging from ropes suspended in mid-air.

Instead, I spend an entire afternoon at White Pagoda Hill, a park overlooking the city. You reach it by riding a cable car over the Yellow River. The air's cooler beneath the walnut trees, where several Chinese men are playing dominoes and sipping beer. Seeing the city from high up heals many things. Viewed from a distance like this, the city gives you the sense it has an almost human side to it; and so, in the heat of the coming summer, I spend a delightful afternoon here, nonchalantly getting drunk on "Eight Treasures Tea," while whiling away the hours, my soul at rest, enjoying this soft quietude right up to the last moment, broken only by the trills of songbirds in cages up in the branches. The Chinese love these birds. Every morning in city parks, elderly gentlemen bring their feathered friends along with them, and the birds engage in veritable singing contests.

I've fine-tuned the next chapter of my journey: I'm going to leave behind Route 312, which I've been following for the last 1,240 miles, then swing south before turning east once again. But first, I stock up: I buy instant noodles and dried fruit for myself, and a new tire for Ulysses, who goes through them at a rapid rate. And tragically, I check my email inbox: it's as I feared, Christophe chose to go home. Then, as soon as he was back, he regretted the decision. Too late. These troubled teens get just one chance—their last; we can't possibly organize a new expedition every week! And I finally have an explanation for the "conspiracy of silence" that I thought I'd fallen victim to: it was a simple miscommunication. My friends had indeed sent replies to my questions . . . but they used a different email address, one I can only consult in France! I'll think a great deal about Christophe over the next two days. His behavior, in some ways suicidal—in any case, which ended in failure—means that once again he stands no hope of reintegration into society. So there he is, sixteen years old, about to enter prison, having missed the one opportunity he had to avoid it.

But did he really want to? In any case, everyone agrees that the two months' walk he did complete has helped him mature. It's really too bad he gave up halfway through.

Prison is on my mind again as I draw near a crowd out in front of the iron gates of police headquarters. There, they've posted the accomplishments of the region's police officers. This apparently highly policed country has its hands full fighting criminal activity: drug and arms trafficking, money laundering, crime, theft, rape. Forty or so images depict all the plagues afflicting China, on par with the problems facing western nations. How those who stray from the straight and narrow are treated, however, is ghastly, for it's designed to set an example. Chinese law enforcement justifies their violent methods by saying that they're "killing the chicken to scare the monkey." Capital punishment is sometimes carried out in public. When that's not the case, photos of the criminal's dead body are posted for all to see. And, in a uniquely sophisticated twist, the police bill the family for the bullet lodged in the condemned man's neck! Judging from the crowd standing before the gates, the Chinese are captivated by all this information. Publications offering detailed accounts of crimes and atrocities are, it seems, very popular, and they all sing the praises of the army and police. Simplistic propaganda that seems to rub the Chinese the right way.

X

THE SACRED RIVER WEI

Heading south out of Lanzhou isn't easy. The trick is locating the street that leads to the cliff overlooking the city. I get lost for over an hour. When I'm finally on the right road, I catch up to an amusing "cart train." Rather than individually pulling their handcarts loaded with fruits and vegetables, farmers have linked all their carts together, one after another, and the entire train is pulled by a horse. A fine example of teamwork. One of the farmers suggests that I attach Ulysses to the convoy, so that's what I do, to the great delight of the farmers looking on. And during those two hundred yards, before the group makes a right turn, I seize the opportunity to inquire about the road I should take. Their information is correct, for I soon spot the first distance marker displaying the road's name: "212."

The road scales dizzying hills. Acrobatic farmers, literally hanging onto to the slopes where no tractor would ever venture, are busily working the red soil with spades and hoes. Here it is, at long last, that rich loess composed of silt snatched from the mountains and desert and carried here on the winds of the Gobi. Those billions and billions of particles sculpted this landscape, deposited through the millennia in thick layers, and peasant farmers finished the work. The pass rises to 2,700 meters (8,860 feet), but a tunnel was cut through, 200 meters below. The toll booth employee forbids me from going in. After an hour of negotiations, tired of fighting, he finally lets me pass, but, he stresses, at my own peril. With my *cheche* over my mouth and my headlamp turned on, I head in for the unlit and unaerated, two-kilometer-long crossing. Traffic, fortunately, is light, for whenever a vehicle approaches, I have to throw myself against the wall: in drivers' minds, neither I nor Ulysses are vehicles, so they refuse to adjust the course they're on, even a little. I'm relieved when I'm finally back outside in the open air.

Beneath a pediment decorated—like everything here—with willow branches, I enter a gleeful hostel, thanks to a flock of playful kids. Yang Yulong, a chubby boy, proudly writes his name for me in pinyin, along with that of his sister, Yang Yufan. Just as I'm about to get going, the kids beg their mother to find me a room. They put me up in a building in the courtyard, but a step away—yet again—from the pig they're fattening. Is this the subconscious place the Chinese think foreigners should occupy? Yulong and Yufan come to my room carrying a bowl, a pitcher of cold water, and a thermos of hot water so that I can wash up; they also bring me a large pot of tea. Yang Yufan simpers as I snap their photo, but her fat-cheeked brother scolds her: doesn't she know that a photograph is for all eternity? You're supposed to show your good side, Yang Yufan! Don't you see?

The next morning, a farmer selling melons comes over and decorates Ulysses with a willow branch. For today is the fifth day of the fifth lunar month: *Duanwu Jie*, the Dragon Boat Festival. In cities near a body of water or river, boats are being decorated for the race. Around here, though, people simply display willow branches in commemoration of the death of Chu Yuan, a poet and government minister in the third century BCE. Appalled at the corruption that reigned in those days (yes, even then!), he committed suicide by throwing himself into the river. And that's how a rather sad event, one that would warrant gatherings of a reverential nature, has given rise to festivities.

Are these young people trying to say that so long as there are honest men like Chu Yuan, there's no need to worry about the future? The unfathomable optimism of youth has transformed the drama of the man's drowning into a joyous festival. The Chinese are not the only ones to do this. In France, on Bastille Day, we dance in the light of paper lanterns to celebrate the monarchy's bloody downfall. In London, in 1605, a group of Catholic extremists (we would label them "fundamentalists" today) smuggled enough gunpowder into the undercroft of the House of Lords to blow the building, the MPs, and King James I himself to smithereens. And today, English youths merrily set off firecrackers on the anniversary of the "Gunpowder Plot." So I'm not surprised to discover, in a village, big-biceped young men carrying colorful statues of divinities on heavy palanquins. Joyfully shouting, they bounce them into the air: it's their way of having the statues participate in the revelry, too.

A couple dozen Muhammadans wearing their distinctive small white hats—we're a few miles from the Muslim district of Dongxiang—look surprised to see the green branch planted on Ulysses. They do not celebrate *Duanwu Jie* and are astonished—or perhaps outraged?—to see a foreigner doing so. But I pay them very little attention, for I have more important things to worry about: whoever planted the signposts at this intersection must have imbibed in a little too much rice wine. According to my map, the city of Linxia looks to be about twenty-two miles to the west. And to the south, thirty miles down the same road I've been traveling, is Lintao. Well, the signs both display identical ideograms, as if Linxia and Lintao were in fact the same city. And the distance? One hundred kilometers (62 miles)!! Even so, I take the road to the south, but only that evening is my mind finally at rest: my inspiration was right.

In the *luguan* where I stop, the condition of the buildings and the lack of dirt in the bathroom attest to the fact that it's been open for no more than six months. People come knocking one by one on my door and, giving me a thumbs up, let me know I'm a champion. They're justified in assuaging my low self-esteem this year. My journey has been uninteresting because the route I'm on is uninspiring and because the Chinese are not openly hospitable like all the other ethnic groups I've encountered since I began my journey in Istanbul. It's true that I was too lazy to learn their language, which makes it hard to meet people. I haven't come across any signs of the Silk Road, and Christophe's journey, in which I had placed a great deal of hope, has ended in failure. There's nothing to celebrate! Most Chinese have never even heard of something called "the Silk Road." But the farther I get from Turfan, having now passed the two-thousand-kilometer mark, the more they express their admiration for what I'm doing. On the other hand, they couldn't care less about the fact that I began my journey in Istanbul. It's as if I'd told them I came from nowhere. From what I can tell, these people have a lot in common with Americans, both in their love of baseball caps, and in how they know very little about life beyond their own national borders.

My next-door neighbors are hungry for company. No sooner have I set down my bundle than I hear a soft knocking on my door, and a young man, as shy as a bride on her wedding day, steps in carrying a slice of rice cake lavishly drizzled with amber honey. A second young man, emboldened by the first, comes to let me know by way of abundant gestures—a thumbs up (of course!), a soccer ball kick, and a raised pinkie—that, although I'm a *faguo* (French) champion, the French soccer team certainly is not . . . for it was brutally knocked off its pedestal in ongoing World Cup competition. Finally, without asking, a third man simply plumps himself down to watch today's game. With wide eyes and open mouth, he looks as placid as a steer hounded by flies.

Though I have nothing to buy, I hang out around the market in the little village of Xintianpu. It's a feast for the eyes, a lovely artist's-palette of fruits, vegetables, and fresh scents. Vendors are eager to perk up sales, so they sprinkle their tomatoes with water, they buff their eggplants and peppers, and they stack apricots, lychees, and melons into pyramids. In the neighboring restaurant, I order a bowl of *mifan* (rice) from a matriarch who gives my hobo's beard, worn-out hat, and stained T-shirt a once-over. She decides to be cautious: three and a half yuan (less than $0.50)—do you have that much with you? I show her a handful of bills. Okay fine. Her fears were groundless, and she can head off into the kitchen.

June 17—I've been walking for two months and have covered precisely two thousand kilometers (1,243 miles). One thousand kilometers (620 miles) a month is too much! I traveled twenty-seven miles again today. I need to wise up. After all, I headed out onto the open road to find wisdom, and to finally see the world. . . . Wisdom? Come on now, let's not kid ourselves: I'm no wiser than I was. To finally see the world? I've perhaps succeeded at that every now and then—when my anguished compulsion to do everything right, to simply "hang in," or to keep pressing on didn't keep me from enjoying the scenery. I know that some force compels me to keep going, something bigger than any one reason, something bigger than my own reasoning. And it's surely this "unreasonableness" within me, which I've put my finger on here, that prompts me to give the poor wretch I come upon—he reminds me of the dead man along Route 312—a one-hundred-yuan note. It occurs to me the following day that there's every chance he'll be accused of having stolen it. Such a large sum in this poor human's pocket is bound to arouse suspicion. I should have slipped him smaller denominations.

I stop for a while to watch an artisan coffin-maker busy at work. His creations are large and tall, with very thick covers are raised at the head like the bow of a tall ship. The boards fit together with dovetail pins. I saw the same joints on coffins exhumed from ancient tombs in Jiayuguan. Techniques are no different here than they were two thousand years ago. The resulting piece is lacquered a beautiful reddish-brown color. But though the coffins are lavish, the sepulchers they're laid in are more modest. The Chinese are buried in sites chosen for perfect *qi*. *Qi* is vital energy. Feng shui masters identify the spots with the best *qi* before a site is selected for a home, temple, or tomb, for instance. But each family can also, thanks to qi, search out wealth (*cai*), happiness (*fu*), longevity (*shou*), or healthy children (*zi*).

For the sepulcher's location, the master designates an ideal spot that will ensure the deceased's eternal happiness. This is why, since there are infinite forms of *qi*, there are tombs all over the place. I saw some smack dab in the middle of a potato field. The tubers had reclaimed the site, and potato plants with white flowers and tender green leaves were poking out of the mortuary pyramids. These pyramids are as simple as can be: they're small earthen mounds no more than three feet high on which large, multicolored paper wreathes are burned on the day of the burial. Upon seeing some mounds like this here and there in the desert, I often wondered whether they were really tombs, or whether a truck had simply unloaded a little excess dirt. A few branches had been planted on the more elaborate ones, or the mound had been covered with a few tiles or stones.

I have to stop and watch a solar oven factory for a moment, too. The ovens in question are parabola-like devices—large, slightly concave cement slabs—on which hundreds of tiny rectangular mirrors are glued. They're designed such that the rays of heat and light they reflect converge three feet above the surface. At that precise location is small iron stand on which a kettle can be set. When properly oriented, this solar cooker can bring water to a boil in only a few minutes. Be careful to avoid getting your hand anywhere near: you'd be instantly burned! The Chinese, who mostly use a highly bituminous and polluting variety of coal, are being encouraged to invent natural energy systems, especially those that harness the energy of the sun. Likewise, the roofs of modern buildings are dotted with heat recovery systems.

June 18. An umpteenth mountain pass to climb since leaving Lanzhou. This one, though, is special, for it marks the divide between two watersheds: one empties to the west, the other to the sea. And the stream located there is, for the Chinese, no doubt the most sacred of all. It's the source of the River Wei, upon whose banks Imperial China first flourished. Little by little, this insignificant rivulet will grow, leading me all the way to Xi'an, which was China's capital city for eight centuries, and the Great Silk Road's point of departure and terminus; and for me, it's the final stage in my long walk.

After the pass, the landscape changes: sparse grass covered in purple and blue flowers springs up between terrace gardens of wheat, peanuts, and potatoes. These rise in steps as far as the eye can see, tracing contour lines like arabesques. I'm surprised to find so much wheat in this country, but then again, this is not southern China, which is entirely given over to rice cultivation. For the northern Chinese, wheat is a staple, primarily in the form of noodles. Some, near the edges of the western deserts, even eat bread, a product of civilizations that availed themselves of clay ovens (the Mongol *tandoor*, known here as the *tandir* or *tavus*), the use of which was spread by the Turks, the Persians, or cousins of one or the other, all along the Silk Road.

Down in a dale, having eaten their fill, some cows ruminate under the watchful eyes of two herders. Pastoral, eternal visions, which can be found in every land. The road snakes its way downhill, separating patches of green from a subtle palette. A heather cock cries out, and the inevitable cuckoo replies. In the China I've traveled through, its two-noted song can be heard everywhere, at any hour of the day. Seated in the grass, I daydream beside a whitewater river rushing to the sea, my eyes lost among the ridgelines of hills that wear apricot trees like Mohawk hairdos. My mind conjures up the legend of the god Pangu, as well as that of the monster Gonggong. Pangu was trapped in an egg that split in two: the celestial vault above, and the Earth below. Pangu Earth-and-Sky grew eighteen feet a day for ten thousand years. What's extraordinary about this legend is how similar it is to the modern infinite-expansion theory of the cosmos known as the Big Bang—named for the initial explosion. The other myth that this little river irresistibly reminds me of, singing as it flows over the stones at my feet, is that of Gonggong. In the beginning, the sky was set on four pillars and everything was stationary. But then Gonggong, a clumsy, horned monster, bumped into one of the pillars, Mount Buzhou, and it collapsed. The Earth and Sky were destabilized and tipped to one side. And so it is ever since that rivers flow east and the stars appear to "flow" west!

Roused from my daydream, I suddenly think how, upon reaching the end of this little river, my long walk will be over. For the very first time, I glimpse the possibility that, after four years, I may actually make it to the end of the road. Victory is starting to seem real. I can already picture myself arriving at the ramparts of Xi'an. From this mountain pass on, instead of counting the distance I've traveled from Turfan, I begin counting down how far I have left to go. And I start thinking how a touch of bittersweet nostalgia will temper my triumph: I felt the same thing when I arrived in Santiago de Compostela after walking 1,438 miles over the course of ninety days. Because arrival is also the end of the dream. And only those who've experienced the adventure of walking themselves will understand why some walkers refuse to wake up and, having reached their destination, turn right back around and head home on foot.

For I set out, I walked, and now soon I will arrive! It suddenly sounds ridiculous to sum up my journey like that. A journey that, while still on the road, I'm unable to see as "an adventure," despite plenty of tribulations, and even a couple brushes with death. Where will I arrive? 7,500 miles farther along, to be sure. But not so changed, in the end, from the person I was four years ago when, light of heart—or rather, with a heart light on apprehension, that is—I rode the ferry across the Bosporus. What have I gained from it all? Fatigue, yes. A rich harvest of visual memories, absolutely! But what else? Let's be fair: there were some real thrills, and a good many simple pleasures.

There's nothing to see in Weiyuan that would surprise a Westerner. "Age-old Chinese culture" disappears in the country's cities, dissolving into planetary conventionality and uniformity. Although the Japanese have preserved their traditions and unique identity while at the same time espousing modernity, the Chinese seem enthralled with the most materialistic country of them all, the United States. They cast off "Eastern wisdom" and demolish traditional neighborhoods to make way for skyscrapers. Tourism turns to its own advantage structures that had survived vandals, thieves, and bad weather, thanks to their sturdiness, like the Great Wall, or their low profile, like certain grottoes. Since tourism is an important source of foreign currency, the country did its best to salvage what it could. But in big cities, entire neighborhoods are still being demolished without any plans to restore them. Kids dress like Westerners, sporting baseball caps and T-shirts, the most highly prized of which are emblazoned with sayings in American English.

I get to know two young women who work at my hotel. Wenhua Ouyang, who speaks a little English, and Hongmei Zhao, accept my invitation to dinner. When winsome Wenhua concentrates and tries to find her words in English, her lips carve out a dimple that give her the look of a young girl. She's twenty-two and is taking university courses, but would like to work in tax administration, a field she hasn't managed to find a job in yet. In the meantime, she cleans rooms here from six to noon every day of the week. Hongmei is about thirty and is married. She's a night security guard. We dine in the hotel restaurant. I'd like to try some local specialties, so I ask Wenhua to pick the dishes. Unfortunately, what she orders is hardly new to the Western palate: bamboo shoots, steamed fish, and eggplant. The bill comes to nearly sixty yuan (roughly $7.50) even though, she tells me, she ordered the least expensive dishes. When I don't act shocked by the amount, she continues: her weekly salary is fifty-nine yuan. Spending it all on one meal is unimaginable to her. Our conversation is rather quiet. She studied English on a computer and has a good mastery of vocabulary and grammar. But her pronunciation is incomprehensible, and naturally, she can't understand what I say either. So, we converse using pens. Hongmei ordered noodles since, Wenhua writes, she doesn't like rice. I express my surprise. In Europe, we're under the impression that every Chinese person eats mainly rice. They suggest that I open my eyes. Indeed, all along the road, I saw mostly wheat fields, and in restaurants, the standard dish consists of noodles. So let's not confuse the Northern Chinese with the Southern Chinese!

Wenhua is engaged to a young man who lives 125 miles away. They plan to marry in three years.

"Why three years?"

"Because my parents think it best for me to wait until we both find jobs, then give it a couple more years."

"Do you always listen to what your parents say?"

"Parents are wise. Children should listen to them."

Well said! I'll have to share this with my own children. To think that parents are wise! Only in China!

XI

SICKNESS

June 19. The owner of the *fandian* I settle into at noon has never met a foreigner. Initially wary, before long he's calling me "big brother" and "*shushu*" (uncle), out of affection and respect. He tops off my meal with a sweet rice dessert that I didn't order, then fishes around in his head for all the English words he knows to let me know: "No money!" He has put me in the large dining room all by myself so he can better keep an eye on me, along with all the servers, cooks, and friends who, under various pretexts, pop in for a quick glimpse of the barbarian. It's all very endearing. But I lose interest when, three hours later, I'm felled by a terrible migraine, a sudden high fever, and uncontrollable vomiting. Did the friendly owner poison his *shushu*? What worries me most is that it's not just a bout of turista, the most common form of food poisoning.

I'm up all night, weakened by spasms and the recollection of the sickness that laid me low in Turkey in 1999, and which forced me on a harrowing ambulance ride back to Istanbul. Xi'an is not far away, but I still have to get there! I actually have a course of broad-spectrum antibiotics with me in my first aid kit, but I purchased it last year, and it has suffered through the infernos of the Fergana Valley and Taklamakan Desert, and spent last winter in my attic. Self-medication, as everyone knows, is often worse than the disease.

I have a note delivered to Wenhua, who's working on one of the hotel's floors, in which I ask her to send for a doctor. A half hour later, she shows up with a petite, doll-mouthed woman who diagnoses

271

me with a digestive tract infection. The doctor indicates, by way of Wenhua's little papers, that she's going to give me two injections. That's a good sign. I didn't wind up with a traditional doctor who would have prescribed toad saliva extract or serpent salad! I tell her that she has to use new needles and syringes: I've read horror stories on the spread of AIDS in China. She comes back a short while later with all her paraphernalia . . . but it's hardly reassuring since she already opened the packages in her office, and there's nothing to prove that she's not using recycled needles. But deciding one way or the other can't wait, so I bare a buttock for the intramuscular injection and hold out my arm for the intravenous one. They use a coat rack to hang the infusion bottle, then the two women exit the room. I'm chomping at the bit. I try to sleep. In vain. And little by little, I'm starting to feel worse, for the diffuse pain that gripped me last night is now growing more specific, and I know it well. Perhaps I do have a digestive tract infection, but I also know that these spasms are the result of a new attack of kidney stones. I still have an agonizing memory of the first, which took place a few Decembers ago, the day after Christmas. Fearing that it could happen again on the road, I've had x-rays taken each year to determine whether some of the stones lining my kidneys might be ready to migrate, resulting in another bout of severe pain. I've twice undergone the tolerable torture of the bathtub where they break up the stones with ultrasound. Today, the attack has set in, and the terrible pain is like a knife in my back. There isn't much I can do about it other than wait for the pressure in the kidney to push the stone out. "Above all, don't drink," I was warned. But the IV is sending liquid to my kidneys. My lady doctor won't be back until late next morning. I can't wait. I pull out the needle planted in my vein. The burning sensation becomes unbearable. Although I don't recall exactly how long the ordeal went on, after one particularly excruciating wave of pain, a feeling of peace suddenly came over me. The stone had passed, taking the pain with it, as if it had been wiped away, expunged, just like that!

When the little doctor pokes her head in around noon, I'm busy closing up my pack. She's alarmed by the nearly full perfusion bag, and a little paper from Wenhua informs me that she's very upset, and cannot be held responsible if I don't get at least two days' rest. But the thought of sitting still in this sad room is more frightening to me than that of falling sick again out on the road. At 1:00 p.m., I'm on my way out of the city; at 3:00, it's raining; and at 5:00, soaked to the bone, I set foot into the filthiest *luguan* imaginable. I take care not to poison myself a second time: dieting, along with tea and water I carefully purify myself, will do me good. Now that I think of it, I was very lucky that I didn't fall sick in 2000 and 2001. But what if my luck has finally run out?

It pours all night long and on June 21, the first day of summer, I leave Shanyang in squalls of icy rain that don't let up until I reach Longxi. The city greets you with a pagoda temple boasting a three-tiered, monster-decorated roof. I rather fancy the covered boardwalk, first of all because it protects me from the rain; and second, because of how strangely its painted beams represent scenes of ordinary life, the work of an unconventional artist: a woman has just finished nursing a child and it dances for joy, another breastfeeds a very old woman slumped on a chair. Other scenes depict fruit picking and harvest time.

At the entrance to the bazaar, a charlatan is all business: first, he has bystanders hold little stones, which he claims to have removed from some of his patients. Today, he's doing what he can to remove the wax blockages everyone has in their ears. His little spiel does the trick: even as he's performing his act, people impatiently line up.

In the not-so-interesting little museum housed in what was once the city's fortified gate, I come across what is, according to Emmanuel Lincot, the French guide I met in Kashgar, a very rare painting. According to him, representations of the human body are extremely rare in Chinese artwork. In this case, the painting depicts a bare-breasted woman decorating a vase.

One manifestation of this modesty is the fact that Chinese women always wear socks. No matter how hot it is out, women never show their feet, even if, say, they're in shorts. They wear little white bobby socks, which don't quite do it for European men. Feet, for the Chinese, are considered highly erotic, and the woman who ventures out in bare feet is, in the public eye, doing something indecent, even obscene.

There are floods in Shaanxi, the province whose capital is Xi'an; over one hundred people have gone missing, and there are apparently a number of deaths. In elementary school, I was taught that continental climates have hot and dry summers. What a curious country, where nothing is the way it's portrayed in my books!

It rains even more overnight. After setting out in a downpour at 7:00 a.m., I reach the first village by 9:00, where all I come to is a fork in the road without any signposts. A young woman with two dimples—dimples have always made me weak in the knees—replies: "Wushan? To the right!" To be on the safe side, I ask the same question of a bicycle repairman: "Wushan? To the left!" Taking a closer look at the map, they're both correct. The dimple-road to Wushan would be more pleasant, for it's probably the less-traveled one, whereas the bike-repairman-road is presumably safer, and I would have no trouble finding somewhere to eat and sleep. If only there were a *luguan* in Yuyang, on the dimple-road!

"There is indeed," the bike-repairman assures me, looking over Ulysses and checking my companion's tire pressure.

The little road is lovely. It runs along a partially decommissioned railroad. A few peasants are busy collecting gravel, a rarity in these loess-rich regions.

When I finally glimpse Yuyang, I'm beat. I wonder whether I didn't overestimate my abilities and should have listened to the doctor. A group of locals watches me draw near, and in the eyes of each one, I see the usual mix of surprise, apprehension, and apparent mute indifference. In China, unlike all the other countries I traveled through, I've failed to come across any enthusiasm, any genuine curiosity that has people thirsting to know the Other, arousing a desire to strike up a relationship. Curiosity here is no more than amazement in the face of peculiarity. Jaws drop at the sight of a foreigner, but no one actually wants to come over and say hello.

"Where is the *luguan*?"

"*Meiyou luguan*."

I sit down on a stone, my legs like taffy. I've just traveled twenty miles and Wushan is twelve miles farther. Do I have the strength? After ten minutes' rest, I half-heartedly start back out. A mile down the road, two friendly peasants stop me. They seem curious!

"Is there no lodging in the village?"

"Yes, yes, there is. Come with us!"

I follow them, full of hope . . . and doubt. On the doorstep of a house they stop in front of, an old woman is bouncing a baby on her knees. She seems surprised, and my understanding is that there's a *fandian* near the train station, but that the *luguan* has been closed for a year.

This time, I'm completely demoralized. I return to the road, my legs like lead: they'd like to walk, but the brain giving them their orders has broken down. All the more so since, before reaching the next city, I'll have to scale a mountain pass at nearly 2,000 meters (6,550 feet). I recall identical situations in years past, when I had to choose from among the many gracious offers to put me up for the night, in the knowledge that I was disappointing those I'd turned down! China seems as inhospitable as France!

And at that very moment, a voice calls out to me. It's the old woman.

"For ten yuan ($1.25), I can put you up at my house tonight."

I could hug her.

The old woman doesn't sleep at home that night: she leaves me her bedroom and heads off to stay with some neighbors. Her daughter and son-in-law and their two children live with her. It's the first time I get to spend the night in a Han Chinese home. Until now, I've seen nothing but hotel rooms and *luguan*. The house has a small foyer, and a minuscule, windowless kitchen. The bedroom I'll be sleeping in is to the right. Covering an area of about forty square feet, it's lit by a window that has a view of the street. Two single beds constitute the only furniture: wooden crates on which mats have been rolled out. Kraft paper has been stapled to the ceiling, the walls were painted before the Flood in obsolete green and are now peeling from all the humidity. Extreme poverty, nicely obscured by two pieces of artwork: one, a good three feet tall, is a portrait of Mao Tse-tung. The other, a poster about the same size, is of religious inspiration. It portrays smiling saint-like figures. In the lower part, two little children astride ducks are handing out banknotes: for the Chinese, prosperity is the highest form of happiness. Completing the panorama, a photo of Deng Xiaoping hangs between the poster and Mao. On the other wall is a map of China's provinces. The room occupied by my landlady's daughter, her son-in-law, and their children—a boy and a girl—looks not much bigger than the one I'm sleeping in. It has a large two-person bed and a piece of Formica furniture. A brand-new color television sits on a chest in one corner. On the walls are several calligraphies and the same map of China's regions as in the other room. In a prominent spot on the large piece of furniture, they've set a picture known the world over: a young boy pulling down his shorts to proudly show what distinguishes him from a little girl; she, meanwhile, is staring at the appendage in question with gravity and wonder, revealing her desire to know more about the facts of life.

The climb from Yuyang to Wushan is steep; the road quickly winds its way to the top. But I have no regrets, for the view is simply breathtaking. I can see the road I traveled, while the village I just left is spread out as in an aerial photograph. Those rows of large-headed nails are apricot trees, and what looks like long stick-lollipops are greenhouses full of melons in the last stages of ripening. The terraced fields form a giant staircase and it climbs to the top of the pass; higher up still, a lamasery taunts me, its oddly-shaped roofs clawing at the sky. In France, you always find monasteries in the most enchanting of places; in China, though, if you're looking for monks, you have to look up to the skies.

Strictly speaking, Wushan is not a city, even though it's in the process of becoming one once again. For the time being, it's under construction. They've bulldozed the old earthen houses where a few poor souls still live, unable to find anywhere else to go. An old woman whose shack was knocked down has sought shelter beneath two boards, and the hopelessness in her eyes sums up the distress of the evicted. The wide avenue that has been laid out is still just a vacant field plowed by bulldozers. Buildings are being constructed shoulder to shoulder for five hundred feet on each side. The only one finished is the hotel where I get a room. To reach it, I have to wade through a puddle of red mud, and Ulysses and I leave what looks like a trail of blood on the reception room's pristine black marble.

It's practically impossible to get any shut eye. Workmen on a construction site nearby work all through the night pouring a concrete floor and, to liquefy it, they use a vibrator which, given the noise it makes and its effect on my nerves, could easily be mistaken for an old-time dentist's drill. The cable supplying electricity to the TV must have run into a backhoe for, without a warning, the thriller I was counting on to help me fall asleep vanishes into a black screen. I was promised hot water by 8:00. At midnight, since it still hasn't arrived, I take a cold shower. And a smart move it was for, in the morning, there's no water at all.

I've been told about fortified villages and spectacular circular compounds, the function and origins of which are unclear. If you look carefully, you can indeed spot one of them a short distance in advance of Luomen: bean-shaped, with a high earthen wall, near the cliff. I'm intrigued by a noise I hear coming from a workshop, so I go to check it out. Craftswomen are carving blocks of jade. The company manager, also a woman, has me visit the showroom where the artists' creations are on display. They're superb. The centerpiece is a junk ship about three feet high that took seven months to make. Light filtered by the noble substance passes through extremely thin sails. I'm captivated by two teacups "specially made for eight treasures tea." They're unimaginably intricate and lightweight. Truly nothing but the essence of jade! I'm strongly tempted to buy them, whatever the cost. My compulsion is linked, no doubt, to the pleasure I've experienced drinking that delightful beverage. But when they show me the box I'd need to carry them in, I give up on the idea.

All day long, the road alternates between paved sections and those that are potholed, stony, and above all dusty. As if done intentionally, as soon as the road reaches a village, the asphalt comes to an end. Trucks raise such great clouds of dust that they seem to swallow up the kids at play beside the road. Merchants hide their stalls beneath large sheets of transparent plastic—turned gray, of course—and its presence only adds to the sad, bleak, sorry state of this would-be village. I even have to ford a river, which makes me suddenly wonder whether I'm still on Route 316. But I'm told that yes, this rutted rural road is indeed the national highway.

I camp in the tiny village of Fandiatou. Children come running. They're really the only ones who still exhibit a little curiosity. A boy who lives nearby tells me he'll boil some water so that I can make my noodle soup. A shrewd little girl comes over with her notebook and English textbook and asks if I'll do the homework she's struggling with. As night falls, a few brats pitch stones at my tent. These are the two faces of China I see every day. Today, on three different occasions, some kids on bikes, but also two adults riding on a tractor, bravely waited until they were far enough away and then yelled: "Go away!" The government, in preparing for the Beijing Olympics, has been broadcasting English lessons on television and has made it a required subject in school. Knowledge can be used for either good or bad: in this case, foreign language skills can be used to either welcome, or shoo away the outsider. It's common knowledge that in China, ever since the Boxer Rebellion, xenophobia still lies just below the surface.

The children head off to bed and I asleep, undeterred by a few locals who, in the middle of the night, draw near my tent to keep an eye on it while loudly commenting on the major event of the day: me. I'm awakened by someone calling out. I want to sleep, and refuse to answer. But then a flashlight pokes past the rainfly and a hand appears holding a bowl of noodle soup. How can I possibly turn it down, although I'm not thrilled at the hour they've chosen and finished my soup only three hours ago! But these people aren't saying "Go away!" so I would be remiss if I didn't honor their "Welcome!"

In the next village, a man and his wife have attracted a crowd. They're melting aluminum and turning it into cookware: ladles, pots, skillets, and more. Residents have brought all their defective aluminum wares. The man purchases these raw materials from them, then sells back to them the objects he casts before their eyes. What's most striking is how many objects lie piled up on the ground, suggesting that every pot and pan in the village wore out just in time for the magician's arrival!

In the fields, farmers have begun harvesting their crops. When I left Turfan, wheat was only beginning to poke through the soil. Little by little, as I've moved along, it has grown tall, and here it has acquired its golden color. Today, it's being cut with sickles. These are unlike French sickles: the harvesters carry the blade separately in their knapsack and only set it at a right angle on the handle when they're ready to work. The blades are very sharp: a farmer proudly had me run my finger along one: if only Chinese barbers sharpened their razors so well!

On the road, I encounter groups of reapers traveling from one village to the next in search of work. Hunched over, they grab a handful of stalks and, with a quick motion, shear them off at the base. They lash each bunch together with two fistfuls of wheat held end to end. The sheaves are rarely left out in the fields. Workers carry them off in the evening on pushcarts. If left in the fields, the farmer sleeps in the grass nearby to deter thieves.

There are a thousand different threshing methods. The oldest technique involves a flail, that is to say a long, wooden pole with a smaller stick attached loosely at one end. It's used to strike the bundles after they've been laid out on a hard, perfectly flat surface. The most modern technique uses a small threshing machine powered by a tractor motor. I've seen only one of these. The sheaf is inserted, then crushed straw emerges from one side and the grain from the other. Between the two are the mechanical wheels. Another ancient technique deploys a grooved stone cylinder hitched to a horse: the animal tramples the stalks on the threshing field all day long. A variant of this replaces the horse and stone with a tractor-pulled trailer. The least sophisticated method consists simply in scattering the bundles over the road. Passing cars and trucks do all the work! The wheat still has to be winnowed though; that is to say, the grain has to be separated from any dust or contaminants picked up on the threshing field. The good grain from the chaff. It's mostly women's work: they're the ones who skillfully handle the winnowing basket, tossing the grain into the air, working, if possible, when the wind is blowing. The wisps of straw blow away, and the heavier grain falls back into the basket. The next-to-last step consists in spreading the clean grain alongside the road or back on the threshing field so that it can dry and harden in the sun; then, at long last, the bags are carried to the miller who, for his wages, keeps a portion of the grain for himself.

I notice that each phase of the harvest—the tilling, harvesting, threshing, and winnowing—is done by hand using tools that must be very much like those Chinese peasants used in the days of Marco Polo. The only touch of modernity: the rubber tires on the handcarts used to transport the precious cargo.

XII

ETERNAL CHINA

After Fandiatou, the road runs along sheer, high cliffs of smooth stone in which thousands of swallows have made their nests. Walking with my eyes to the sky so that I can admire the birds' airborne arabesques, I suddenly stop, dumbfounded. There, in the middle of the cliff, over a hundred yards up, a temple emerges from the solid rock, seemingly inlaid in the wall itself. A providential woman selling incense agrees to keep an eye on Ulysses, and I head off to explore. I follow on the heels of a couple of women with two children. They've just purchased several small red candles, a package of incense, and a few sheets of paper. A path winds its way through the trees, then makes a quick climb up toward the cliff. After we arrive at the foot of the vertical wall, we ascend a stairway teeming with armies of *scolopendra*. Is this arthropod known for its piety? Millipedes in France don't launch assaults on French churches, as far as I know! But perhaps Buddhist temples, of which I know next to nothing, are more appealing to them? I take my time going up, first of all because I have great respect for the fervor of these fabulous mini-dragons, but above all because I burned out my thighs climbing a minaret in Iran, and have, ever since, been keenly aware of the fact that the muscles I use for walking, which are now perfectly broken in, are not the same ones I use for climbing. So I avoid taking any risks.

Whether I look up or down, the wall's height and verticality are impressive. The stairway seems like it will never end. The two women stop in a first grotto containing three statues; one statue wears a deep grimace. The women light a small red candle and add it to those already burning. Then, holding several sticks of smoldering incense in their conjoined hands, they prostrate themselves several times. Lastly, they set a strip of paper on fire and toss it into the wind; it goes up in flames, sending pretty wisps of smoke into the air before falling back to the earth.

These little pieces of paper are, in fact, being sent to the deceased. They symbolize money. The dead cannot be left destitute! In the south of China, people print fake currency, houses, and furniture on brightly colored pieces of paper, which are then burned for use by the departed, so that they can enjoy a little comfort in the afterlife.

In all, fourteen grottoes have been hollowed out of the cliff. The largest contains a Buddha and two bodhisattvas—saint-like individuals who have foregone nirvana for a time in order to help humankind. An altar has been erected at the center of the room. A large bowl is piled high with fruit: they are offerings from the faithful. The monk in charge of the premises' upkeep takes two apricots from it, and hands them to the two kids. One large cavern is unique as it has just one figurine: entirely black, its shoulders are draped with what resembles a shawl of tree leaves, and two horns decorate its forehead. This is the divinity known as Shen Nong, the divine farmer. As generous as Fuxi and Nügua, it is he who invented agriculture, for human beings, having grown too numerous, were dying of hunger.

He holds in his hand a round disk, the Bagua, or trigram, decorated with nine symbols. At its center is a circle inscribed with two signs: Yin and Yang. Around them are eight figures that represent the entire Universe.

Yin and Yang symbolize life and are different without conflicting with one another. They're black and white, but do not stand for good and evil. Yin is a female principle: restful, dark, even numbered. Yang is active male energy: bright and odd numbered. Rather than being in opposition, the two signs are complementary. Thus, over the course of an entire day, there is Yang (the day) and Yin (the night). Each sign of the Bagua, positioned in a circle around the central symbol, is made up of three lines, either solid or broken. Three solid lines represent the sky, pure Yang. Three broken lines represent pure Yin, the Earth. Between the two extremes are six figures composed of the same solid or broken lines representing water, fire, lakes, thunder, mountains, and the last one, both wind and wood. These very simple signs can stand for many other things as well, such as a family of eight across three generations, a season, a quality, or one of the eight directions of the compass rose. When the Chinese want to know what the future holds, they practice divination by consulting the trigrams.

The two women, along with many other people, go from one grotto to the next, skipping none, and at each station they repeat the same motions. On the way back down, in a cavity carved into the rock, I'm surprised to discover a spring gushing from the rock wall. The statues are modest, made of stucco and plaster. Most are blackened by candle smoke. On the other hand, the clothing they have on must be changed regularly, for it's clean. I'm moved by the deep faith that seems to brighten the faces of these people, and by the peace and quiet prevailing in this place. I notice that visitors are so absorbed in prayer that no one even so much as glances at the valley, which is magnificent from this vantage point. It stretches off to the horizon, diligently gardened by all the ant-like farmers I see busy at work in the square plots. Of all the colors, the gold of wheat stands out most.

Six miles farther along, there are more and more grottoes, a good fifty of them. The most impressive houses a ninety-foot-tall seated Buddha carved directly into the rock. Locals call the place "elephant mountain." Unlike the one I just visited, it's not a place of worship, but a museum of closed grottoes, part of China's national heritage. And I become conscious of the fact that the permanency of the country's past resides more in the worshippers' rituals at the first shrine than in the duly registered, centuries-old statues, displayed behind bars here.

I stop in Gangu only long enough to have lunch, then dash off toward the mountains. A steep climb lifts me up from an elevation of 1,200 meters (3,940 feet) to a mountain pass at 1,700 meters (5,580 feet). At the top, I behold a view so powerful that it completely dazzles me: I let go of Ulysses and drop down onto the grass where I sit for a good hour, staring out at the spectacle, overcome with emotion.

The road in this location is perched atop a hill, and the view to the south, north, and east extends out to distant hills awash in periwinkle haze. From here, wherever I look, I see thousands of terraced plots. Large or small, some truly tiny, they're planted with wheat, corn, chili peppers, and fruit trees. In this extraordinary garden, from the depths of the dales to the heights of the hills, not a single square foot, not a single square inch goes unplanted. Now that the sun has returned, the colors compose a brilliant palette. I'm instantly in communion with all the men and women who created this work of art. How many billions of shovelfuls, how much sweat did it take to transform these naturally treeless mountains into such sumptuous gardens? How many generations, how many centuries did it take these humble farmers to create this masterpiece, this scene of infinite splendor? The Great Wall? Big deal! The pyramids of Giza? What of them? The work of art here before me—created without bloodshed and without violence—is greater by far! The artists of this fabulous scenery are simple peasants, armed with shovels and a willingness to bow their noble heads out of respect for these summits so that they can eke out a livelihood for themselves and their fellow human beings.

Here, before my eyes, is Eternal China. Indeed, for an eternity, since time immemorial, this work of art has been continuously improved and beautified. It enrages me to think that "Great Works" are recognized as such only if achieved through blood and tears— that they're valued only in proportion to the grief they've caused— whereas the masterpiece of many lifetimes I now behold before my eyes figures nowhere in travel agents' brochures. But the agents surely have their reasons. Would anyone be willing to pay to come here and admire this work of art? UNESCO will never declare Kilometer 2,649 along Route 316 a World Heritage Site. This magnum opus was created neither to defeat an enemy nor to immortalize a great leader, it serves only to feed people. To be sure, no emperor, no general ever commanded these peaceful and generous troops who, armed with only their shovels and regardless of how long it would take, moved and transformed mountains so vast that my eye cannot capture them all. Their virtue and mettle were the sole engines of this master-piece. The Great Wall is falling victim to the ravages of weather and graffiti; temples are succumbing to wars, by and large of a religious nature, destroyed by time and men; but these terraced gardens grow more beautiful with each passing year: they are living, ever-changing sculptures, covered spring after spring in flowers, wheatgrass, and the promise of fruit. Behold the world's greatest museum!

Will the exploitation of the deserts and the advent of mechanized agriculture spell the end of Dongsanshipu's terraced gardens? If so, then nature will reclaim what was once hers. For what could tractors ever accomplish out here in these vertiginous, fragile plots? It would be unthinkable to allow diesel engines to disrupt the calm grandeur of this place.

Filled with wonder by so much beauty and unable to let go of it, I nibble on a hunk of bread—probably made of flour from wheat grown right here—along with some raisins from Turfan. My stomach is empty, but my soul is full. When I once again pick up Ulysses's tow bar, I feel like singing. The fervor of the faithful in the temple this morning, and now this extraordinary sight, have together finally revealed to me Age-Old China, not the one hidden behind a struc-ture that's been given a facelift or slathered in make-up to please tourists, and which requires a tour guide to visit. Here, there's no need for a cicerone: the people and land, like hard work and pride, speak for themselves.

At the top of the pass, I run into a farmer on his way back up to the village pushing a handcart heavily loaded with wheat. He walks between the shafts, guiding the vehicle as it's towed by a cow led by a young boy. A little calf is freely prancing about; the convoy turns down a path running between two terraced plots, adjusting its speed to match the animal's leisurely gait.

At Guanzizhen, the *luguan* where I sleep smells of manure, sandwiched as it is between a horse stable and pigsty. The single room they've given me doubles as a tool shed, and every now and then the owner or his son walks in without knocking. They pay attention to me only as long as it takes them to snatch the money I give them out of my hand, and they even fail to reply when I bid them *zaijian* (goodbye) as I head out at the crack of dawn. In the village main street, I buy myself ten meat- and vegetable-stuffed steamed rolls prepared by a family that works together in a production line to meet demand. There's enough energy in a breakfast like that to carry me sixty miles! So this twenty-six-mile leg to Tianshui should be all but effortless, especially since I've decided to take two days off once I get there. It's a city of two and a half million and is, in reality, two cities, although they both go by the same name: the one I'm just getting to is Tianshui-City, aka Qincheng, and eleven miles farther is Tianshui-Station, which is also known as Beidao.

For my first day off, I visit Fuxi Temple. Fuxi, as you'll recall, was the husband of Nügua, who was both his wife and sister, and the mother of the first human beings. Stepping inside, the visitor leaves the noisy city behind and enters a world of silence. I roam through the four buildings, which, like all museums, house manuscripts, objects, pottery—there's even a five-thousand-year-old vase—but since all the signs are in Chinese, I feel as though I'm missing something. Illustrations by a modern painter portray the arts Fuxi taught humans in scenes of hunting, fishing, and ranching. In myth, he is the very first emperor and also supposedly taught medicine; other texts, it has been noted however, attribute that gift to Shen Nong. Heaven only knows. . . .

Some workmen are crafting timbers nearby for use in the construction of a small pavilion to be assembled at the temple's entrance. I spend an hour at the work site, for it's a veritable living museum of ancient technologies. Tree trunks arrive and are sawed by two men tugging on a long saw known as a "misery whip," equipped with a handle at each end. Other craftsmen are hewing timber with what looks like an adze, consisting of a wooden handle with a large square of oak-wood fitted with a sharpened blade. Lastly, the building's pieces are finished off with a two-handled planer, which allows the workman to apply greater force. It's once again a glimpse into the past. There's not a single electric or mechanical device to disrupt the silence of the temple nearby. People worked no differently ten or twenty centuries ago.

For day two, I decide to play the tourist and visit the famous grottoes of Maiji Shan, one of the four most revered Buddhist shrines in all China, located approximately twenty-five miles to the southeast of Tianshui. I hire an English guide since no French speakers are available. Ms. Lee is twenty-one. She has a charming smile, a small beauty mark on her lip, and is more than happy to answer each of the thousand questions I uninterruptedly pull from my bag. There's time for that, too, since, to get there, we first have to go by bus from Qinchen to Beidao. At the station, we board a second bus, but there aren't enough passengers. To make the trip cost effective, the company drops us off out in the middle of nowhere and sends a minibus to pick us up. At the entrance to the grotto premises where visitors have to pay, we learn that new rules went into effect that very morning and now everyone, tourists and Chinese alike, must purchase a ticket. The locals are outraged: they can't be forced to pay just to go home! But the guards are unflinching: it's the new rule. Deliberations drag on for so long that I fall asleep. Ms. Lee wakes me up when we reach the foot of "wheatstack mountain," the name local farmers have given the place on account of the rock massif's shape.

The 194 grottoes were carved between the third and fifth centuries, during the Wei and Jin Dynasties, when Silk Road trade was booming. They're relatively well preserved, likely protected by the site's sheer walls, which made them inaccessible. Historians still wonder exactly how the sculptors managed to carve two large Buddhas onto two of the mountain's faces. One theory is that their builders piled logs up to the top of the ridge, then removed them little by little as work progressed. From afar, the mountain looks like a chunk of Swiss cheese and bears some resemblance to Paris's Pompidou Center with its corridor-stairways connecting one floor to another. I grumble a little—as any self-respecting Frenchman would—since, in order to preserve the statues, gratings have been placed at the entrance to each grotto. The sunlight from outside creates such a contrast that it's impossible to see anything, and the flashlight I've brought along is of no help. Despite a statement forbidding the use of cameras, as the "self-respecting Frenchman" I am yet again, I snap a picture of one extremely elaborate Buddha. The smiling figure is seated cross-legged with one hand raised, of which three fingers are missing. Paint residue on the statue and in the niche hints at the splendor of the predominantly blue original colors.

Looking out at the surrounding countryside, it's easy to see why the builders chose this particular site. The view extends out over a patchwork of forest-covered hills. Whether returning from the desert or preparing to enter it, Silk Road traders would have found a divine site here where they could prepare themselves either to face the worst, or to recover from having just survived it. In this paradise, they must have also more readily opened the drawstrings of their purse to either thank or propitiate Providence. The surrounding area is bursting with flowering hibiscus and albizia, a plant also known as "rose curtains." Its flowers, to my mind, look like long feather eyelashes that grow red at the tips.

Leaving Tianshui-Qincheng at the break of dawn, I take a very wide avenue that has only recently been completed. Elegant city girls lazily pedal along on bicycles, which they've rigged with parasols in order to protect themselves from the sun.

Is there a problem the engineers have yet to solve, or has construction been delayed? Large concrete electric poles still lie here and there along the avenue. A distracted bus driver forgot they were there. His vehicle has literally planted itself on top of one of the pylons.

At 10:00 a.m., I seek shelter from the sun and walk along a wall for the sacrosanct apple ceremonial. I smile at a tramp passing by on the other side of the road. He stops, recognizes one of his own, and crosses over to me. He shakes my hand but never lets go of a string to which he has attached a deck of cards. Then, shaking his head, he goes his way. This eventless encounter oddly puts a smile in my heart. Probably because it makes me feel a little less alone.

I had a lot of trouble finding a *luguan* in Ba Yang. I got slowed up because the distance markers abruptly disappeared. Without my GPS, I have a hard time figuring out where I am and which way I need to go. At each fork in the road, which, fortunately, are not too numerous, my only option is to wait for someone to come by so that I can ask for directions to the village where I'm planning to spend the night. Once there, I tend to my health by going to bed early. But at the crack of dawn, I'm awakened by the loud cries of a crowd. I jump into my shorts and head out to see what's up. The large square behind the house, though empty last night, is now filled with hundreds of people: farmers loudly chatting, shouting out to one another by dawn's first light. There are peaches everywhere. In carts loaded down with brimming baskets; in willow baskets hung from a pole and carried by two people on their shoulders; in wicker dosser baskets. They're all here with the precious fruit they picked last night in the vast orchards I traveled through, intending to sell it to wholesalers whose trucks are parked every which way. The buyers move from one vendor to another, trying to spot a good deal, poised to rush over and buy the very best. I remember seeing people trading horses at fairs when I was a child. Techniques used here are quite similar to those of the livestock dealers of Normandy's markets. I watch the participants and surmise what they're saying:

"How much are you asking for these?"

The husband stops talking. It's his wife who answers. She tosses out a figure.

The buyer scowls disdainfully:

"My dear woman! At that price, New Year's will come and go and you'll still have your peaches!"

And with that, he turns around and heads off to see another seller. Same exchange, same pouty face. Several minutes later, he's back to see the first couple. The sellers say nothing, they simply wait. The buyer pushes aside the largest fruit sitting at the top of one of the baskets and, plunging his hand deep down, pulls out a small peach.

"And to top it all off, they're puny little things! These won't sell."

The woman argues her case. Her fruit is superb. She grabs a few, squeezes them, and holds them under his nose.

The man makes a new offer.

The woman counters.

The buyer shakes his head "no" and walks off a second time. Ten yards away, he spins around and comes back, offering yet another price. Now everyone knows: it's take-it-or-leave-it. The woman agrees, her husband never having said a word.

The fruit poured out into piles is weighed then placed in crates and promptly loaded onto trucks. The same scene plays over and over, a hundred times, two hundred times, in every corner of the square. And new carts arrive single file, blocking traffic. The loaded trucks force their way through, horns blaring continuously. Other buyers seem to specialize in fruit that's overly ripe or too small, to be used in syrups and juices. This is the region's only livelihood. And the way everyone feverishly goes about this business proves just how vital the orchards are to the population's prosperity and welfare. Here, people know they won't die of hunger. As I turn to leave, a buyer presents me with a gift: a handful of large, velvety fruit.

A second track is being added to the Xi'an-Ürümqi railroad: the single line can no longer accommodate all the passengers and freight heading to Xinjiang. The construction site is enormous. Building this line was one of the first projects the communists embarked upon after their rise to power. Today's regime wants a faster way to move the immense region's mineral wealth east—especially petroleum. The current line forces descending convoys to make short runs— then pull off onto a sidetrack—to let upward-bound convoys pass. It takes the Xi'an-Ürümqi Express forty hours to cover the 930 miles of straight-line track between the two cities, with freight trains taking twice as long. What's more, the line often runs along mountainsides, where landslides are a constant threat. What's being built here is colossal. In the narrow valley where the Wei River, the highway, and the old railroad are already tightly packed, there's precious little room left. And encroaching on farmland is out of the question, for this is China's breadbasket. The future line's passengers will either ride continuously atop viaducts, or in the darkness of tunnels.

Near a worksite where I arouse the workmen's curiosity, one of them comes over to me and offers me a handful of banknotes! I finally grasp that he'd like to buy Ulysses. I burst out laughing. I'm not like those who sell off their friends! Out of curiosity, I ask him how much he thinks my companion's worth, but seeing that I'm not serious, the man beats a hasty retreat.

The girl who sets foot in the restaurant I decided on gives me quite the shock: her head is shaped just like that of a statue I photographed in Maiji Shan, especially her strongly angled, almond eyes, which pull back toward her temples. Ms. Lee, my guide, told me that the Han Chinese didn't much appreciate that particular face shape, and so it was a short-lived fad in statuary. How unfortunate! This fawn-eyed girl seems to bring together all the elements that, deep down in my heart, I call beauty.

In Tianshui, the hotel receptionists make me change rooms three times in three nights. Since I graciously acquiesce, and no doubt to compensate me for all the bother, for my last night, they put me up in the top-floor royal suite but charge me the same rate as before. Three rooms all to myself, sofas as deep as the waters of the Yellow River, and armfuls of flowers on the tables!

July 1—If I'm to trust my map, the distance from Tailu to Jiaochuan is seventeen miles. I've just traveled nineteen and people tell me I still have six miles to go, adding that there's no hotel in the city. The fact that Xi'an is now near has calmed me down. Instead of pushing on as I normally do, I decide that nineteen miles is enough. I order myself a hearty meal, take out the manuscript of *Rosa*, and spend several hours with my now-familiar characters. The thought that I'll soon be at my destination has a dual effect on me. Happy to be so near Xi'an, I'm tempted to double the distances I travel in order to get there even faster. At the same time, I haven't felt this relaxed since leaving Istanbul. I have until around noon on July 14 to make my flight for Beijing. And since I'm well ahead of schedule, were the opportunity to arise, I wouldn't at all mind taking a full day off to poke around a bit, or maybe even strike up a new friendship.

I continue to descend toward the plain. Today, my altimeter reads 900 meters (2,950 feet) and, as I lose some of the benefits of elevation, I increasingly feel the heat. Especially since there isn't the slightest breeze in this narrow valley. In some spots with room for the Wei River only, travelers of yore had to head down into the riverbed in order to keep going. Today, the train and the road pass through tunnels. I wonder whether the bed of the river wasn't safer, despite being rocky and muddy in places. I hate tunnels. They terrify me. I recall in particular what a nightmare it was to make my way through a tunnel in Iran in early June 2000: I was pretty sure I wouldn't make it out alive.* The one I have to go through today is a full mile and a quarter long. There's no lighting. I practically run from one end to the other. A truck barrels in, its horn blaring nonstop, which, amplified by the confined area, literally deafens me. I wave my flashlight to let him know I'm there, for of course, there's no sidewalk: no one dreamed that anyone would ever try walking through! The truck makes no attempt to slow down but does, fortunately, hug the tunnel wall.

---

* See *Walking to Samarkand, op. cit.* Chapter 3.

July 1 is the anniversary of the CPC, the Communist Party of China.*
I expect to see rallies, but there are none. Of course, I'm passing
through minuscule villages only, places unlikely to be swarming with
Party members. But with sixty million of them in all, the CPC has
ways of ensuring that there are good Chinese citizens everywhere!
Still, it has better things to do than celebrate: it's gearing up for the
National Congress in the Fall, during which it's said member num-
ber one, Jiang Zemin, will step down.

Four truck drivers come into the restaurant where I've just finished having lunch. They're hungrier for company than for the platter of stir-fried noodles that appeared on their table without them
even asking, and they invite me to join in. I try to explain—the hand
gesture of tapping one's stomach is understood in every country—
that I've just finished eating my own meal, but no dice, I have to pick
my chopsticks back up. The owner brings other platters out onto the
table and I'm saved by Chinese tradition, since everyone partakes
freely of the shared dishes. That way, I can pretend to honor the
food being offered while only having a few nibbles. The one breach
of tradition, though, is that we eat while conversing, whereas the
Chinese usually eat first and talk later. "Conversing," though, is a bit
of an exaggeration. I smile a lot; I nod in agreement without really
knowing what I'm agreeing to. These are odd encounters, and yet
they're somehow comforting: I've gotten to know all too well during
this journey how social isolation can throw your morale off—as in
the case of my veritable paranoia with respect to Seuil—and how
sometimes it can just plain throw you off.

I take a rest day in Meixian. Taking into account the fact that I'm
ahead of schedule, I now expect to reach Xi'an on July 11. Since
my plane for Beijing is the fourteenth, I'm in no hurry. I revise my
walking schedule for the umpteenth time, and now have only sixteen
miles a day to travel from here to the end. A stroll in the park.

---

* TN: First celebrated July 1, 1921.

Once again, I'm caught off guard by the hotel bathroom, though I should be hardened: at the sink, when I turn on the cold tap, the water—by some mystery no law of physics can explain—comes pouring out of the ceiling, and it does so through a grating, such that I can't locate the leak. Someone ought to write a guidebook to Chinese hotel bathrooms in order to help travelers avoid hidden traps like this. If someone tells you "there's hot water," believe what you want, but whoever's making the statement bears no responsibility for it. If someone tells you "there'll be hot water between 8:00 and 10:00 p.m.," take it to mean "between 10:00 and 10:15." And since everyone's eagerly waiting for it to be turned on, because it's shared, at best it will be lukewarm. If they tell you "the toilets flush," though you claim otherwise, tired of fighting, they'll eventually send up a workman. He'll stand on the toilet seat, fish around for a string in the tank near the ceiling and give it a firm tug. And water will come pouring down, under the maintenance man's scoffing gaze. As for the floor's blackish marbling, those are not the veins of fancy tiling, but—more prosaically—hairs left by generations of female occupants that have, over time, become encrusted.

I arrive in Meixian on the eve of university entrance examinations, slated for July 7 and 8. There's a deluge of candidates. May the most intelligent and most brilliant win, as they say. I've been given to understand however that dunces helped along by influential members of the Party automatically pass for geniuses in the examiners' eyes. The faucet-shower hotel, where I miraculously managed to find a vacancy, is swarming with future students, crammed three or four to a room. They're here from all the neighboring towns. Exams will be held in the hotel's large conference rooms, rented for the occasion. Other sites have been requisitioned in town. This year, the Chinese university system is accepting 2,700,000 students, a new record. Candidates number eight to ten times that figure.

Having settled in beneath a small arbor to do some writing, a young woman comes over and sits down beside me, book in hand.

She's studying English out loud. She mangles an irregular verb and, eager to start up a conversation, I correct her. One of her girlfriends, then five, then ten, come to join her. There's a little mumbling, a few introductions, some hesitations. . . . A professor, greeted with great respect by the young women, is amused by the situation. "Chinese young people," he tells me, "work very hard at English. In terms of reading and writing, they're almost fluent. But they have trouble with pronunciation and never get the chance to practice with native speakers. These girls don't understand what you're saying, but if you were to write it down, they'd have no trouble reading it." I think of Wenhua, with whom I communicated using little pieces of paper. The man confirms what I heard, that only twenty-five percent of primary schoolchildren go on to "middle high school" (*collège* in the French educational system). And they're the ones who eventually attend university—if they pass the exam, that is. He tells me that when he was a student, he worked from 5:00 in the morning to 11:00 at night every day.

I express my surprise that there are fewer girls than boys taking the exam.

"Do the Chinese still prefer male children?"

"In cities, people have no preference today regarding their child's sex, some are even delighted not to have a boy. But in the countryside, the birth of a girl is still a catastrophe. Who will honor the ancestors and take over the farm? There's no social security for the elderly in this country. Not to have a male child is to live in the fear that, when old, you'll fall into poverty."

It's a well-known fact that there are more men in China than women. The rural population that prefers boys represents 85 percent of all Chinese citizens. Are there still cases where daughters are murdered after birth? Apparently not, but induced abortions do reportedly take place when it has been determined that the baby will be a girl. Abductions of women to serve as the spouses of isolated farmers are by no means unheard of, despite attempts by authorities to crack down on the practice. I'm surprised to learn that, in spite of the one-child policy, the population continues to grow.*

"For the moment, according to experts, it continues to increase and will do so until it reaches 1.5 to 1.6 billion individuals. The rise can be attributed to improved hygiene."

In my head, I silently scroll through the string of *luguan* I've been in of late, but say nothing . . .

"And where are you going to put all these people?"

"That's a real problem. China's population increase is amplified by rural depopulation. Together, the two trends have led to a short-age of housing. Quite often, three generations have to squeeze into a tiny space. The shortage is exacerbated even more in that, as people grow richer, they want to live in more spacious houses. So we have to build millions of new houses and apartment buildings."

Reflecting on these conversations and a few others I had previously, I arrive at the conclusion that, though regimes change, China itself remains "eternal." Confucianism has left its mark on all aspects of Chinese society. In Confucian society, wives venerate and obey their husbands, younger siblings defer to their older brothers and sisters, and sons submit to their fathers. Young people owe respect to their elders and average citizens must show regard for Party members. The result is that nothing changes. Everything is as it should be in a social structure paralyzed by a whole series of barriers. When you're at the top, barring some powerful grass-roots movement as befalls China from time to time, you can be pretty sure that that's where you'll always be. And so, anxious to profit from the system, the Communist Party, which took power by denouncing Confucianism, has come to terms with it today.

China reveals its best face to early risers only. As soon as the sun comes up over the horizon, a nation of hard-working individuals

---

* TN: In 2015, thirteen years after Ollivier's walk, the Chinese government amended this policy to allow two children per family.

invades the streets. Children pedaling to school, followed by working men and women. But before all those, in every city and town,
small-scale vendors take over the sidewalks. You get the sense that
the Chinese never eat at home. Should you need convincing, the
crossroads at the center of Meixian ought to do the trick. The Han
Chinese not only breakfast here, but they lunch, play, shop, conduct
business, have their shoes repaired, meet up with friends, and dine
in these few square yards, which constitute the true heart of the city.

Keen on making sure their customers are comfortable, savvy
shopkeepers bring a table and chairs on their delivery tricycle or
handcart, well before the sun is up. Although in France I never skip
my tea, toast, and butter, here I stuff myself with donuts dripping in
grease, loaded with enough energy to carry me till noon and beyond.
The vendors' meals go for one or two yuan each ($0.09 or $0.18)
and consist of *youtiao* (braided dough fried in oil), little steamed rolls
stuffed with onions and meat, onion crepes, and what are, to my palate, incredibly spicy cold noodles. Delicious broths are also served.
If only Chinese men and women didn't clear their throats and spit
at every turn, for me, there would be nothing not to love about the
morning street ambiance here!

As soon as the last breakfast customers finish their meals by wiping their mouths with toilet paper (used here and elsewhere as nap-
kins), carts and tricycles loaded with fruits and vegetables pull up
and take over the sidewalks: a traveling pastry chef riding his bike,
a cobbler who sets his sewing machine up next to someone selling
sunglasses, several little shoeshine men, and a farm implement man-
ufacturer all nonchalantly rub elbows with one another.

As afternoon drags on, these vendors move out and new carts
and tricycles arrive to unload gas stoves and barbecues full of live
embers. The newcomers plug cords into outlets in nearby shops to
power their freezers or colored lamps atop long bamboo poles. The
night market is setting up. The pungent smell of heavily sulfured
Chinese charcoal soon wafts over the central crossroads which, after
nightfall, sparkles with a hundred lights and echoes with a thousand

sounds. Long tables have been set up where entire families or groups of friends sit down. There's no escaping the night market's conviviality; lone individuals like me are few. Chinese dining is a communal feast. In terms of food, the choice is endless. Lamb kabobs; hot noodles—cold noodles; stuffed or grilled breads, some cooked over coals, others steamed; pork; sandstone pots filled with vegetables, meat, or eggs and served piping hot; fish that has been either grilled or poached in a court-bouillon; vegetable fondues cooked right at the table; melons sliced with large knives upon request. And it all takes place in an incredible din: conversations and laughter; the ding of tricycles as they make their way through the thick of the throng; the cries of children playing between the tables; and the holler of merchants. The ground is strewn with garbage given how everyone throws what they're done with onto the ground: bones, leftovers, papers, the tea leaves left in cups, and on and on. In the heat of this summer night, outfits are light. Women wear shorts and form-fitting blouses, or long, diaphanous dresses; the men have pulled their pant legs up to their knees and rolled their T-shirts to their armpits, displaying their round bellies with pride. In modern China, it's better to be a have than a have-not.

Though Chinese women bankrupt themselves buying clothes, they spend very little on makeup, with the exception perhaps of lipstick. Their natural peach skin tone is something our female companions in the West achieve through the liberal application of foundation and blush. The most coquettish Chinese women lighten their faces with rice powder and never venture out into the sun without a parasol. It's extremely rare for them to curl their jet-black hair. I've seen few heavyset women, and none obese. Most are quite thin and "saddlebag fat," which European and American women obsess over, is unheard of. Small breasts, small buttocks. They look great in pants and lovely in long dresses. On the other hand, shorts or miniskirts are not their strong suit, as their legs most often lack grace and, furthermore, are covered in socks, without which even the boldest Chinese woman wouldn't dare step into the street.

Han women are very acquisitive. When Deng Xiaoping declared: "To get rich is glorious!" indicating that there should be no shame in getting rich, his words fell upon two billion receptive ears, and today, his compatriots want for themselves above all wealth and longevity, life's two joys.*

I've hit on an infallible way to tell the Muslim Hui Chinese apart from the physically similar Han Chinese. Among the Hui, when you go to pay for a meal in a restaurant, the person who takes your money is a man. When the restaurant is run by non-Muslims, it's always a woman who brings the bill and pockets the money.

The morning of July 8. It's muggy out. I didn't sleep well, so I decided to leave the hotel at 5:00 a.m. I'm not the only one who barely slept a wink. Out in the courtyard, a few young people, each with a book in hand, are trying to memorize entire pages in the last few hours before the start of the exam. I notice two young women, hand in hand, pacing up and down the street and quietly singing—no doubt their way of staving off nervousness.

The sun is barely above the horizon and already the streets are swarming with people. Before long, I've left the small city, but the road is lined with an almost endless chain of houses. Agricultural workers are out in the fields cutting wheat with sickles. There are no more natural areas. Every square foot of land is cultivated. The groundwater here is just below the surface. Poplar trees line the road. Beyond them, crops occupy all the space. The corn is taller than I am, and it now bears kernels ripe enough such that, here and there, street vendors are hawking corn on the cob to passersby, steamed or grilled.

The road runs alongside fields that are directly below me on my right. I spot a roof with upturned corners, and curiosity compels me to scale a small, steep dirt path leading to a temple. The monk who

* TN: Whether Deng Xiaoping ever uttered those exact words (in English or their equivalent in Chinese) is unclear; the spirit behind them, though, is undeniably his.

takes care of it is having breakfast with his wife. They offer me bread
and a bowl of very spicy broth made from a starch and vegetable base.
The man, whose face radiates peaceful loving-kindness, the hallmark
of the just, has me visit their cave dwelling and the temple, which
contains a statue of Buddha and two bodhisattvas. Dozens of little
fabric figurines, sewn and painted by my hosts, hang for sale on display racks. Some are dressed in Tibetan garb, others in contemporary
outfits.

In Zhouzhi, I'm told there's an Internet cafe, but given how early it
is, I expect it will be closed. As I'm leaving the hotel, they tell me
it's open around the clock. At 5:30 in the morning, I discover an
atmosphere there that's straight out of the film *Gambling Hell.* In a
large, smoky room filled with rows of computers, some young people
lie asleep, crammed onto a large sofa. Others have dozed off on their
crossed arms while still sitting at their screens, which display images
of killers frozen in firing position. The younger Chinese generation
is crazy about video games like this, in which players, with whom
they identify, move freely through a virtual world while enemies pop
up at every turn. They draw their guns once per second, filling the
room with automatic weapons fire and exploding grenades. Barely
awake, still caught up in their dreams, they start tapping away at the
keys and the killing starts all over again. Oh, what brave little boys!
Yet another fine example of what to expect from future generations.

I'm now only forty-seven miles from Xi'an and my feet are itching
to be done. Still, I take a long break to contemplate a fascinating
spectacle: three dentists busy at work. Like everyone else here, they
operate their business out in the street—or very nearly so. The space
they work in is just off the roadway, a step down from the level of
the blacktop, about three or four yards away. It must have once been

* TN: *Macao, l'enfer du jeu*, a 1942 French film directed by Jean Delannoy, and
released in the United States in 1950.

a street shop, for its walls fully open up to the outside. Drawings tacked on the wall call attention to the calamities awaiting those who fail to regularly avail themselves of their toothbrush, or of this place. Bicycles and scooters are parked every which way. A bike that likely belongs to one of the men of the trade leans against the back wall of this "dental office." Customers, friends, or parents who accompanied the patients being worked on wait in chairs inside the shop, or stand just outside. A young woman whose hand is trying to calm a dreadfully swollen cheek is pacing up and down the sidewalk, bedeviled by her pain, oblivious to the world around her. The three practitioners work side by side. Two of the patients are lying on inclined dentist's chairs with their heads tilted back. To operate, the surgeons—dressed in tank tops, like their customers—wear protective masks over their mouth and nose. Pliers and needles are their only tools. Among those waiting, no one says a word, mesmerized as they are by a spectacle in which they themselves will soon be the actors. Each passing truck stirs up a cloud of dust, and it settles over the resigned congregation. I recall the professor who told me that health standards in China had improved! Still, unlike the peoples of Central Asia, nearly everyone in China uses a toothbrush.

Chi Gan Hui passes me up on his bike, brakes, then begins firing questions at me in very offhanded way: what am I doing here, where do I come from, where am I going? He's still a young man, sporting a T-shirt, shorts, and those ubiquitous black slippers on his feet. He wears his salt-and-pepper hair in a crewcut; a receding hairline has laid bare most of his forehead. As soon as he finishes reading my little papers, he invites me to his house. He lives in a village only a short distance away; in fact, its first houses are visible from where we stand. We take a dirt path to a little house with a wall around it. A tiny cement courtyard leads into three rather large rooms. In one corner is a loom that Chi uses in his spare time, which he enjoys thanks to a job as a rice wholesaler. He tells me he has a son who lives and works in Baoji. When I compliment him on his fitness, he tells me that he and I are the same age, and then he performs several exuberant tai chi moves—those carefully called-out, precise, and healthful figures that comprise a "meditation in motion," which I've seen people perform in parks in large cities. He invites me to join him in his rather frugal meal: two tomatoes he washes off in a bucket of water and a slice of dry bread. The man is brimming with amiability. Without worrying much about whether I understand, he tells me stories, half in words and half in mime. One of these involves soldiers. He's standing at attention in front of someone very important whose name he utters: Mao. Then, he goes off to get a medal bearing the image of the late charismatic leader and ceremoniously presents it to me as a gift. We take a short rest, and when I finally drive home to him the fact that I have to get going, Chi insists on coming with me: he pulls Ulysses while performing a kind of dance as we make our way down the road, until we reach the village's last houses. We've spent only two hours together, but when it's time to say farewell, we're both choked up from the joy of the encounter and embrace like two old acquaintances. I watch him walk away and it suddenly occurs to me that I've just said farewell to the last of the many friends I've made on my Silk Road journey.

I've dawdled too long this morning and now I have to walk in the heat of the day. The asphalt is melting beneath my feet. I'm dripping with sweat despite sucking on salt lozenges, and I gulp down liter upon liter of water, filling my water bags up along the way from the pipes feeding irrigation canals. As I enter Ganhezhen, a sign proclaims "XI'AN – 46 KILOMETERS" (29 miles). Above the house of a woman everyone in the street apparently adores, I rent what, either out of the goodness of my heart or laxity, I'll call a "room." The woman hounds her son to bring me a bathing suit, then leads me a short distance away to a large cement basin in which perhaps fifty kids are splashing about. The weather's so hot and humid that I dive in head first. It must be that I'm getting very near my objective for me to take such risks: first Chi's poorly washed tomatoes and now a swim in this murky water, which clearly hasn't been changed all summer! A week ago, I would never have dared such a thing. But, between dying from the heat right this very moment or from dysentery tomorrow, I've made my choice. I'm floating now not only in this mucky water, but also in that misty, unreal cloud that one might call "the end of the journey."

As I lie down to sleep, anointed with a thick layer of repellent to ward off the mosquitoes attracted by the nearby basin, I reflect on the fact that, in two days, I'll have completed this long, solitary walk, begun four years ago. I still have a hard time believing that the end is near. The heat is stifling and the relative cool of the swim has long since worn off. I have trouble sleeping, especially because someone on a nearby worksite is operating a drill nonstop. Chinese civil engineers never shut off their machinery. Just two more days. I repeat that sentence over and over to myself like a litany, but the words have no meaning, they fail to penetrate my cerebral cortex. I turn over on the plank serving as my box spring and wonder: what does reaching the end of the journey really mean? For the moment, all I can picture is a black hole. Will I feel called to something new, something even richer? Or will it be the beginning of a descent into some terrifying unknown? I recall how disappointed I was when I came upon the distance markers announcing the end of the Way of St. James. I retaliated on the first one by peeing on it, thirty miles before entering Santiago de Compostela. Right this minute though, in the muggy night, I feel instead like I'm about to drown.

Yet I had set a goal for myself, just one, and it wasn't much: to try and understand why I felt compelled to walk like this. I'm not sure I've found an answer; I mean that, probably, on the contrary, I'm no closer to understanding the reasons why than on the day I first set out. Something—a force greater than I—spurs me on. Is it curiosity? Absolutely. But my guess is that curiosity is not my primary driving force. More like a desire to be alone, for in solitude there exists fewer untruths, fewer social grimaces, and greater inner truth; we are also more present to the vast mystery of the world, more open to the miraculous moment of the encounter. But in that case, the journey should never end: it should be life itself, not just a parenthesis, long or short, in the course of life. . . .

Rereading these words scrawled last night in my journal, I feel they shed virtually no light whatsoever on my would-be "adventure." I'd like to say: I travel—I walk—because a hand, or rather a breath, as mysterious as elusive, is pushing me from behind. In order to find myself increasingly alone, increasingly naked: closer—at least I'd like to think so, anyway—to what I believe to be my truth . . . which apparently gallops faster than I do, and will never let me catch it! The winds of the desert and of the steppe—although they quite often made me suffer, I have, in the end, come to love them. They are in the image of what I'm looking for, and which words—my words, in any case—are unable to capture. The winds of the steppe have never needed words. We're a little bit alike, these winds and I: we've befriended emptiness and silence. We have no idea why we travel along, but we're aware that we have to keep on sweeping through space, even if there's no point to it—or rather, even if there *seems* to be no point to it. One fine day we head home and take a momentary break. Friends say: he has mellowed a bit; he has calmed down. Life goes on, whether we journey or stay put; for it, too, has to keep *moving*. For everything, in the end, may be nothing more than a journey.

At 6:00 in the morning, the village of Ganhezhen is beginning to stir as I walk back up main street in order to get to the highway. Almost everyone slept outside. The melon vendor who sells me a watermelon thinks to himself how his day is off to a good start: he rolled out of bed—a mat just a few feet from his stall—and right away had a first customer! On the sidewalks, lying on boards, blankets, or directly on the ground, people are all curled up, still sweetly dreaming. A woman on a pile of rags is asleep with her hand on the belly of a naked toddler who, with eyes wide open, watches me pass, not making a sound. They'll all have to wait until tonight to once again enjoy a little of the cool, clammy air that helps lull them to sleep in the depths of night.

It feels good to walk. Then, ever so softly, a little devil murmurs in my ear: "Just twenty-nine miles to go! Why wait until tomorrow when you can be at the end of the road *tonight*?" In vain, I shake my head to tell him no: but the little rascal won't give up, he keeps badgering me. And so, in spite of myself, pushed by the Demon of Walking who pumps me up with powerful bursts of endorphins and gets me feeling high, I pick up the pace. My guardian angel, after bringing me all this way, keeping me safe and sound from so many perils, says over and over, but to no avail: "With the heat brewing today, you really ought to take it easy." It's a barely audible voice, whereas that of the silver-tongued imp rings out in my head: "Twenty-nine miles is no big deal, you've done it before. Then tomorrow, the following day, and the one after that, you can kick back and relax!" It's a one-sided contest. "Weren't you supposed to acquire wisdom by the time you reached the end of the road?" my cherub moans, deeming me ungrateful for all the services rendered. But it's no use, and little by little my strides grow long. The battle's quickly over, the tempter's victory complete. Now that that's settled, let's get going! Today, July 10, I'll have my first glimpse of the Walls of Xi'an, come what may!

And the cost is high, as high as the rising temperature! By 8:30, I'm dripping in sweat. By 9:00, perspiration is pouring out from under my hat and streaming down my face and neck, trickling along my torso and the length my back, then seeping between my buttocks until it finally pools in my boots. I take off my T-shirt and wring it out, squeezing a half pint of sweat from it, then put it back on so that it soaks up more of the water that is simply making a quick trip from my water bags to my skin by way of my stomach. Every fifteen minutes, I repeat the process.

Around 3:00 p.m., just outside the city, I spot the first factories through a smoggy haze. I'm choking from the dust, the heat, and the smell of smoke and diesel. Back when I was running marathons, I noticed how exercise heightens one's sense of smell. Although it can't block the odors, the cotton mask I fashion for myself does, at least, filter out some of the dust. When I stop for lunch in a small bistro,

I'm gasping for breath, awash in sweat, and my muscles are loaded with toxins. A compassionate waitress brings me a pan of clean water in which I rinse my T-shirt. She then hangs it on a wire in the yard and returns it to me ten minutes later, completely dry. The sun can burn and injure you. It can even kill: an English-speaking customer tells me that the radio just announced that a farmer died from sunstroke, and officials are calling on everyone who has to work outdoors to be extremely careful. What a day I picked! I think I hear my angel sneering: "I told you so!" But is there any way to stop now without losing face? I resolved to wind things up today, so let's get on with it.

Stepping out of the restaurant, the scorching air sets my lungs ablaze; it's as if the oxygen had already been sucked out of it. The only people out on the streets seek shelter beneath the plane trees. They scramble past the trenches and piles of dirt that the roaring bulldozers, spitting hellish smoke, leave behind them. Is there a single city not under construction in all of China? Condemned to walk on the roadway, the heat wears me down, trucks blast me as I go by with their fiery, burnt-diesel breath. The diners one table over told me: "Ximen? (the western gateway to the Old City) Five kilometers!" (3 miles). The sign this morning proclaimed: "XI'AN – 46 KILOMETERS." I've gone forty without stopping, so the figure seems about right. I could wait until 6:00 p.m. for the heat to let up a little. But no, with only five lousy kilometers left, let's get going! I can hardly wait to be done and finally see first Ximen and then Zhonglou, the Bell Tower of Xi'an. To shield my skin, I swap my T-shirt for my sole surviving long-sleeve shirt, sweat having turned the other one to tatters. It has excessively long sleeves, and I pull them down to protect my fingers from the sun. The thermometer reads 108°F. I've experienced worse, but the heat was never this muggy. It makes me nostalgic for the bone-dry 126°F heat of Iran's Dasht-e Kavir I experienced two years ago.[*] I take small steps, my gaze fixed on the far end of the avenue where, before long, I ought to catch my first sight of Ximen.

---

[*] *Walking to Samarkand: The Great Silk Road from Persia to Central Asia, op. cit.*

Xi'an is surrounded by nearly nine miles of high, well-preserved, crenellated fortifications. The walls are fifty feet at the base and forty at the top. They form a square. Each compass point is marked by a gate surmounted by a citadel. Once I pass the western gate, I'll have four or five kilometers (2.5 or 3 miles) to reach my final objective, in my sights for four years now: Xi'an's Bell Tower, which rises at the heart of the Old City. If I'm to believe what I've been told, I was only six kilometers away from it. Now five, four, three, two . . . but still no Ximen. My endorphins have thrown in the towel and the large cold sore disfiguring my lip has begun throbbing once again. The hot weather crushes me; the simple act of lifting my boots from the melting asphalt is no minor achievement. I put up with the noise of the gasping trucks, so I don't have to hear my guardian angel's sniggering. At a busy intersection, I let myself drop to the ground beneath a large plane tree, not far from a small group of chattering old men seated on the edge of the sidewalk. Once I've caught my breath, I risk asking a question.

"How much farther is Ximen?"

"Straight ahead, four or five kilometers!"

I leave Ulysses with them the time it takes me to go buy a can of juice in a nearby shop. The keeper can't understand why I don't want an ice-cold drink: how strange these big-noses are! Here's one who walks when there are cars and drinks beverages warm off the shelves when there are refrigerators!

Getting back under way, I'm hobbling even more than before. My left knee hurts and a plantar wart under the big toe of my right foot that has been bothering me for some time suddenly flares up like wildfire. I had better reach my destination soon, I'm coming apart at the seams! But I'm so focused on my objective that even if they told me that my legs were going to fall off tomorrow, I'd just keep right on going. I hum "Ximen, Ximen!" to myself to stoke the fire in my belly and put some strength back in my calves, but the gate remains hidden in the hot haze at the far end of the straight avenue. The sun's beating directly down, trapping the large trees' shade at their feet. Is what I'm feeling that infamous fear of success?

I try not to think that this is the end—it's too depressing. But I know that before long—in an hour, a day, in an eternity too short—I'll find myself waking up from a dream that has been my life over these past four years. The Silk Road doesn't go on forever, and I'm nearing kilometer zero.

Afterward, later on, I'll figure all that out. On the road, I'm in the moment. Just stop thinking and walk! Just one more kilometer, then another, and another. . . . Emerging out of the dust are impetuous trucks, and people on bicycles protected by parasols pedaling in slow motion, only fast enough to keep from falling over.

"Ximen?"

"Straight ahead, four or five kilometers!"

I could almost strangle the young watermelon merchant with a shaved head who kindly answers me while trying to entice me to buy a dust-covered slice of his fruit. There's no way I'm going to stop now! And I'm done asking how much farther it is, as the replies I get are too depressing. With a jerk, I get Ulysses rolling again while taking a greedy sip from my water bag's straw. I'm soaked in sweat and it makes my feet burn with every step. One more stride, then another. That damned Western Gate is eventually going to come into view. I stop for a moment to contemplate several large buildings with oddly-shaped roofs to my right; leading to them is a wide alleyway lined with monumental statues representing men in long robes from the Tang period. Is it a museum? No, just a movie set now open for visits. Little peddlers want to talk me into some postcards printed with scenes from the film, whose name I can't read. Behind a gatehouse near the entrance, I take off my shirt and put back on my now-very-dry T-shirt, which starts absorbing sweat once again.

Feeling more comfortable, I change tactics. Fed up with chasing down Ximen, I decide to take my time, to wander around, to enjoy myself and unwind. I pause to nibble on some dried fruit and photograph a young cobbler napping in a canvas armchair, his sock-covered feet perched on the stool intended for his customers' use, surrounded by all his tools, among which proudly sits a sewing machine that must date back to a distant dynasty.

I've purged all sense of urgency now. I've invented an excuse. Ximen may be evading me, but I'm already in Xi'an, so no more running! After striving for four years to reach my goal, now I dread reaching it. I sit down for a short break on a tiny rectangle of grass and lean back against the smooth trunk of a flowering hibiscus. There, I try to visualize the three days ahead. Three back-to-back free days in China: that hasn't happened since I left Turfan! I thumb through my guidebook, wondering which sites to visit, which tasty dishes I might try in the Muslim Quarter. Will I pay the soldiers of the Terracotta Army another visit?

Back underway for about ten minutes, suddenly, there she is: the citadel atop Ximen, the West Gate, with her haughty white facade and gray-tile roof! She was playfully hiding behind a few plane trees. I wish she were prettier, to more fittingly celebrate our encounter. Before me is a long, rectangular, four-story building, each level perforated with a dozen or so neatly aligned windows. Except for its pagoda roof, it would look a lot like a fire station back home. To its right, I spot the crenellations of the sentries' walkway. I set Ulysses's tow bar against the railing of a bridge straddling the moat. There, a man wearing a wide-brimmed hat is fishing, stock-still. Pedestrians walk past me, eager to escape the pounding heat in this shadeless spot. I ask a young man to take my picture in front of the monument. I want to capture this moment—one I still can't believe is real. A few minutes later, I'm towing my two-wheeled companion toward the Bell Tower. Once again, I couldn't avoid asking for directions. Tired as I am, getting lost and having to walk farther than necessary would be unbearable.

"Straight ahead, four or five kilometers!"

I know the drill. There's no point in losing my cool. These are the last "four or five," after the first *twelve thousand*. All the more reason to savor them, to relish each and every step! On my right and my left, factories have recently made room for large apartment buildings and offices, some still under construction. The city and its metropolitan area have a combined population of nearly seven million; all those souls have to be housed. So buildings are going up everywhere, raised by tall tower cranes. Industry powered the former Imperial capital's revival, but tourism is really what got things started. The discovery of the buried Terracotta Army nearby, considered one of Ancient China's two wonders, draws a constant flow of tourists from every corner of the planet. It's yet another example of a marvel preserved for 2,200 years from human folly by a layer of dirt.

I'm soon walking in the same way that the Chinese are pedaling: slowly, lost in the haze of waking from a protracted dream. I blot out the Chinese men in tank tops scurrying over to the watermelon vendors; I pay no heed to the little old goateed men who, squatting on their heels in a circle in the shade, busy themselves in endless games of chess. I walk blindly toward the east, and my reverie takes me back through these past four years. After the millions of random steps that brought me here, now the faces and landscapes of this immense road parade before my eyes, both the good and the not-so-good moments. Turkey and all the wonderful people I met there: Selim, the philosophical woodsman; Behçet, the loving grandfather who still sends me letters written with a Sergent-Major dip pen;* and Arif, the *muhtar* of Erence. Of Turkey, I still vividly recall the Kangals that would gladly have devoured me and the dazzling sight of Mount Ararat at dawn. Of Iran: Taiebe and Karim, my friends from Tabriz; Ahmet, from Qazvin, along with his old friend who was so amazed that I still had my teeth; the joy of a night spent alone in a caravansary; and my dear friends Mehdi and Monir, those big-hearted artists from Mashhad, who carry within them all the great culture of their country. I have by no means forgotten my stay in a garden of earthly delights at the Uzbekistan border; nor Bukhara and Samarkand; the

---

* TN: The *plume Sergent-Major* was a brand of dip pen used to teach handwriting in French schools from the 19th century until the 1960s.

horsemen and frozen heights of Kyrgyzstan; Soltanad and Tokon; the Sunday market in mesmerizing Kasghar; nor little Mr. Liu. My entire circle of Silk Road friends reappears all at once to welcome me here at the foot of Xi'an's Bell Tower, at the end of this legendary road. They're the flesh and blood of it, they bring the story to life. People marvel that I've been able to walk this entire road alone—but I was hardly ever truly alone. They all drop by, my companions for an hour or a day: the women who stuffed my pack with delicacies, fearing that I might die of hunger; the men who offered me their friendship and a warm, fraternal hug when words failed to convey our mutual affection. All these faces, peasants, emotions, fears, and joys experienced so intensely over the course of the past four years now march before my eyes as I go the final distance beneath a relentless sun, for salutary shade is nowhere to be found.

What will I feel beyond the Bell Tower? Probably a touch of pride, perhaps even a little vanity, but I'll have to be careful not to pat myself too hard on the back! There's no denying, though, that I'm quite likely the only man to have traveled the entire Silk Road—alone and on foot—in its entire two thousand years of history. It's no small feat!* And yet, if someone were to ask me at this very moment what I came in search of, I'd tell them: "the next chapter." When the time came for me to retire, my first thought was that it was all over. But I made a fresh start. I had gotten ahead of myself, just as I suspected. And I've found myself. I didn't wear myself out—I regained my strength! Four years ago, on the little square of the *Milione* in

---

* Some of my thoughtful readers from Japan have rightly set me straight with respect to this little touch of hubris. Between 1994 and 1996, the young Japanese walker Ichiro Omura (24 years old) traveled the entire route in two stages and told of his odyssey in a book published in Japanese in 2004 (ISBN: 4-8396-0166-6). Also published in 2004 is the travelogue of the slightly older Yoshitaro Nakayama (born in 1957) who, heading out of Xi'an . . . ran all the way to Istanbul between June 2000 and December 2001: perhaps we even crossed paths! (ISBN: 4-635-28061-6). My friend Jamel Bahli—an absolutely extraordinary runner who, among other things, traveled from Tierra del Fuego to Alaska—also ran several extensive portions of the Silk Road, although not the entire route. So many people have traveled this mythical road!

Venice, which witnessed the return of Marco Polo, I wondered what this third chapter in life might be like, a life begun at an age when common sense says you should retire. And now young people are surprised and amazed by an undertaking that they themselves wouldn't dare attempt. So why not just keep on going? The Bell Tower is but a stopover; I did not find wisdom here, but what I did find is the strength—or the madness—to go on with my journey on Earth.

Lost in thought and future plans, I meanwhile polished off the last stretch of avenue I was walking down. And suddenly, there it is, in the middle of the intersection directly ahead: the tower, Zhonglou, my Bell Tower! Four floors rising 120 feet into the air. Visitors wander about beneath its pagoda-roof awnings. Built in the fourteenth century by the first emperor of the Ming Dynasty, while Xi'an was still the unrivaled opulent and prestigious City of the Silk Road, its large bell, located on the first-floor balcony, once announced the hours of the day to the city's inhabitants. Today, the bell rings out constantly, for visitors can't resist coaxing a low-pitched sound from its large bronze barrel.

I settle in at one of the nearest hotels and ask for a room with a view of the tower. Stepping out of the shower, I hurry over to stare at it from the window, but I feel no emotion. I go back into the bathroom, stand in front of the mirror, and repeat to myself: "You did it, old buddy! You did it!" But I don't recognize the man in the mirror, and I don't believe a word he says. Reality is unreal.

In other respects, the fatigue of this final day has wiped me out. I nevertheless muster the strength to head over to an Internet cafe and send a message of liberation to Paris—"I made it!"—along with the address of the hotel where I'm staying. It's 8:00 p.m. in Xi'an, 1:00 p.m. in Paris. I limp back to my room. I return to my station in front of the mirror. I try out the magic formula once more: "You did it!" but I still can't believe it. The thought, however, that I won the race against visas and bureaucrats excites me a bit. Not all that much, though, for I suddenly nod off, vaguely aware of having accomplished something big.

I'm jolted awake by the phone. A certain Mi would like to talk to me. She's waiting for me in the lobby.

Mi Re Rong is a petite woman with short hair and high cheekbones, barely visible beneath a long flower dress. She speaks perfect English and tells me she represents a Chinese organization for international cultural exchange. A young Chinese woman who introduces herself by the English name Ellen arrives shortly thereafter. The pair, tipped off by mysterious sources, either friends or journalists, had already set the wheels in motion yesterday evening, and now whisk me away for a series of press briefings. Newspapers, television, radio stations: I spend the entire day in interviews, and then in the evening, Abel Segretin arrives, Beijing correspondent for Paris's *Journal du Dimanche*, who made the trip from the capital just for the occasion. TV cameras and photographers are especially interested in checking out Ulysses, whose wings I had folded up, but who now poses unabashedly out in front of the Bell Tower. The final shot, snapped at midnight, leaves me feeling more exhausted than my thirty-four-mile walk did yesterday. Mi picks me back up on the morning of July 12 for a photo session with Wang Ping, a photographer for the *Xi'an Evening News*. Befuddled by all this Asian fame, I have my portrait taken on the city's west side next to an immense sculpture representing camels and camel drivers, a place where caravans once gathered as they prepared to leave for the West. My heart is set on visiting the Giant Wild Goose Pagoda, still haunted by the shadow of Xuanzang, a man with an extraordinary destiny, and one of China's greatest heroes. His story takes us back to the seventh century. Once upon a time, a baby was abandoned in a cradle on the Luo He River, and was picked up by some monks. This little Moses became a monk himself, then left on a sixteen-year journey that would take him over the Pamirs just south of Torugart Pass and all the way to the East Indies. He returned home with Buddhism's founding texts, transported on the backs of twenty-two horses, and he would spend ten years—until his death in 664—translating them into Chinese. The Giant Wild Goose Pagoda was built to safely house these manuscripts. At the same time, Xuanzang dictated *The Great Tang Records on the Western Regions*, which centuries later inspired one of China's all-time bestsellers, *Journey to the West*, written during the Ming Dynasty. It's attributed to Wu Cheng'en, and is the eastern equivalent of Marco Polo's *Description of the World*.

People stop me in the street to shake my hand. Waitresses ask me to pose for souvenir photos. Little notebooks are held out for me to autograph. Are all these smiling, slanted eyes trying to tell me that they admire me, that I'm some kind of celebrity? For the first time since arriving in Xi'an, I realize that I've accomplished something verging on a real achievement. I would even start to think I was Superman if it weren't for a sudden, providential case of diarrhea, contracted that same evening in a Muslim District restaurant by the name of "Prosperity-Fortune," which forces me to spend my last day in Xi'an in my room, ironically illustrating the words that quickly come to mind whenever I'm tempted by a little misplaced pride: *vanitas vanitatum, et omnia vanitas*.

EPILOGUE

> If you only want to get somewhere, you can ride in a post-chaise.
> But if you want to travel, you must go on foot.
> JEAN-JACQUES ROUSSEAU,
> *Emile, or On Education.*

As I wrap up my Long Walk narrative and turn my attention to several new projects, I have a confession to make: I didn't carry off this 7,000-plus-mile journey, begun in 1999, entirely alone.

Four years ago, I embarked on what was quite literally a crazy adventure. All alone and, I thought, old. A recent retiree, I felt what all men and women must feel when their social existence undergoes a sudden, radical change. Only yesterday, I was a journalist in love with my profession—although it had taken a turn which increasingly had me questioning the validity of exercising it—in an increasingly anxious, breathless world. I had a place, a name, a *raison d'être*.

Then, all of a sudden, I was a "pensioner," a welfare case, for all intents and purposes—a ship without a rudder, heading nowhere. Without love as well, since the one I loved was no more.

Throwing myself onto the Silk Road was like throwing a bottle into the sea. To survive. People wondered what I was looking for so far afield. Could I have told them "a reason to live"? Success was the furthest thing from my mind. My chances of reaching my destination were, I believed, next to nothing. How could I have been so pretentious to think—at my age, alone, on foot, and over such a terrifying distance—that I might actually pull off a caper that no one, as far as I knew, had ever even tried, let alone completed? I was

315

like a swimmer who, struggling for air at the bottom of the pool, kicks with his legs in an effort to return to the surface. I couldn't breathe. On that day, on this side of the Bosporus, even though it had occurred to me that it may very well cost me my life, I wasn't ready to die. I mean, I wasn't resigned to being nothing. I had to get moving. So long as they're alive, human beings need to move.

With the journey behind me now, I know that, though the heathen that I am eventually triumphed over peril, my success was the result of several miracles performed through the punctilious and kind intercession of an attentive, hard-working, and unfaltering guardian angel. But I also owe a great debt of thanks to my readers, surely the envy of many an author. Since the first of these three travelogues was published, I've received a steady stream of friendly, enthusiastic, and even downright panegyric letters of support. When sickness, heat, thirst, fatigue, a lapse of courage, or some other twist of fate had me thinking that there'd be no shame in throwing in the towel, their silent presence injected at just the right moment the determination I needed to push on. Readers have often told me that they felt as if they were walking by my side. It was no impression, it was reality! Without their presence, how could I have ever managed to enjoy—or simply tolerate—what was at times such intense loneliness?

Finally, a word about Seuil, the association I run along with a number of friends (some of whom are marvelous "retirees"). I would like to say how much these young people—who, in trouble with the law, managed to walk to their own freedom or are getting ready to do so—also helped me push on to the end. Western societies, unlike those through which I traveled these last four years, marginalize "old" people, since they are no longer "productive" members of the system. It also excludes (and sometimes imprisons) young people who get a little carried away in asserting their existence and who wind up breaking rules that no one ever teaches or explains. They're treated so badly by adults and/or society that they seek to settle the score. How good it would be if the two groups, both young and old, could reach out to one another and break free from their respective ghettoes, affirming side by side their rightful place in this anguished world.

When Michel Serres was asked whether people should listen to their elders, the philosopher replied: "Not only will they be listened to, but they may be listened to more than anyone else, as this century draws to a close. All they have to do is make their voices heard. People treat culture nowadays as if there were no time for it. Culture requires time, culture requires experience. Old people hold in their hands all the cards needed to bring a little beauty back to a world growing uglier day by day." *

Walking takes time, too. And to my mind, that lovely word "culture" embraces several other less obvious concepts such as friendship, fraternity, or simply listening and understanding. As I complete this book, I'm also completing my long and beautiful Silk Road journey. But it's not an ending. Only a new beginning.

Come on! Let's get going!

---

* Michel Serres, Danièle Sallenave, and Anne Meert, *Un si grand âge* . . . (Paris: Centre national de la Photographie, in collaboration with the Ministère de la culture et de la communication, 1986). TN: Michel Serres (1930-2019) was a French philosopher whose writings grapple with issues such as death, time, science in the modern world, communication, and . . . angels.

APPENDICES

证　　明

　　法国驻华大使馆证明，Bernard Ollivier先生，1938年01月11日出生于法国芒什省Gathemo，持第00HZ04417号护照，2000年11月22日签发于巴黎，有效期至2005年11月21日。Bernard Ollivier先生徒步穿越丝绸之路，目的是锻炼身体和丰富文化，也是为了推进人民的友谊和欧亚两洲的历史关联，促进东西方文化与文明的相互了解。Bernard Ollivier先生的此项计划得到了法国驻华大使馆的全面信任。

　　鉴于以上原因，法国驻华大使馆谨请所有相关行政部门和人民解放军为其提供帮助和协助，为他徒步在中国境内穿越丝绸之路提供方便。他的行走路线是老丝绸之路，从新疆维吾尔自治区的土尔朵特山口到吐鲁番盆地。

　　法国驻华大使馆事先感谢为Ollivier先生成功穿越丝绸之路提供帮助的所有部门。

　　特此证明。

毛磊

法国驻华大使

318

AMBASSADE DE FRANCE
A PEKIN

REPUBLIQUE FRANCAISE

ATTESTATION

L'ambassade de France en Chine certifie que M. Bernard Ollivier, né le 11 janvier 1938 à Gathemo (département de la Manche), titulaire du passeport n°00HZ04417 délivré le 22 novembre 2000 à Paris, valable jusqu'au 21 novembre 2005, parcourt à pied la route de la soie en poursuivant un objectif sportif et culturel, et dans le but de promouvoir l'amitié entre les peuples, les liens historiques entre l'Europe et l'Asie et la connaissance réciproque des cultures et des civilisations. M. Bernard Ollivier a toute la confiance de cette ambassade dans son projet.

Pour ces raisons, l'ambassade de France en Chine prie tous les services concernés de l'administration et de l'Armée populaire de libération de porter aide et assistance à M. Ollivier et de lui faciliter le passage à pied sur le territoire chinois, sur l'itinéraire de l'ancienne route de la soie, entre la passe de Turugart et l'oasis de Turpan, dans la région autonome ouighoure du Xinjiang.

L'ambassade de France remercie par avance tous ceux qui auront contribué à la réussite du projet de M. Ollivier.

Attestation établie pour faire et valoir ce que de droit.

Pierre MOREL
Ambassadeur de France en Chine

THE FRENCH EMBASSY   **THE REPUBLIC OF FRANCE**
IN BEIJING

ATTESTATION

The French Embassy in China certifies that Mr. Bernard Ollivier, born January 11, 1938 in Gathemo (Department of the Manche), holder of passport № 00HZ04417 issued on November 22, 2000 in Paris, valid until November 21, 2005, is traveling the Silk Road on foot for both sport and culture, and with the goal of promoting friendship among peoples, Europe and Asia's historical ties, and mutual understanding among cultures and civilizations. Mr. Bernard Ollivier has the full confidence of this Embassy in carrying out his endeavor.

For these reasons, the French Embassy in China requests that all the relevant services of the Government and of the People's Liberation Army provide aid and assistance to Mr. Ollivier and that they facilitate his passage on foot through Chinese territory, following the itinerary of the old Silk Road, between Torugart Pass and the Turfan Oasis, in the Uyghur Autonomous Region of Xinjiang.

The French Embassy would like to thank in advance all those who aid in the success of Mr. Ollivier's undertaking.

This attestation has been drawn up for the appropriate legal purposes.

Pierre MOREL
French Ambassador to China

BIBLIOGRAPHY

Before setting out each year, I spent a great deal of time reading books and consulting maps. There is no way I could cite them all here. Several, however, became my bedside books, and their authors my mentors, who either preceded me or traveled right along with me on the silken road.

Anquetil, Jacques. *Routes de la Soie, vingt-deux siècles d'Histoire: des déserts de l'Asie aux rives du monde occidental.* Paris: J.-C. Lattès, 1992.

Boothroyd, Ninette, and Muriel Détrie, eds. *Le Voyage en Chine: anthologie des voyageurs occidentaux du Moyen Âge à la chute de l'Empire chinois.* Paris: Robert Laffont, Collection "Bouquins," 1992.

Boulnois, Luce. *La Route de la Soie: dieux, Guerriers et Marchands.* Geneva: Éditions Olizane, 2001.

Cable, Mildred, and Francesca French. *The Challenge of Central Asia,* London and New York: World Dominion Press, 1929.

Cagnat, René. *La Rumeur des steppes: Aral, Asie centrale, Russie.* Paris: Payot, Collection "Petite Bibliothèque Payot/Voyageurs," 2001.

Drege, Jean-Pierre. *Marco Polo et la route de la Soie.* Paris: Gallimard, Collection "Découvertes," 1998.

Fleming, Peter. *Courrier de Tartarie* followed by an interview with Ella Maillart. Translated from the English by S. and P. Bourgeois. Paris: Libretto Nº 80, 2001. First published 1989 by Phébus (Paris).

Gonzalez de Clavijo, Ruy. *La Route de Samarkand au temps de Tamerlan (1403-1406): relation du voyage de l'ambassade de Castille à la cour de Timour Beg.* Translated from the Spanish and commented by Lucien Kehren. Paris: Imprimerie nationale, 2002.

Gorshenina, Svetlana, and Claude Rapin. *De Kaboul à Samarcande: les archéologues en Asie centrale.* Paris: Gallimard, Collection "Découvertes," 2001.

Hopkirk, Peter. *Bouddhas et rôdeurs sur la route de la Soie.* Translated from the English by Clarisse Beaune. Paris: Picquier-poche, 1995.

Jan, Michel. *Le Réveil des Tartares: en Mongolie sur les traces de Guillaume de Rubrouck,* rev. ed. Paris: Payot, Collection "Petite Bibliothèque Payot/Voyageurs," 2002. First published 1989.

Jan, Michel, ed. *Le Voyage en Asie centrale et au Tibet: anthologie des voyageurs occidentaux du Moyen Âge à la première moitié du XXe siècle,* rev. ed. Paris: Robert Laffont, Collection "Bouquins," 2001. First published 1992.

Kehren, Lucien. *Tamerlan: l'empire du seigneur de fer.* Paris: Payot, 1980.

Le Breton, David. *Éloge de la marche.* Paris: Métaillé, Collection "Suites," 2000.

Le Fèvres, Georges, and Paul Pelliot. *La Croisière jaune: expédition Citroën Centre-Asie.* Paris: L'Asiathèque, 1991.

Maillart, Ella. *Oasis interdites: de Pékin au Cachemire, une femme à travers l'Asie centrale en 1935.* Preface by Nicolas Bouvier. Paris: Payot, Collection "Petite Bibliothèque Payot/Voyageurs," 2002. First published 1937 by B. Grasset (Paris).

Moorhouse, Geoffrey. *Le Pèlerin de Samarcande: un voyage en Asie centrale.* Translated from the English by Katia Holmes. Paris: Phébus, 1993.

Morier, James. *Les Aventures de Hadji Baba d'Ispahan,* rev. ed. Translated from the English by Elian J. Finbert. Paris: Phébus, Libretto Nº 40, 2000. First published 1983 by Phébus (Paris).

Pirazzoli-T'serstevens, Michèle. *La Chine des Hans: histoire et civilisation.* Paris: PUF, 1982.

Polo, Marco. *Le Devisement du monde. Le Livre des Merveilles.* Translated and edited by A. C. Moule and Paul Pelliot. Paris: Phébus, 1996.

Rubrouck, Guillaume de. *Voyage dans l'empire mongol: 1253-1255.* Translated from the Latin and commented by Claude-Claire Kappler and René Kappler; photographs by Roland Michaud. Paris: Imprimerie nationale, 1993.

Teilhard de Chardin, Pierre. *Lettres de voyage: 1923-1939.* Paris: Grasset, Collection "Les Cahiers rouges," 1956.

Telmon, Priscilla, and Sylvain Tesson. *La Chevauchée des steppes: 3 000 kilomètres à cheval à travers l'Asie centrale.* Paris: Robert Laffont, 2001.

Valéry, Philippe. *Par les sentiers de la Soie: à pied jusqu'en Chine.* Paris: Transboréal, 2002.

Vambery, Armin. *Voyage d'un faux derviche en Asie centrale: 1862-1864.* Paris: Phébus, Libretto № 293, 2009. First published 1994 by Phébus (Paris).

Van Dis, Adriaan. *Sur la route de la Soie, terres d'aventure.* Translated from the Dutch by Marie Hooghe. Arles: Actes Sud, 1990.

Vayron, Isabelle, and Xavier Vayron. *Échos d'orient: visions de glaneurs de musiques.* With two CDs. Paris: Transboréal, 2001.

GUIDEBOOKS

Introduction à la route de la Soie. Geneva: Éditions Olizane, Collection "Guides," 1995.

Lonely Planet Turkey. Lonely Planet, 1998.

Lonely Planet Iran. Lonely Planet, 1999.

Lonely Planet China. Lonely Planet, 2000.

Lonely Planet Central Asia. Lonely Planet, 1999.

Iran. Nagel's Guide. Edited by Paul Wagret. Geneva: Nagel Publishers, 1974. Although published before the Islamic Revolution, this is a gold mine of information.

Bonavia, Judy. *Introduction à la route de la Soie: de Xi'an à Kashgar, sur les traces des grandes caravanes.* Geneva: Éditions Olizane, 1995.

AUTHOR'S ACKNOWLEDGMENTS

Over the course of my long walk, hundreds of people generously offered me their help, support, and encouragement. I am deeply grateful to them all. There are a few people I would like to mention by name:

- –Philippe de Suremain, French Ambassador to Iran in 2000
- –Pierre Morel, French Ambassador to China until May 2002
- –Ms. Mi Re Rong (Xi'an) and Mr. Liu Ming (Beijing) of the China International Culture Exchange Center
- –M. Xian Zhao Shang and Ms. Fang Yumei (Xi'an)
- –Mr. Wang Ping, talented photographer with the *Xi'an Evening News*

I would like to send a special word of thanks to my guardian angels of the *Rue des Boulangers* in Paris, and my dear friends at the "Orients–Sur les Routes de la Soie" Travel Agency, who, through a little of their amazing Internet magic, sent help and reassurance whenever, between Istanbul and Xi'an, I found myself—a poor walker all alone in the vastness of Asia—confronted with nasty bureaucrats, or when solitude was too much to bear. Émilie, Sofy and Sophie, Pascale, Claire and Anne, Jean-Jacques and Anthony—thank you all from the bottom of my heart!

ABOUT THE AUTHOR

Six days into his retirement, in April 1998, depressed and heartbroken since the death of his wife years earlier, his children now well into adulthood, Bernard Ollivier set out to hike the Way of St. James from Paris, France, to Santiago de Compostela, Spain, hoping to figure out what to do with the rest of his life. At journey's end, nearly 1,500 miles later, he returned home with a two-fold plan of action: first, he would help troubled young people find their place in society through the act of walking, just as he had done for himself; and second, he would embark on yet another of History's great roads. In April 1999, he set out to walk the entire 7,500-mile length of the Great Silk Road, and, the following year, he created Seuil, an association dedicated to helping young men and women run afoul of the law set out on accompanied long walks as an alternative to prison.